Defining Dominion

STUDIES IN MEDIEVAL AND EARLY MODERN CIVILIZATION
Marvin B. Becker, General Editor

Charity and Children in Renaissance Florence:
The Ospedale degli Innocenti, 1410–1536
　Philip Gavitt

Humanism in Crisis: The Decline of the French Renaissance
　Philippe Desan, editor

Upon My Husband's Death: Widows in the Literatures
and Histories of Medieval Europe
　Louise Mirrer, editor

The Crannied Wall: Women, Religion, and the Arts
in Early Modern Europe
　Craig A. Monson, editor

Wife and Widow in Medieval England
　Sue Sheridan Walker, editor

The Rhetorics of Life-Writing in Early Modern Europe: Forms of
Biography from Cassandra Fedele to Louis XIV
　Thomas F. Mayer and D. R. Woolf, editors

Defining Dominion: The Discourses of Magic and Witchcraft in
Early Modern France and Germany
　Gerhild Scholz Williams

Women, Jews, and Muslims in the Texts
of Reconquest Castile
　Louise Mirrer

The Culture of Merit: Nobility, Royal Service, and the Making of
Absolute Monarchy in France, 1600–1789
　Jay M. Smith

Clean Hands and Rough Justice: An Investigating Magistrate
in Renaissance Italy
　David S. Chambers and Trevor Dean

"Songes of Rechelesnesse": Langland and the
Franciscans
　Lawrence M. Clopper

Godliness and Governance in Tudor Colchester
　Laquita M. Higgs

Defining Dominion

*The Discourses of Magic and Witchcraft
in Early Modern France and Germany*

Gerhild Scholz Williams

Ann Arbor
The University of Michigan Press

First paperback edition 1999
Copyright © by the University of Michigan 1995
All rights reserved
Published in the United States of America by
The University of Michigan Press
Manufactured in the United States of America
⊗ Printed on acid-free paper

2002 2001 2000 1999   4 3 2 1

A CIP catalogue record for this book is available from the British Library.

Library of Congress Cataloging-in-Publication Data

Scholz Williams, Gerhild.
   Defining dominion : the discourses of magic and witchcraft in early modern France and Germany / Gerhild Scholz Williams.
     p. cm. — (Studies in medieval and early modern civilization)
   Includes bibliographical references and index.
   ISBN 0-472-10619-8 (hardcover : alk. paper)
   1. Witchcraft—France—History. 2. Witchcraft—Germany—History. 3. Magic—France—History. 4. Magic—Germany—History. I. Title. II. Series.
BF1582.S36 1995
133.4′3′0943—dc20   95-13470
                                                                                 CIP

ISBN 0-472-08619-7

*To Hildegard Ebersbach Scholz†,
Marianne Scholz, Verena Williams Weber,
and Jessie C. Weber*

Acknowledgments

Although my work on the discourses of magic began several years ago, this book owes its completion to the generous gift of time afforded by a DAAD Fellowship (Summer 1991) and a Fulbright Senior Scholars Grant (1992–93). The year was spent at the Institut für Europäische Kulturgeschichte, Augsburg University. Over the years I was able to use the resources of the Oettingen-Wallerstein Collection (Augsburg University) and of the Staats- und Stadtbibliothek at Augsburg, whose staff, led by Dr. Rupp and Dr. Gier, respectively, was always available for expert advice. I am grateful for the support given to my work by Augsburger colleagues Jochen Brüning, director of the institute, and Johannes Janota, whose initial invitation prompted me to pursue research in witchcraft and magic at Augsburg. Cornelia Weber (Kulturinstitut) and Ruth Meyer (Augsburg University) provided valuable assistance during my year in Augsburg.

My work has benefited from the encouragement and comments of many colleagues and students. I would like to thank those of my students who explored some of the topics of this book with me in seminars on magic and travel literature. The Interlibrary Loan Division of Washington University's John M. Olin Library provided reliable and prompt assistance with the numerous and often arcane requests for materials, many of them centuries old and located in libraries throughout Europe. Early thoughts on this topic surfaced in various talks and papers over the past years; I thank my colleagues at Washington University in St. Louis, Craig Monson, Lynne Tatlock, as well as Alexander Schwarz (Lausanne), Horst Wenzel (Berlin), and Wolfgang Haubrichs (Saarbrücken), for the opportunity to explore the early stages of some of the ideas elaborated in the following pages. Harriet Stone (Washington University) contributed critical commentary and stylistic queries that resulted in a sharpened focus and clearer language for the benefit of the reader. Thanks as well are due to Elaine Tennant (University of California, Berkeley), C. Stephen Jaeger (University of Washington), Steven Ozment (Harvard University), H. C. Erik Midelfort (University of Virginia), Merry Wiesner-Hanks (University of Wisconsin, Milwaukee), Steven Rowan (University of Missouri, St. Louis), and the anonymous readers of this book for their attention and support.

When—alongside the duties of department chair—I accepted the appointment as associate provost at Washington University, the indefatigable and diligent support of my graduate assistants, Frank Wagner, Elizabeth Ambrose, Elisabeth Waghall (the latter two by now also colleagues in early modern German studies), and the electronic wizardry and meticulous note checking of Richard Langston made timely completion of the manuscript possible. No one could have wished for more professional and congenial associates.

Finally, since this is—in part—a study of women's struggle against prejudice and destructive science, I would like to remember my friends and colleagues, past and present, in the United States and abroad, and especially the women of my family, whose intelligence, courage, perseverance, and fear-defying laughter have inspired my life and my work. To them I dedicate this book.

Contents

Abbreviations xi

1. Introduction 1

2. Magic and the Myth of Transgression:
   Mélusine de Lusignan by Jean d'Arras (1393) 23

3. Magic and the Science of Man and Woman:
   Theophrastus Bombastus von Hohenheim,
   called Paracelsus 45

4. Magic and Gender: The Struggle for Control in the
   Witchcraft Tracts of Kramer, Weyer, and Bodin 65

5. Magic and the Margins: Pierre de Lancre 89

6. Magic and Religious Diversity:
   The Discourses of Belonging and Exclusion 121

Notes 147

Works Cited 201

Index 229

Abbreviations

Peuckert's edition contains the following works by Paracelsus, which are cited in the text with the accompanying abbreviations:

AR	"Zehn Bücher der Archidoxen"	1:333–448
BA	"Bertheonea"	1:1–21
BG	"Das Buch von der Gebärung der empfindlichen Dinge durch die Vernunft"	1:21–64
DS	"De sagis"	3:439–62
GW	"Der grossen Wundartzney"	2:385–440
LA	"Liber Azoth"	5:337–91
H	"Herbarius"	1:241–97
LB	"Liber de summo et aeterno bono"	4:166–85
LF	"Liber de fundamento"	3:1–37
LH	"Liber de homunculis"	3:427–39
LI	"Liber de inventione artium"	4:325–53
LME	"Labyrinthus medicorum errantium"	2:440–97
LN	"Liber de nymphis"	3:462–98
LNA	"Liber de nupta"	4:81–103
MI	"De causis morborum invisibilium"	2:187–284
OP	"Opus Paramirum"	2:1–187
PA	"Das Buch Paragranum"	1:495–584
PS	"Philosophia sagax"	3:37–406
QT	"Quinque philosophiae tractatus"	3:406–27
RP	"De religione perpetua"	4:148–66
VA	"Liber de votis alienis"	4:353–76
VH	"De virtute humana"	4:224–35
VL	"Liber de longa vita"	1:469–95
VP	"Volumen Paramirum"	1:168–297

1
Introduction

"The importance of the witch-hunter's manual, the *Malleus Maleficarum*, published in 1486, has been exaggerated."[1] With this opening statement from the twelfth chapter of his influential and still much cited study, *Europe's Inner Demons: An Enquiry Inspired by the Great Witch-Hunt* (1975), Norman Cohn emphasizes two concepts that frame a historical perspective. According to Cohn—and corroborated by H. C. Erik Midelfort's and Edward Peter's pathbreaking studies—at the time Heinrich Kramer's *Malleus Maleficarum, the Witches' Hammer,* was published, the witch phenomenon had already assumed all of its characteristic dimensions.[2] Moreover, the effect of the handbook on the Great Witch-Hunts was negligible, since these historical events did not begin until almost a century following its publication. Situated too far after one event and too long before the other to be of serious consequence, the *Malleus* is, in Cohn's and, less stridently, Midelfort's views, a work undeserving of much of the attention it has received.

Cohn is certainly correct about the pre-*Malleus* formation of the image of the witch. On the other hand, he and Midelfort underestimate the importance of Kramer's publication, which was the first document in handbook form to bring together judicial, social, and anthropological aspects of the witch phenomenon. With the printing of this tract, the medieval and early modern public's diffuse fears of witches were articulated as an urgent threat. The author stated authoritatively, using strong and dramatic language, that if the illicit behavior of women called witches were not curbed and if it were not countered vigorously and decisively, individual souls as well as communities would be at risk. Although written in difficult Latin and, by Midelfort's description (*Witch Hunting in Southwestern Germany,* 5), rarely mentioned in German sermons and trial records, it was Kramer's stated intent to make the tract widely available to a literate public and to inspire the appropriate authorities to act against the perceived menace.

Cohn misreads the events separating the publication of the *Malleus* from the most virulent persecutions, which began around 1563. He misjudges—as do, to some degree, Midelfort and André Schnyder,[3] the most recent *Malleus* critic—the role of this text as the impulse and impetus of these later events. When we survey the relationship of magic to witchcraft in early modern Europe, it becomes clear that the metamorphosis of the witchcraft phenomenon can be divided into a pre- and a post-*Malleus* period. It is undeniably the case—legal, intellectual, and social influences on the witch phenomenon notwithstanding—that this tract was of fundamental importance to the process of witch persecutions in Europe. Its influence waxing and waning during the sixteenth century, the *Malleus* also reflected the changing role, interpretation, and influence of those aspects of magic that relate to women and to witchcraft.

On the basis of selected, demonstrably widely read, even popular and influential texts, the present work studies the varieties of magic relating to the construction of the witch as it materialized during the early modern period. Among them, the *Malleus* was, while not the only text to influence learned and lay attitudes toward magic, decidedly one of the most important. It put woman into the center of a destructive discussion and did not permit her to leave this place until, more than a hundred and fifty years after it was first published, doubts about the efficacy of the handbook and about the ability of the judicial system to establish just and fair trials in matters of alleged witchcraft began to outweigh the text's authority.[4]

Still, owing to its ubiquity in the witch tracts of the late sixteenth century, it determined to a not inconsiderable degree the direction that the witchcraft debate was going to take. Drawing on the Scholasticism of the Middle Ages and the humanism of the Renaissance, the sixteenth century built on a rich epistemological tradition when it created the multiple discourses that helped to articulate the approach of modernity. In the context of this study, discourse denotes two things: the medium of textual and semiotic transmission; and the interpretation, hermeneutics, of what has been transmitted. Discourse does more than identify the spoken or the written word: it also stands for the whole spectrum of cultural signs, for different narrative voices that gave form to magical impulses in different narrative and instructional settings.[5] It stands for the range of discourses available to the writers as they communicated with their readers in a shared and coherent mental universe.[6]

In this study I am identifying three such discourses: the most important, the one that will be present in all the ensuing discussion, is the discourse of magic as it relates to women and witchcraft. The two other discourses treated here will be shown to depend on magic, to be influenced and shaped by it, sometimes directly, sometimes indirectly; these are the discourses of discovery and of religious diversity and dissidence. All three discourses interpreted and demarcated what was known in order that they might provide articulation for what was unknown; these discourses defined the encounter of early modern people with antagonists internal and external to their contemporary culture. Those accused of being witches and those condemned as religious dissenters and suspected of being dissimulators or even nonbelievers—atheists—were viewed as hostile internal forces. Distant cultures and foreign peoples brought near by the discoveries in the New World represented threatening encounters with external forces. Together the narratives about, and invectives against, this trio of maligned objects—alleged witches, the natives in the New World, and the religious dissenters and dissimulators in the Old World—expressed the antagonisms, anxieties, and ambitions of early modern thinkers as well as their intellectual reflections on the identification, containment, and/or elimination of the marginalized groups.[7] That is, narratives furnished the language that would report and, in a second, more important step, interpret the events, placing the participants within an epistemological context, assigning them a significant place within early modern social codes. The intrusion into early modern life of demonology, discovery, and religious diversity, dissidence, and unbelief had the happy effect of assimilating what was new, strange, or totally unfamiliar into the established discourse of the familiar.[8] This din of competing discourses was accommodated and organized with the help of the printing press: all the while the proliferation of texts on witchcraft, the discoveries, and dissidence articulated and continuously adjusted the majority position of those who, according to Michel de Certeau, "ha[d] the power of naming in [their] own discourse a dissident formation and of excluding it as marginal."[9] The cosmology and epistemology of magical thought provided the conceptual tools, the discursive raw material, for the narrative conquest; it enabled the coming to terms with, and the marginalization of, the strange, the unfamiliar, and the feared.

This study will look at magic as an intellectual and cultural language, as a discourse that gave expression to the early modern mentality as it struggled to articulate the extraordinary, the forbidden, as it strove to extend further the limits of knowledge. I will examine magic as it attempted to control and confine woman, whose propensity toward satanic dalliance threatened not just her soul but the health of the body politic. I will show that during this period, specifically between 1550 and 1620, people sought to operate in a world whose limits could be transcended by magical means, whose history could be influenced by magical persons, and whose New World became old under the influence of the Enemy, Satan, who had been living across the ocean long before people first set foot on its shores. Furthermore, this study will explain how magic was eventually attacked and reduced to marginality by those in power.

At about the same time, between 1540 and 1680, a growing movement toward various forms of religious libertinism, skepticism, and even atheism initiated a debate among intellectuals and educated—that is, literate—lay people about the existence of God, the divine economy of retribution, and the nature of heaven and hell.[10] During the course of this debate, a whole new vocabulary of religious dissension and disbelief found its way into the early modern discussion on religiosity and social discipline.[11]

Defined as an act of aggression against the community, against the state, demonic magic as well as libertinism and unbelief had to be prosecuted by those who exercised the discourse of authority: physicians, lawyers, and magistrates. Such controlling, even punitive, discourse could be directed against opposing intellectual and social equals, as was the case in the witchcraft debates between Jean Bodin and Johannes Weyer and their partisans. It could be directed as well against those who were unwanted and feared: women and others in the margins of society; strangers in the New World, people who had only recently, in 1537, been pronounced human by the decree of Pope Paul III.[12] These discursive acts were employed to stabilize social order and to purge society of its nonconforming members while protecting areas of privileged scientific inquiry, all in the name of religious orthodoxy, social order, and scientific advances. However, the dichotomy between the licit and the illicit and the threat of stepping across the thin line separating them never disappeared. Even as relentless a jurist as Bodin tried to preserve a bit of space where the licit could be practiced by differentiating between magic, which, in the words of his German translator Johann Fischart, was "Erkendtnuß Göttlicher vnnd Natürlicher sachen," and its satanic counterpart, "Teufflische Zauberey" ("Vom aussgelasnen wütigen Teuffelsheer," 66).

During the first decade of the seventeenth century, the French magistrate and witch hunter Pierre de Lancre found such differentiation difficult, if not impossible. He thus distinguished himself from the physician and magus Theophrastus Paracelsus von Hohenheim. During the first half of the preceding century, Paracelsus had avoided the controversy as best as he could, in part by raising magic to the status of divine inspiration and reserving its practice for the truly blessed. By contrast, the little-known writer of the French prose *Mélusine* (1393), a text written a century and a half prior to the identified period, saw magic manifest itself in the workings of history and in the life and un-death of his female protagonists. Mélusine's metamorphosis from the active fairy founding mother of the powerful house of Lusignan into a satanic succubus in sixteenth-century tracts signals the shift in magic's emphasis. It suggests the difficulty that the adept experienced in separating licit magic from its illicit, demonic twin. Mélusine's story will serve as my pre-*Malleus* example of magical energies at work; it is a frame text for the historical context that I explore.

It is accepted practice in the research on magic as science, *scientia magica,* to stress its special philosophical and theological closeness to religion. Magic emerged from a dialogue of religion with itself, or, as Kurt Goldammer declares, from a theological and philosophical reflection about secular matters that concerned religion.[13] During the fifteenth century, magic included all forms of the "natural" sciences, all theories of the universe and man's and woman's place in it, and much philosophical and theosophical speculation on the grand design that connected the highest good, God, with the least of the elements in one uninterrupted chain of mutual dependence and existential reassurance.[14] The proximity of magic and religion, however, was also part of the struggle for dominance among science, philosophy, and theology. It affected the anthropology of early modern men and women, their relationship both to God and to each other. Magic and religion shared a context in which "coherent cosmological assumptions about agents and causation" bound together the categories of "ritual" and "real" in the experience of people.[15] Magic and religion were part of common history and the shared presence in humanity's relationship with the numinous. They have affected the view of women, strangers, religious outsiders, dissenters, and heretics since the dawn of time.

When setting sail in the direction of unknown shores, the early modern people took assumptions about magic right along with their religious rituals. Moreover, the suspicion of magic, of satanic allegiances, was always present when zealous men accused each other of religious dissidence in post-Reformation Europe.[16] Magic and religion have been considered two aspects of the same emotional debates about ideology. This book will show that magic's relationship to politics is equally compelling, and that belief in magic and religion was frequently supported by unbelievers as indispensable tools to uphold public order.[17] Magic's rich epistemological tradition influenced the Christianization of Europe,[18] the birth of modern science,[19] the view of woman, and the genesis of the witch craze.[20] It has survived as a form of natural philosophy—a mystical kind of magic—in modern esoteric and New Age thought. As historians have studied magic in the context of its perpetual and dangerously close associate, witchcraft, they have concentrated their attention on size, reasons, and origins of the witch craze in an attempt to isolate its geographic, economic, religious, political, and cultural roots.[21] Historians also have pondered the fact that alongside magic as science and divine philosophy, the fascination with, and fear of, the darker side—i.e., satanic magic and witchcraft—has persisted throughout the centuries.

In spite of the exalted position that magic attained in the circle around Marsilio Ficino in fifteenth-century Florence, as among the students of Pietro Pomponazzi in turn-of-the-century Padua, one cannot help but be struck by the negative turn that the debate took in the second half of the sixteenth century, when all branches of learning—the natural sciences, law, medicine, theology, philosophy, and politics—became deeply entangled in the debate over natural magic versus satanic witchcraft.[22] The known world had grown larger, but it also appeared increasingly precarious as satanic forces rallied in the New World and in the Old to attack the forces of orthodoxy. Scholars searched for answers in the very language of magic.[23] Magic's place in this complex semiotics of early modern culture explains contemporary interest in the subject. Indeed, magic ushered in an astonishingly energetic period of intellectual engagement as it sought to answer what Gary Tomlinson calls the "epistemological challenge of magic's enduring role in Western tradition."[24]

In addition, magic flourished in a time that witnessed a pronounced passion for juridical discussion and reform. It likewise produced a great deal of what today we might call existential anxiety, *angst*.[25] Those who sought access to the secrets of *scientia magica*, to the perennial tradition of esoteric wisdom, were always aware that their search poised them somewhat precariously between the licit and the illicit. Agrippa of Nettesheim, Giovanni and Gianfrancesco Pico della Mirandola, Ficino, Girolamo Cardano, Trithemius of Sponheim, and Paracelsus—to name only the most notorious—wrote extensively on magic. Yet each of these writers on occasion also expressed feelings of ambivalence, indeed even hostility, toward the magical sciences.[26]

As I examine the discourses of magic in several texts spanning roughly two hundred and fifty years, 1400–1650, my investigation into magic's discursive varieties will be confined to texts that rapidly went through multiple editions and/or frequent, often immediate translations, and that are cited and discussed in later works studied here. These texts are the appropriate vehicles for my investigation because they articulate religious beliefs, scholarly concerns, and political imperatives in a discursive context and in a conceptual space that was accessible to a great number of people, learned as well as lay.[27] They provide historical, fictional, scientific, and didactic structures for the articulation of what was often strange, new, and therefore feared.

This period witnessed the publication of some of the most famous documents reflecting both the diversity and the conceptual and intellectual vigor of the occult sciences. Giovanni Pico della Mirandola's hymn to the godliness of man, the *Oration on the Dignity of Man* (1484), was published three quarters of a century after the prose *Mélusine* (1393) and only a few years before the publication—sanctioned but not supervised by the Holy See—of the *Malleus Maleficarum* (1486). I have chosen Jean d'Arras's prose history, *Mélusine,* the tale about a fairy who, in spite of her magical nature, is not yet thought of as truly diabolical. This is the most comprehensive version of the tale; later French and German adaptations/translations reduce considerably its narrative and magical complexity.

In 1563 the Dutch physician Johann Weyer wrote *De praestigiis daemonum,* attempting to alter the direction of the magic/witchcraft controversy. He intended to move the discussion about women as witches away from the deadly equation magic/witchcraft/satanic pacts, which the *Malleus* had authoritatively established. Witchcraft, Weyer argued, was to be treated as a pathology rather than as satanic possession. Paracelsus's short tract on witches, *De sagis,* written decades before, during the mid-thirties, had explored the same theme but remained incomplete and without much of an echo. While it was clearly not

8   *Defining Dominion*

Weyer's intention, his defense of women accused of witchcraft turned the spotlight with renewed and deadly intensity on Kramer's *Malleus Maleficarum,* which—although not forgotten—had remained in the background during the religious and social strife that dominated the early and mid-century.[28] The *Malleus Maleficarum* will be identified as the text that precipitated a profound, albeit belated, change in the witch discussion, the clear turning point in the overwhelming gendering of the witch phenomenon. I will examine selected writings by Paracelsus, notably the *Philosophia sagax,* as well as tracts on witchcraft by Lancre, the *Tableau de l'inconstance des mauvais anges et demons* (1612).[29] The dispute between Weyer and Bodin carried out in the *De praestigiis daemonum* and the *Démonomanie des sorciers* will serve as an example of the intellectual, religious, and juridical antagonism that generated massive written commentaries and did much to bureaucratize and prolong the persecution of women as witches. Several editions and translations of Weyer's *De praestigiis daemonum* appeared in quick succession, causing considerable debate in scientific and juridical circles.[30] Bodin answered Weyer's call for the decriminalization of witchcraft by publishing the treatise *La démonomanie des sorciers* in 1580. A German translation/adaptation by Fischart, a German jurist as well as a writer and translator, from Strasbourg, followed immediately, in 1581. It extended Bodin's influence—prompting my use of this translation—into Germany, where the magistrates consulted the Fischart translation alongside the *Malleus Maleficarum* as law manuals during the witch trials at Rottenburg/Sonthofen (1586–87).[31]

Bodin's book on witchcraft, which recommends relentless and thorough prosecution and punishment of alleged witches, has puzzled modern readers because he is also known and well respected for his *Six Books on the Republic,* published in 1586. Modern scholars have been as generally uneasy about Fischart's enthusiastic and decidedly partisan translation/adaptation, finding it difficult to square his eagerness to hunt the witch with his apparent bent for the satirical, manifested in his translation/adaptation of François Rabelais's masterpiece *Gargantua and Pantagruel.*[32] Bodin's *Six Books* remains one of the most compelling articulations of the theory of the absolutist state. Scholars have been even more confounded by Bodin's composition—thirteen years after the *Démonomanie*—of the *Colloquium Heptaplomeres,* a libertine, even deist tract, which Bodin's contemporaries appeared to have read, copied, and circulated among themselves. This book on religious tolerance has been compared with Gotthold Lessing's play *Nathan der Weise* and was not published until the nineteenth century.[33] It seems that Bodin's involvement in the witchcraft discussions did not affect his religious skepticism, lending credence to my thesis that both discourses, far from being mutually exclusive, touched and influenced each other.[34]

In the course of my readings, I will have the opportunity to mark the influence of magical concepts on the perceptions and actions of the discoverers and conquerors of the New World. In the end, I mean to discuss the implication of the fact that the panic over the presence of satanic magic among women in certain areas coincided with the post-Reformation crises of religious diversity and dissidence. I will suggest that the relationship between the discourses of magic, religious dissent, and discovery contributed to a polyphony of discursive options that—toward the end of the sixteenth and early seventeenth centuries—determined who occupied society's center and who was forced to move to, or remain at, its margins. The division between those who stayed within orthodoxy and those who fell into heterodoxy will be reflected in the interplay of these three discourses. My assumptions are based on the premise that magical thought—although centuries old in its basic tenets about the relationship of magic to man and woman and to the universe—exerted a rich and varied influence on the culture of early modern Europe. Waxing and waning through the centuries and reaching its highest pitch in the public discussions, scientific expansion, and social panic between the years 1550 and 1670, magic does not conform to Michel Foucault's concept of the episteme as a new and epoch-making epistemology or to his concept of an archive, that is, a paradigm that transcends centuries and surfaces occasionally with disruptive force.[35] Significantly, magic is both of these concepts at once: a discourse of contemporary violence, fears, and marginalization in the context of a century-old cosmology and theology. Nor can magic be characterized by a sudden paradigm shift, as Thomas Kuhn defines changes in mentalities and epochs.[36] Its presence in Western European consciousness can best be understood in the context of Hans Blumenberg's theory of epochs, which pairs the evolution of scientific curiosity with the Copernican *Wende*,[37] or what Amos Funkenstein has called "a new approach to matters divine, a secular theology of sorts."[38] Against Kuhn's paradigmatic shift and its lack of continuity, Blumenberg argues that positions were changed within a conceptual framework that remained functionally intact. Blumenberg insists that partial epistemological changes not only are bearable but can also more readily be accepted as plausible. The epistemological change in the thinking about magic in the course of the sixteenth century conforms to Blumenberg's postulate.

The spiritual and linguistic crisis of the latter half of the sixteenth century, discernible in religious upheavals, persecutions, and geographic discoveries and conquests, led to a crisis in representation, to what Walter Haug terms "experimenting with the conditions that enable a narrative action to make meaning plausible as a category of social conceptual ideals."[39] The discourses of magic and witchcraft, religious dissidence, and discovery challenged our ability to imagine, to think, in politics, religious traditions, history, and language. They converged upon and contradicted each other, sometimes violently.

I will focus my attention on the epistemology of magic as an old and perennially new metaphor for knowing beyond knowledge. It will become clear that the sixteenth century did not progress from a magical to a more rational universe. Nor did the belief in magic necessarily predispose men toward the persecution of women only. New World natives were slaughtered regardless of their sex or age; dissidents, maligned or attacked by self-proclaimed champions of orthodoxy, no matter of which kind, were almost always men. Midelfort has found that the larger the trial, the more diverse the accused (*Witch Hunting in Southwestern Germany*, 195). In the later stages of the persecutions many of the witches were children.[40]

Still, due to the fear of heresy, magical knowledge and witchcraft were merged in juridical and theological *summae* that pronounced authoritatively on the religious, political, and social danger of satanic witchcraft, whose major perpetrators—on the whole—were women. When religious dissidence and dissimulation cast doubt over the most cherished spiritual certainties, and when the discoveries opened previously unknown spaces and it appeared that Satan had established his rule even there, an already existing administrative apparatus composed of secular and church authorities was set in motion that led within a very short time—not all at once but in less than a century—and with lethal inevitability to the largely gendered application of magical beliefs and the victimization of women. During the same time, licit, white magic remained by and large a male preoccupation, an intellectually privileged scientific exercise even among religious dissenters. Popular and/or black magic admitted mostly women to its practice. These were women who, near the end of the sixteenth century, found themselves persecuted by public opinion, by judicial procedures, and by practices of social control. By this very propulsion, moreover, they moved ever farther away from the authoritative protective discourse of learned orthodoxy.[41]

It is important to keep in mind that the great number of female victims cannot hide the fact that information about these women is also, as Joan Scott defined it, "necessarily information about men...denoting cultural construction of gender, which is a social category imposed on a sexed body."[42] Striving for ever greater insight into a realm of knowledge that was created by them in the first place, the men who wrote the texts at issue here also talk about themselves, give information not just about their relationship to history, law and order, and sexuality but also about their curiosities, anxieties, passions, and fears of the end of history, of the unfamiliar, of death. The aspects of life controlled by gendered dichotomies are deeply embedded in the ideological frameworks and social institutions of early modern Europe; they provide ways to encode and decode meaning and to predict and understand social interactions. The dichotomies of gender are also those of the Christian faith; they represent also the basic tenets of magic—good and evil, Adam and Eve, Eve and Mary, Christ and Satan. They are ultimately expressions of a single, gendered dichotomy: the flesh that is woman stands opposite the spirit that is man. The antagonism of *scientia magica* (the spirit) and satanic, black magic (the flesh) found its most virulent and violent expression in the institutionalized hatred and fear of women.[43]

My task is made difficult by the fact that at this time, specifically between 1550 and 1620, the marginal, where it concerned religious or magical issues, became a moving target. Determinations about who was in—orthodox in faith, licit in the practice of magic—and who was out—heterodox, illicit—depended increasingly on the individual's ability to shape and to participate in the language of a chosen and therefore privileged group. The fact that women, especially the old and the poor, represented a large and constant group at the margins, that they most often lacked the ability to distinguish the fine line separating licit from illicit, meant that more than anybody else they were susceptible to being pushed beyond society's protective orthodox boundaries. The precariousness of "woman's" place, the threat of exclusion brought about by an accusation of witchcraft, had as much to do with the social realities of the late sixteenth century as with women's inability to participate in the protective and sophisticated languages of power, that is, in the discourses of philosophy, theology, jurisprudence, and scientific magic. The dichotomy between the simplicity of the witchcraft definition/accusation and the circuity and sheer textual mass of the learned discussions and publications on the subject makes it clear that to survive in this society was to belong; and to belong meant having power and control over the insider's language. The ability to dissimulate, to practice what one did not believe, was yet another way to keep control.[44] The study and practice of licit magic was one way to exercise this power. As the peoples of Europe made ready to enforce religious, economic, social, and military dominance over the New World, magic provided a pivotal, for the natives frequently deadly, sign system by which to identify, prosecute, judge, and destroy difference. The alleged witch, the religious dissident, and the native in the New World shared the experience of being objects acted upon by those who presumed power over them. Those in power were, upon closer inspection, as much afraid of losing control as they were insistent upon dominating for the sake of the early modern notions of political order, social control, and religious orthodoxy.[45]

On the Nature of Magic

It is not the intention of the present study to rehearse the history and development of magic.[46] Such research has been accomplished by many scholars on whose expertise I drew while preparing this project. The following outline, however, is intended to provide an introduction to the magical concepts important to my thesis.

By magic, I refer to a sign system that, if accepted as having real and considered principles and powers, shares with religion the characteristic that it speaks to the common people and to the educated elite from the same assumptions but not with the same language. This dichotomy will be apparent when Mélusine's historiography of magical beings is compared with Paracelsus's magic anthropology, and when the witch tracts of Kramer, Weyer, Bodin, and Lancre are compared and contrasted with each other. Like religion, magic was accepted as a linguistic and ritual totality.[47] It presupposed the existence of a knowable, closed, and finite universe where all was not yet revealed but upon which the exceptional mortal, the magus, or the witch was permitted—or dared—to cast an occasional tantalizing glance. Whether popular practice or learned inquiry, magic had developed its own explanatory discourse, which affirmed—against all assertions to the contrary—that natural and demonic magic "were at opposite ends of the moral spectrum, but [that] they were epistemologically indistinguishable."[48] Magic was always associated with curiosity, either negatively or positively. In fact, throughout the early modern period, the praise or condemnation of the magical arts is a reliable measure by which to judge the writer's attitude about experimental science or exploration of the unknown. The secularization of the notion of *curiositas* had become singularly important for the secularization of culture—that is, for the waning of the power and influence of the magical worldview.[49]

As long as it remained in force, magical thought provided the illiterate with the mental resources to help cope with the world, while for the learned it opened avenues of comprehensive and universal inquiry. Examples of the former are presented in Carlo Ginzburg's research on the night-riding *benandanti* of the Italian Friul and in Gustav Henningsen's study of the "white women" of Sicily.[50] The voluminous publications of magi, such as the Picos, Agrippa, and Paracelsus, represent the stuff that fed the fascination of the literate public. Although the earth and the universe were always threatening and challenging, the learned lay public was convinced that they could be dominated and controlled with the understanding and the assistance of magical ritual and science.[51] Paracelsus knew, as did the majority of his contemporaries, that magical knowledge was a form of perpetually widening and deepening universal remembrance, a way of comprehending with increasing clarity what, prior to the moment of knowing, had been clouded by ignorance. This process was understood to be a continuous, God-willed unveiling of hidden wisdom.[52] To experience the world was to know God. For the discoverers and conquerors of the New World, this "theologizing" of experience served as a major impetus for undertaking dangerous voyages and as an explanation for their perseverance even in the face of grave mental and physical tribulations. The New World became the site for renewing the Divine Covenant; realms of magical experience hidden behind the vast sea were made visible and tangible.[53] And finally, it became yet another arena for acting out the religious confrontations and upheavals besetting the Old World.[54]

Magic also presupposes a belief in a fixed system of relationships and confidence in the efficacy of their functioning. Awareness and use of magic depended on the practitioner's linguistic competence and on the understanding that complex magical codes governed and influenced universal energies and potential behavior.[55] Situated in a realm beyond the quotidian, although always remaining part of it, magic created the sense of a superior reality, of an existence beyond the reality that ruled the everyday. Magical discourse could mark the ascendancy of a dynasty or its demise; it had the power to open the door to a knowledge never dreamed of and unimagined. Participation in this superior reality led to perpetual conflicts regarding individuals' access to its privileges. The educated and aristocratic elite's attempts to guard against admission to its practice always ran counter to its ability to exclude the ignorant, especially and most importantly women, who were judged to be beyond reason's control.[56]

Magic is always, even etymologically, associated with *Macht* ("power"); it shares with mysticism the wish to gain access to superhuman realms of knowledge and experience. It differs from the mystical experience in one important aspect, however. Magic seeks control—over people, animals, the weather, the stars. Mysticism, on the other hand, places control into the hands of a higher power. Thus, while magic potentially seeks control in whatever form, it also epitomizes a power perpetually at risk, a power spinning out of control.[57] Consequently, injunctions against the unauthorized use of, or even acquaintance with, magic and the apologia for the correct and licit use of this science constituted a topos in scholarly writings throughout the Middle Ages and the early modern period.[58] The inherent contradiction between the desire to communicate and the simultaneous need to keep secrets—a contradiction that has always characterized the practice of the magical sciences—led to the development of artificial languages, the construction of codes, the founding of secret societies, and the relentless pursuit of those believed to be in the possession of such secrets, namely, people accused of being witches.[59] In the hands of these alleged witches, magic was believed to have changed from the divine science into a "semantics of deceit," a "rhetoric of seduction."[60]

Early modern intellectuals viewed language in terms of what today we would describe as a performative system that accomplishes social acts. In the case of magic, this system consisted of signs that were part of a secret language called forth from the hidden source of knowledge. Whoever was familiar with its letters, its numbers, and its cosmological associations could initiate contact with God or with Satan.[61] Magical discourse—whether in the form of numbers, language, or ritual—was a unifying symbol for the indulgence of the senses and the enjoyment of worldly beauty, a sign of the quest for wealth and political power, for the attainment of infinite knowledge. It could lead the virtuous, ceaselessly searching, and solitary magus to the very height of divine illumination. And it could pit the discourse of an irrational and uncontrollable femininity against the rational discourse of masculinity.[62] The texts to be examined here bear signs of each of these categories.

In her comprehensive study *The Rise of Magic in Early Medieval Europe* (1991), Valerie Flint shows that much of European magical knowledge and practice was the result of a multireligious and multicultural symbiosis. It was sanctioned by the church during the early years of the Christianization of Europe in support of efforts to consolidate spiritual and temporal power. Flint finds supporting evidence for this synchretism in legal, doctrinal, literary, and scientific sources, in saints' lives, as well as in schoolbooks, glosses, and in miracle books of late antiquity and the early Middle Ages. Flint confirms that all elements in the early modern relationship to magic, be they self-consciously scientific and philosophical or stridently heretical—those that strike the modern reader as so typical for the Renaissance—were already present in much earlier texts. She finds that accusations of malevolent magic and witchcraft were then, as later, "clustered in the areas of ambiguous social relations."[63] Her examples show that several hundred years later, during early modern judicial proceedings, secular laws were often more severely punitive than church sanctions.[64] Flint hypothesizes that the apparent similarity in approaches to magic and witchcraft in two so dissimilar periods was the result of ecclesiastic need: the not yet securely established *ecclesia* was forced to rely on the religious constraints and ordering structures enforced by local priests and shamans so that its own organization might gather strength in the safety of their protection. The necessity of not squandering its strength in pointless and potentially devastating conflicts with local belief systems was more compelling, in the judgment of the young church, than was its need to erase unorthodox practices and effect immediate and total conversion. Still, the church remained understandably wary of newly Christianized chieftains whose willful and overly assertive exercise of power they could not let pass entirely unchecked, lest this power threaten the church's own religious and political agenda. The woman who allegedly ate human flesh and the woman who, because of her "masculine behavior," ruled over her husband were cause for grave concern and subject to punishment, much as they were to be in the *Malleus Maleficarum*. However, the measures sanctioning such behavior were—in comparison with later tactics—astonishingly lenient.[65] The hour of the *Malleus* had clearly not yet arrived, even if Bishop Hincmar was convinced that witches were prevalent during his time and that most of them were women.[66] Flint shows that during the early years of Christianity, much transfer of magical practices from one belief system into another took place, especially in the area of healing practices. Love magic, inducement of abortions, and conjuring of the dead were—not surprisingly—rigorously and vigorously opposed, even though in most cases this opposition did not lead the accused to the stake.

The translation of magical practices from biblical, patristic sources—as well as from pre- and non-Christian ones—into the context of early medieval Christian mentalities was successful primarily because theology, cosmology, and the sciences agreed on the nature and construction of the cosmos, man's and woman's place in it, and on the ambiguity implicit in exercising control over both.[67] Living in and being part of the universe, the macrocosm, humanity, as the microcosm, reflected all its constituent parts within themselves: the bond between human psychology, Christian truths, and cosmic order was the major theme of the religious and philosophical debates of late antiquity and early Christianity. To it was added much Egyptian, Jewish, and Near and Middle Eastern esoteric thought in the guise of ancient, pre-Mosaic, proto-Christian, secret religions: the *prisca theologia*.[68] The association of universal order with magical words and numbers and, conversely, the conviction that improper and illicit use of magical discourse signaled transgression and disorder made magical practices at all times a privilege, as much feared as sought after.[69] Magical powers could—with the help of divine sanction or satanic subterfuge—change states of being, as was the fate of the fairy Mélusine de Lusignan. Similarly, when women flew through the night air to join their Dark Master at the sabbath, their bodies seemed to stay behind in the conjugal bed. Magical utterances and ritual could establish relationships between things and powers, as happened in alchemical practice; between people, as in love or hate magic; and between humans and spirits, as when succubi or incubi tormented mortal men or women.

Arcane knowledge divided the world into insiders and outsiders. Outsiders always legitimate insiders; keeping others out identifies and privileges those who remain in what presumably is the circle of entitlement and power. The magus rejected, even persecuted, the witch in an effort to create a space in which he could practice the hidden arts unencumbered. A wise and cunning woman might remain feared but unchallenged for a time. If the environment shifted, that is, if there occurred an unexpected death, an illness, a bad harvest, or a quarrel, her status could change precipitously. To counteract her alleged persecution of neighbors and friends, the jurists and theologians persecuted her.[70] They tried to extract from her hidden knowledge about satanic experiences.

To accept magic as a system of transcendence as well as of immanence meant that all people, educated or illiterate, shared the understanding of the efficacy of its signs, its semiotics. This semiotics was larger than the searching individual. The witch trials and the legal and medical tracts that regulated their proceedings confirmed yet simultaneously condemned the signifying power of magic. The Spanish inquisitor Alonso de Salazar Frías and Lancre represent such a dichotomous reaction to the witch problematic. During the first decades of the seventeenth century, both men participated in the Basque witch hunts at the Spanish and French sides of the border. The proceedings led the increasingly skeptical Salazar to formulate rules that effectively reduced the burning of women as witches in Spain. On the other hand, Lancre, looking at the same kind of "evidence," became more and more convinced of the increasing danger of the witch infestation, not only in the Basque region but in all of France.[71]

The texts to be considered in this study distinguish carefully between intellectual magic and common superstition. As will be seen in the jurists' tracts on witchcraft and in the great synthesizing efforts of such scholars of magic as Paracelsus, language dealing with the magical arts was clearly gendered: masculine and licit signified the divine word; feminine and illicit referred to the satanic utterance. Where the boundaries between licit and illicit magic appeared blurred, as in the case of the writings of the century's great magicians, anxiety over such ambiguities can be heard in the very language employed, language that situated magic firmly between the poles of self-confident scientific and religious pronouncements and fervent apology.

Methodology

To comprehend the significance of magic in the cultural discourse of the sixteenth century, one has to accept the presence of knowledge about magic among the people at all levels of society. This knowledge reflected not only familiarity with the practice of magic but also caution, fear, and curiosity toward such practice.[72] The universal presence of magical thought in early modern European culture can be best understood in terms of the discursive context that George Lakoff calls *experiential realism*. Magical thought could dominate the later Middle Ages and early modern period so decisively because it assembled theology, science, philosophy, cosmology, folk wisdom, and witchcraft in its purview. This assemblage of disciplines and realms of knowledge resulted in a comprehensive cultural semiotics, a nexus of discourses that promised its practitioners control as well as transcendence. According to Lakoff, experiential realism is characterized by four assumptions: a commitment to the existence of the real world; a recognition that reality places constraints on concepts; a conception of truth that goes beyond the internal coherence of an idea; and a commitment to the existence of a stable knowledge of this world and of the universe.[73] Experiential realism determines the ways in which the mind forms the categories and the classifications that help to articulate, organize, name, and accept as true an individual's interactions with society. It represents the totality of our beliefs. This concept has little to do with inalterable precepts of philosophical, scientific, or even theological doctrine. Rather it demarcates when and why mental constructs such as magical practices and witchcraft or religious dissidence and unbelief are thought to be true and accessible to certain people under certain very specific conditions; it indicates when these constructs lose their power and are replaced by others.

During the early modern period, magical beliefs were intelligible to the majority of people, even though different groups coming from varied educational and social backgrounds did differ in their understanding of its precepts. Magic was neither a "false physics" nor the faulty observation of nature.[74] Discussing the history of mentalities as practiced by French historians—Robert Muchembled, Jean Delumeau, and Robert Mandrou among them—Stuart Clark turns to Ludwig Wittgenstein's "On Certainty" to help explain the problem of magical phenomena from a cultural vantage point. Clark insists that the "ritual" and "real" are not separable categories of experience in early modern culture. Therefore, rituals were practiced (and tracts written) in the context of intellectually coherent cosmological assumptions about agency and causation and in the expectation of real, not spurious, efficacy.[75] The centrality of early modern cultural semiotics, the status of the comprehending and participating subject, and the coincidence of language and social order provide the basis for Lakoff's experiential realism as they do for

R. Howard Bloch's epistemologically based assumptions about the reality of magic.[76] How practitioners in a variety of cultures and historical periods approach magic is first and foremost a discursive decision, where discourse is understood to be the collection of words, cultural facts, and linguistic elements beyond the level of words—but not existing independently—that converge and intersect. According to Wolfgang Neuber's study on the discourses of early modern travel literature, these are modes of representation influenced ("geprägt") by older linguistic models that the new discourse cannot leave behind, even when—indeed, especially when—they are employed to describe the totally unprecedented, the heretofore unknown.[77] The way that the early modern observer describes an unfamiliar reality—a new people, a magical practice, or an unorthodox belief—is prefigured in the increasingly complex discourse, which must articulate layers of cultural, scientific, and theological difference, dissidence, and social change.[78]

In this context, experiential realism becomes an appropriate tool for investigating magic's discursive structure and epistemological potential, a form of criticism that affords access to perceptions of the real, of history and memory, and of narrative forms. The concept of experiential realism accommodates the old within the context of naming the new; it thus makes experience—intellectual, social, sexual, and religious—the foundation for conceiving what can be acknowledged as real and constructing its articulation. Examining the rhetorical structures of travel discourse, Neuber reformulates Eugene Vance's speculation that the relationship between magic and rhetoric is quite direct. Vance finds this connection to be the natural consequence of a mental attitude that assumes the power of human beings to impose control on cosmic forces by means of either linguistic or symbolic instruments. This power or language resides in the strength of persuasion, by which man is able—on account of his exulted position in the universe—to exert control over the most enigmatic and mysterious forces of nature and the cosmos.[79]

The early modern obsession with the comprehension and systematization of what was known of witches, their movements, and their powers has much in common with the evolution of early modern cosmography in the wake of the subjugation of the Americas and Africa. In both cases, practitioners and theoreticians struggled to harmonize reports by those who experienced phenomena (navigators and conquerors; witches at the sabbath) with what had been transmitted in ancient texts; to reconcile the seeing and "writing" eye with the reading eye; and to submit tradition to experience and produce an understanding of what can be accepted as true.[80]

Magical discourse and cosmographical discourse, not unlike Neuber's rhetoric or Vance's oratory, are marked by conceptual and structural stasis as well as continuing intellectual evolution. This fact underlies the repeated assertions that—as far as the basic ingredients of magical beliefs are concerned—nothing much new was added between antiquity and the early modern period. What eventually culminated in the witch hunts was more the result of new and destructive ways of rearranging and associating available knowledge than the discovery of new information.[81]

Beyond signifying the new within the old—the evolution of biblical and hermetic magic within early modern urban and rural culture—discursive conventions also denote restraint. Reviewing Neal Gilbert's reflections on Renaissance ideas of method, de Certeau concurred that it was characteristic for Renaissance thought to construct rules (of usage) rather than reveal laws.[82] These rules consist of linguistic, cognitive, and moral constraints imposed on the speaking subject.[83] As one looks at the discourses on witchcraft, such constraints appear curiously ineffective; they become judgments—more often than not, gender-specific ones—leveled with the fatal precision of juridical and theological authority against the subject who has been identified as a witch. Her "seductive Otherness" places her outside of the orthodox majority, which—holding the power of naming and rule making—also has the power to declare her, the New World native, or the religious dissenter to be marginal.[84]

Meaning, in magic as in all other intellectual and linguistic contexts, is created through choices. The learned magus or the witch chose to attain information, gain power, inflict damage, or simply impress cohorts. Frequently these choices were responses to mental and intellectual crises. The witch craze, the reforming movements, and the discoveries are three such cases in point, as is the establishment of a founding legend for an aristocratic family. Considered in this way, the variety of magical discourses serves as a significant register for cultural transformations because magical inquiries and practices combine to form a system of "principieller Denkbarkeit" (things that can, in principle, be thought).[85] Magic as a set of discursive options simultaneously transgressed and confirmed general patterns of social and moral control. That is, it symbolized at once all forms of social deviance and revolt, all striving for excellence and divine favor, as well as the systematic imposition of a bureaucratic control whose thoroughness and brutality has been justly seen as an avatar of totalitarian regimes in later centuries.

The experiential reality of magic determined its creative as well as its destructive potential in the minds of real and imagined practitioners. Magic bound together history and myth, encouraged bold scientific speculation, and brought about changes in the practice of physical and mental health. Finally, the ability to write and/or to read notwithstanding, magic inscribed the body with as yet another discourse to be deciphered by the gaze of inquisitors and magistrates, who searched it for signs of yet another truth, that of satanic association. In the end, because of the inability to separate scientific magic from satanism, magic bore within its cognitive structures the very seeds that brought about its eventual marginalization and consequent dismissal as an authoritative scientific discourse. It had summoned the powers of great masculine minds to devise a system of judicial inquiry and political control that, more than anything else, indicated the great importance that magic and witchcraft had assumed in the minds of early modern men and women. Significantly, the belief in witches subsided, and their destruction ceased at the same time that magic lost its authority in the minds of its learned practitioners. Equally significantly, the belief in witches wound down as the conviction diminished that a reliable and just system of laws could be devised to ajudicate cases of witchcraft, and as accusations of libertinism and atheism lost much of their marginalizing threat.[86]

2

Magic and the Myth of Transgression: *Mélusine de Lusignan* by Jean d'Arras (1393)

Magic accompanies the history of the noble house of Lusignan from the outset. Its dynastic catalyst comes from several meetings between women with more than natural powers and men to whom these women offer assistance during periods of extreme personal crisis. The men accept the women's offers, thereby shifting the established ordering structures of the family and of the text that tells their story. Among the mysterious meetings of various couples, Mélusine de Lusignan's meeting with her future husband, Remond, nephew of the conte de Poitiers, bears the farthest-reaching dynastic and narrative consequences. However, it is by no means the only one affecting the tale of this exceptional family. Soon it becomes clear that at stake in the meeting are profound alterations in the power relations among the nobility of the duchy of Poitiers, alterations that benefit Mélusine, Remond, and, later, their progeny.

A variant of the tale of Amor and Psyche, *Mélusine* presents the ancient motif of a supernatural woman meeting a mortal man. The plot is quickly summarized. Mélusine's mother, Presine, lost her husband, Elinas, after he had transgressed the interdict that she had imposed before their marriage. In due time, Mélusine marries Remond. She, too, imposes an interdict before assenting to the union; Remond must promise never to seek out his wife's company on Saturdays, nor to learn her whereabouts on that day. He agrees, in part because he falls under the spell of Mélusine's beauty and courtliness, but also because he is despondent over having inadvertently killed his lord and uncle, the conte de Poitiers, in a boar-hunting accident.

As Mélusine promised the inconsolable Remond, wealth and happiness are soon theirs: much land, many castles and towns, and eight male children—most of them born with a disfiguring physical mark—will ensure the survival of the dynasty. The family idyll ends abruptly when Remond is provoked into an insanely jealous rage after his brother, the conte de Foretz, intimates that Mélusine might be seeing a lover during her Saturday absences. Remond breaks his promise and goes in search of his wife. He finds her—half fish (in other versions, half snake or dragon), half woman—in the bath she built for her Saturday retreat. Remond immediately regrets his deed, yet he conceals his knowledge from his wife. Aware of his trespass, Mélusine does not make him answer for it until one of their sons, Gieffroy au grant dent, kills his brother the monk Fromond in a fit of anger. Gieffroy burns the Mallieres monastery, murdering all its inhabitants. Hearing about this crime, Remond publicly accuses Mélusine, claiming that she bears responsibility for Gieffroy's action because of her "witch" nature. Deeply hurt, Mélusine discloses that she must leave the disconsolate Remond. She disappears into the world of the spirits after recounting her story in the presence of the court. Now Remond understands that in her marriage to a mortal man, Mélusine had sought forgiveness of her own sin: the murder of her father, Elinas. Had she died in a Christian marriage, she would have gained an immortal soul, the guarantee that her sin has been forgiven. Now the couple must separate. But Mélusine predicts that the house of Lusignan will live on in Mélusine and Remond's sons and their progeny.

The story of Mélusine was immensely popular among early modern readers. Jean d'Arras's version (1393), under discussion here, was followed by a French verse adaptation (1400). The Bernese nobleman Thüring von Ringoltingen produced the often copied popular German prose translation of the verse-*Mélusine* by Couldrette for the margrave Rudolf of Hochberg, the Duke of Neuchâtel, in 1445. It is now believed that both the Jean D'Arras and Coudrette texts go back to an earlier source.[1] From her initial appearance in late medieval literature and through the twentieth century, Mélusine has been a popular heroine of history and fiction and has received a great variety of scholarly attention. Many early modern writers mention her tale, a fact that prompted me to examine this text.[2]

Accompanied by portents and strange events—seemingly chance meetings at a magical fountain in the woods, astrological signs, an accidental murder, interdicts, and secret sources of wealth—the lives of the protagonists Mélusine and Remond, their parents, and their progeny are surrounded by an aura of the exceptional, the magical. This aura lends to events of the story—the encounters in the solitude of the woods, the ensuing marriages, and their lives together—a feeling of precariousness and even dread, an impression sustained by the narrator's frequent explanatory and warning asides.

Jean d'Arras wants to tell a true history ("vrayes histoire"). In the service of Jean, duc de Berry, he reconstructs a family history that also becomes the history of several exceptional women—of Mélusine; of her sisters, Mélior and Palestine; of their mother, Presine; and of the decidedly unmagical Dame de la Val Bruiant.[3] This founding myth tells a story about marriage, courage and valor, betrayal, and salvation lost. Moreover, it tells of magical powers, secrets, and human transgressions that mark the women's fateful relationships to men, be they father, husband, or son.

Transgressio means to go beyond, to trespass, to sin; in Latin it appears as *violatio, peccatum, delictum*.[4] Transgression presumes limits. In one of his early articles, Foucault formulated a definition to which he returned in much of his later work: limits and transgressions depend on each other in the totality of their existence.[5] Transgression was programmed into the Christian creation myth from the beginning: the first human act of transgression—the eating of the apple from the Tree of Knowledge—had been preceded by Lucifer's proud and fateful transgressive gesture of rebellion against God. Hubris had tempted Lucifer to think himself as powerful as God. Hurled from the vaults of heaven in a gesture of divine avenging violence, he and his minions fell to the farthest corner of the cosmos, into hell, whereupon God filled the empty space with his favored creation, humankind. From the start, this indirect yet undeniable proximity to the rebellious Lucifer predisposed humankind to disobedience toward God.[6] Positioned as universal mediators, man and woman are of the earth yet instructed to rule over it. Made in God's image, they discover in their existential ambiguity the seed of their disobedience.[7] The Fall and subsequent expulsion from paradise are as much signs of election as of satanic seduction: Christ died on the cross to redeem God's creature.

A strong exegetical and apocryphal tradition suggests that the Fall stands for sexual desire, which brought sin into paradise.[8] It is said that Adam and Eve saw their nakedness and covered themselves with leaves; their punishment for eating from the Tree of Knowledge was hard work, sexual desire, the curse of painful childbirth, and grim death.[9] Human forfeiture of paradise and the subsequent procreative burden of lust and pain brought death into the lives of the first parents. With it came also the wish to conquer death through knowledge, that is, to return to God through faith and/or the practice of divine magic.

This attempt to atone for transgressions through faith and with the help of magical knowledge governs much of the fate of Mélusine and her family. The women's magical nature does not violate Jean d'Arras' promise to tell a "true story." Its veracity is assured by family history and by the castles, churches, and monasteries erected by Mélusine and her sons, all still there to be admired by d'Arras's and Ringoltingen's compatriots. Jean d'Arras tells an extraordinary story in which the natural and the supernatural join to form a narrative of love and loss, human death and un-death in the never-never land of the spirits who inhabit the space between the moon and the earth. This tale of human action and failing, of supernatural signs and events, establishes historical meanings and legitimates the future.[10]

Linking magic with transgression in the history of a noble family constructs two levels of narration: the verisimilar and the true or real.[11] Together these discourses form the experiential realism of this dynastic myth. Integrated into a narrative about events believed to have taken place, myth becomes history, which, in turn, affects dynastic identity. As the result of this transmutation, the experiential realism of the narrative becomes politically, socially, and intellectually acceptable to its culture. It not only defines and sets the standards of language and behavior, but it determines as well when individual or communal transgressions can be absorbed into the prevailing system of sanctioned activity, or when they prompt the expulsion of the offender. In other words, the experiential realism of a given culture determines whether violations of the established order become acceptable behavior or—in cases where such adaptation is not an option—whether they be punished.[12] Adding to the cultural poetics of neo-historicists and expanding on Haug's formal and structural narrativity, experiential realism emphasizes the influence that culturally specific mental categories—magic being one—exert on people's notion of reality.[13] To appreciate this difference is to understand that the Lusignan history is legitimated by its prehistory; its virtual reality is affected by the magical nature of the women characters, whose actions alter the history of the family. The later experience—that is, the historical role of this noble house—validates the myth retroactively: reality fashions myth.

The symbiosis of magic and history functions so effectively in this text because of the energizing effects that magical forces exert on people and their actions. These forces dominate Jean d'Arras's world. In his view, the cosmos is a closed universe formed of the small world, humankind, and the large world, the whole of creation, filled with extraordinary events and actions. God's works are wonderful, and much is possible in his world. Thus Jean d'Arras and earlier commentators of this tale are not the least bit troubled to encounter a woman who as lover, wife, and mother bestows exceptional gifts on those closest to her. Extraordinary, even magical knowledge and powers, have their place in this cosmos; they influence significantly medieval and early modern anthropology.[14] Woman plays her role as much in nature as in theology, myth, and history. However, there are limits. Stories of Mélusine and women like her also show that it is unacceptable for such creatures to govern, unchecked by males, over their realm and their people. Nor can they exert power and rule over men indefinitely; limits are enforced by interdicts that—even though they are imposed on men—in the end serve to control the actions of the very women who utter the interdicts. Although magical forces empower women to accomplish acts that amaze, frighten, or anger mortal males, they also confine them in an invisible prison constructed by the everpresent threat of discovery and betrayal. In this, as in other respects, such women do not differ much from other creatures that share their world but whose substance differs from theirs. These are the "monsters," that is, the giants, ghosts, and elemental spirits that inhabit the sublunary sphere. Small wonder that at a later stage of the tale's evolution, Mélusine is assigned to the category of "devilish succubus," as we read in one of Martin Luther's *Tischreden*.[15]

Presine and her three daughters, Mélusine, Mélior, and Palestine, bear the burden of transgressions not initiated by them but whose origin is lost in the dawn of time. Their need for redemption by mortal men introduces them as actors into time and history, a history that must repeatedly and inevitably disappoint them.[16] Remond's verbal aggression[17]—his accusation that Mélusine might be consorting with demons, that she might owe her talents to satanic magic—and her inability to defend herself against this assault by breaking out of the interdict's confinement make it impossible for her to act in her own interest without first having to solicit male assistance. Mélusine's sovereignty extends to all that she oversees, yet not to herself. Her first and only expression of affirmative but uncontrolled action—her revenge for her father's broken promise to her mother, Presine—condemns her to a space from which she can only be redeemed by entering into marriage with a mortal man.

She will depend for her deliverance on a husband whose ignorance of this fact makes him as vulnerable as she to the vagaries of fortune. She must suffer knowingly the betrayal of her unsuspecting husband, after which she must abandon her hope for salvation until the end of time.

The ambiguity of the Mélusinian moment, this amalgam of history and magic, can be divided into three narrative elements that overlap, interconnect, and modify the interpretation: the view of the world that legitimates the action of all participants; the conflict of loyalty, such as Remond might feel toward his brother and/or wife, and how such conflict affects the compulsion to act; and, finally, the effects of both of these elements on the narrative's concepts of truth and narrative coherence. Taken together, these discursive traits authenticate the narrative's structural intertwining of magic and history; they form its experiential realism.

At the beginning the narrator insists that his chronicle takes place in the real world familiar to his patron and his readers. The paratactic narrative structure of the prose text leads the reader directly through the action, whose veracity is scientifically and theologically confirmed by the authority of Aristotle and the Apostle Paul:

> La creature de Dieu raisonnable doit entendre, selon que dit Aristote, que des choses invisibles, selon la distinction des choses qu'il a faictes ça jus, et que par leur presence de leur estre et nature le certifie, si comme saint Pol le dit en l'epistre aux Rommains, que les choses qu'il a faictes seront veues et sceues par la creature du monde. (2)[18]

The factors motivating the action and the narrative impetus have a logical and—within the medieval and early modern worldview—acceptable order. The proximity of quotidian reality and the magical, the wondrous, does not diminish the veracity of the tale for the narrator and/or the reader. The narrator's repeated exclamations about future calamities heighten the narrative tension without denying or disputing the efficacy of magic in his narrative universe. When Remond meets a beautiful stranger at a fountain in the woods, the reader knows that it is Mélusine, whose father had also been mesmerized by the angelic voice of a beautiful woman at a mysterious fountain in the woods.[19] The doubling of this motif heightens the story's tension and deepens its mystery. At the first fateful meeting, Presine had agreed to become Elinas's second wife, provided that he promise never to seek her out in childbirth. Quite in passing, the name of Mataquas, a son from Elinas's first marriage, is mentioned: "qui estoit filz du roy Elinas, [et] la haioit moult" [who was the son of King Elinas and who hated her much] (9). This casual but foreboding introduction belies the important narrative impetus centered on this son. He will do nothing less than plot the destruction of the second marriage in an effort to secure his inheritance. At the time of Presine's lying-in, Mataquas exploits his father's joyful impatience. Announcing the birth of three girls, he urges his father to join his wife in her chamber:

> Il s'en vint devers le roy son pere et lui dit: Ma dame la royne Presine, vostre femme, vous a apporté les trois plus belles filles qui oncques feussent veues. Sire, venez les veoir. (9)[20]

Elinas rushes to Presine's bedside, only to find that he has lost her forever. He has transgressed the interdict that Presine had made the precondition of their marriage.

It is impossible to determine with any certainty what kind of taboo is contained in the interdict that Elinas has broken. One can only assume that it is sexual. Though an interpretation of the king's penetration of the chamber as rape is tempting, it is difficult on the basis of the textual evidence.[21] Still, support for this claim might be found in the underlying theme of sexual transgression and in the fact that the interdicts invoked against Presine's daughters reflect comparable sexual ambiguities.[22]

Immediately following Elinas's trespass, Presine takes her daughters and leaves the court to raise them at the home of her sister, Morgana, La Dame de l'Isle Perdue, King Arthur's sister, "pour ce que nulz homs, tant y eust esté de foiz, n'y sauroit rassegner, fors par aventure" [in order that no man ever would find her, except by chance] (10). Fifteen years later, viewing their patrimony from the top of a high mountain, Presine reveals Elinas's betrayal to her daughters:

> Filles, veez vous la le pays ou vous fustes neez et ou vous eussiez eu vostre partie, ne feust la fausseté de vostre pere, qui vous et moy a mis en grant misere sans fin jusques au jour du Hault Juge, qui punira les maulx et essaucera les biens. (11)[23]

Mélusine, who is described as being the oldest of the three, suggests to her sisters that they do what their mother had not done—that they avenge their father's treachery in their mother's place. She does not hesitate to do what—in the context of her noble self-image—is the only right thing to do: she counsels revenge. Mélusine's quick anger is prompted as much by her father's transgression, now many years past, as by her painful realization that she and her sisters have lost the ease and the honor of court life [grant aise et grant honnour] (11). Her reaction fits the family pattern of male behavior: her father, Elinas; her father-in-law, Hervy de Leon; her husband, Remond; her son Gieffroy; and finally her grandson Guion d'Armenie all suffer the consequences of uncontrolled rage. Remond loses his natural reason [raison naturelle] in a fit of rage at the news of Gieffroy's fratricide; in this moment of intense anger and parental suffering, he fails to control his language. He cannot help but cry out the truth as he sees it: that his son's terrible temper—and by implication, Mélusine's character—have demonic attributes: "Or est [Fromond] destruit par l'art demoniacle, car tous ceulx qui sont forcennez de yre sont ou commandement des princes d'enfer" [Now [Fromond] has been destroyed by demonic force, for all those who are overcome by anger are at the bidding of the princes of hell] (255).

Surveying Elinas's realm from afar a generation before her daughter's misfortune, Presine sets in motion the events that will affect Mélusine's fate. Fifteen years after Presine's flight to Avalon, she explains that she had denied herself vengeance for Elinas's trespass because she still loved him. More importantly, had Elinas lived to a peaceful end, he would have passed on to his daughters his human nature [nature humaine]: he could have given them a soul.[24] An extraordinary irony lies at the heart of the punishments that Presine imposes on her daughters: these righteous, impatient, quick-tempered, vengeful young women, who are guilty of the most violent and socially destructive transgression—patricide—are condemned to wait patiently for men who, ignorant of their roles in this salvific drama, must release them from their curse. Mélusine must live her life in fear that her husband might breach his promise; Mélior, la Dame de l'Esprevier, must await deliverance by a man of her lineage; and Palestine, locked away in a mountain, must guard her father's treasure until her knight arrives. Only then will this treasure be freed to finance the reconquest of the Holy Land, the ultimate gesture of redemption.[25]

According to Presine's command, Mélusine's retribution is the most harsh: "Tu, Melusigne, qui es l'aisnee et celle qui deusses estre la plus congnoissans . . . je te donne le don que tu seras tous les samedis serpente de nombril en aval" [You, Mélusine, who are the oldest and the one who should have been the most discerning... I am bestowing on you the gift that, on Saturdays, you will be a serpent from the navel downwards] (12–13). Mélusine understands the severity of the curse. Under the weight of its burden, she changes; henceforth she will play the role of the wise, active heroine of her family history.[26]

During Remond's first encounter with Mélusine at the fountain, he meets a very different woman from the one who had sinned so terribly. Remond had just killed his uncle, Conte Aimery, in a fateful hunting accident. The count was an extraordinary man, a wise ruler, a passionate hunter, learned in the arts, and especially well versed in astronomy:

> ... contes Aimery fu un tres vaillans homs, et qui ama toutes noblesces et fu ly plus saiges d'astronomie qui feust a son temps ne depuis Aristote. Car, si comme dit l'ystoire, par ce temps nulz n'osoit faire apprendre ses enfans nul des vij. ars.... Et pour lors estoient les sciences chier tenues et prisiees plus qu'elles ne sont ores. (16)[27]

Just before his demise, Aimery—not knowing that he was speaking about himself—predicted the death of a nobleman at the hands of one of his vassals. Aimery's interpretation of a strange apparition in the night sky momentarily becomes reality. In an effort to defend his uncle against an onrushing boar, Remond picks up the spear that had fallen from the count's hand and points it toward the animal. Sliding off the boar's hide, the spear strikes the count in the navel [par my le nombril], killing him instantly. Realizing his misfortune, Remond all but loses his mind; numbed by his pain and guilt, he rides through the woods, not knowing where he is, or what time it might be. When he comes upon the fountain, he is startled by what seems to be an apparition that acts and sounds like a perfectly courtly woman. She addresses him by his name; she comforts and counsels him. He in turn accepts her counsel as well as her offer of marriage. Her beauty and his desperate situation compel him to agree at once to all that she proposes.

Mélusine's loveliness, her unexpected appearance, the strangeness of her court, and her magical knowledge mark her as extraordinary in every respect. But in spite of her apparent gifts, it becomes clear that she, too, has her limitations: she must confine her operations to fit within the feudal system of justice and order.

Her magical advice—"quant il le vous aura accordé [to grant Remond a favor for faithful service], si lui demandez autant de place en ceste roche et en ce desrubant comment un cuir de cerf pourra enclourre..." (31)[28]—assures quick land gain.

She also instructs Remond to ask the new, young conte de Poitiers for a letter and seal to ensure for future generations the possessions of land that Remond acquired in such a strange manner: "...et de ce prennez bonnes lettres et bonne chartre seellee du grant seel de la dicte conté et des seaulx des pers du dit païs" (31).[29] Mélusine can scheme and plan, but she cannot assure the prosperity of her family without recourse to the legal procedures of the feudal order, to the signs and rituals that make contractual agreements binding for all time. Magical powers can create historical realities, but these realities lack legitimation if they fail to find their place within human ordering structures.

In the world of this tale, the male protagonists have two clear modes of action available to them. If they are guilty of transgressions and show remorse, forgiveness will be granted—a very simple application of Christ's promise to his people. This is the pattern followed by the males of the house of Lusignan, most notably Remond and Gieffroy. The second model presents a less charitable and more archaically legal solution: transgression leads to prosecution in the form of a public pronouncement of judgment that is immediately executed. The punishment may even take the form of an immediate death sentence, as in the case of the treacherous vassals at the court of the king of Bretagne. The vassals had conspired against Remond's father, Hervy, and driven him into exile. A generation later Remond comes to demand and is granted justice.

Almost all male members of the Lusignan family—Hervy, Remond, Gieffroy—commit a grave sin: they murder in a fit of rage. But they also, almost instantly, regret their actions, repent, and seek forgiveness. Outsiders to this group—Hervy's enemies at the court of the king of Bretagne, the giants whom Gieffroy slays, the adversaries of Mélusine's sons—follow the second pattern of immediate, severe punishment. The economy of Christian salvation works perfectly for the first group; a more archaic pattern of retributive justice settles the fate of the second.

The female protagonists, Presine and her daughters, suffer a different fate. A life-size marble likeness of Presine arrested in a state of perpetual watchfulness and vengeance stands guard over Elinas's tomb. In her arms Presine holds a stone tablet, on which is written the history of her husband's transgression and her daughters' revenge and subsequent punishment. As the keeper of the family history, Presine points to the future. Contrition and repentance promise salvation at the end of time. Historical progression passes to her grandson Gieffroy. Entering the tomb, he reads the story and learns about his mother's fate and about his uncle's deed. The tablet also reveals that if the preordained happens, the Lusignan progeny will regain the Holy Land (265, 266).

Mélusine does her best to make this destiny come true. Although her impatience and vengefulness have caused her father's death, she now guides Remond's destiny and that of her family with a sure and calm hand. She manages their legal affairs; she builds castles, monasteries, and churches; and she bears eight sons, all but two of whom are born with a disfiguring sign announcing to the world their exceptional parentage. Mélusine's building and birthing affirms that her family's history will evolve as the heavenly portent read by Aimery had predicted. She is an extremely active mother and ruler. With her husband's acquiescence—indeed, encouragement—she disregards the boundaries between male and female categories of action, even though the everpresent interdict and the dependence on Remond's unquestioning acceptance of her Saturday absences keep these boundaries forever before the mental eye of the audience.

The interdict plays two significant roles in the unfolding story: it symbolizes the taming of unfettered sexuality within marriage; and it appears as a signal of social control in a situation that might be considered threatening to the very order of society, namely, that a woman with magical powers has the ability and the political understanding to restructure feudal realities in the interest of her family's future and her own salvation. Ultimately, the interdict forces Remond to acknowledge and accept his wife as different, as occupying—at least on Saturdays—a space where he cannot follow or control her.

Mélusine's activities are not limited to the management of the economy and the politics of her realm. When she tells Remond to go and avenge his father, she also redresses injustice done to the previous generation. Following her advice, Remond demands recompense from the king of Bretagne for the loss of his father's patrimony. After killing the king's nephew, who had conspired against him, Hervy fled the realm, never to return and forsaking all his possessions. Shortly thereafter, he, too, found love and comfort in the company of a "belle dame" at a fountain in the woods:

> ... ilz s'entramerent, et lui dist la dame moult de confors. Et bastirent ou lieu et pays desert pluseurs fors, villes et habitacions firent, et fu le pays en assez brief temps assez peuplez.... Or advint qu'il ot entre

la dame et chevalier une riote... elle se party de lui soubdainement. (15)[30]

After the mysterious lady's disappearance, Hervy married the daughter of the conte de Foretz, whose land he inherited. Through his father's liaison with the lady, Remond's life had been touched by the presence of a magical woman and by a quarrel [une riote] even before his conception. While neither the identity of the lady nor the cause of the quarrel is ever disclosed, the meeting and separation lead to Hervy's marriage and to Remond's birth.

When Remond, at his wife's counsel, appears before the king of Bretagne and demands that justice be done to his late father and to him, he is every bit the valiant knight and the wise ruler. He proceeds cautiously and according to the law of the land, which he knows to be on his side. He does not demand vengeance but justice, "le bon droit, la bonne justice" (60). To assure his success, Mélusine gives him two rings upon his departure. The rings play no role in his action; they merely mark Remond's exemplary virtue and remind us of Mélusine's extraordinary powers.

In spite of their disfiguring marks, Mélusine and Remond's eight sons are distinguished by exceptional beauty and manliness. The marks that all of them bear, acknowledged by the admiring public as a sign of election, of special grace, represent—as the reader knows—Mélusine's magical nature, her satanic markings. Gieffroy's terrifying boar's tooth directly links Remond's unintentional killing of his uncle with the family's rise to power and wealth. While the other sons' birthmarks do not diminish their chivalric virtues, in the case of Horrible, the magical forces active in the mother's family are revealed in horrifying, satanic potentiality. He is born with three eyes—one in the middle of his forehead—and with a personality so murderous that he kills two of his nurses before he reaches the age of four (80).[31] The precarious balance between order and chaos, between magic that benefits and magic that has the power to destroy, becomes painfully and dangerously visible in this violent child.

Mélusine knows that this son's existence jeopardizes the family's future. When she prepares to leave her family forever, she orders that Horrible be killed by suffocation and given a Christian burial. A torment to himself and a danger to those around him, he nevertheless obtains from his mother the solace of church rites, something Mélusine sought in marriage and lost due to an outburst of male temper. As ruler and as mother, Mélusine shows the wisdom that empowers her to recommend an action that would be murder, were it not for the obvious threat that this child poses to the family's prosperity. The chaos lurking under the surface of familial order occasionally demands gestures of archaic justice if it is to be kept under control.

Mélusine's activism does not end here; in an extended instruction on knightly conduct—a thoughtful, pragmatic, wise *Ritterspiegel*—she confers on her sons her political and practical good sense, her piety, and her economic farsightedness. "Droit et raison" [law and reason] and "raison et justice" [reason and justice] mark her words to Guion and Uriens, the two sons first to leave Lusignan in search of adventure in the war against the Infidel. Remond expresses his great respect for his wife's wisdom when he grants their sons permission to leave: "Par foy, dame, se il vous semble que ce [seeking knightly glory in the service of a noble cause] soit chose qui soit bonne a faire, si en faictes a vostre voulenté" (83).[32] Mélusine's words to her sons take the form of an initiation speech, usually reserved for the father or a close and respected male relative. Though not a rhetorically formal address, her speech touches on all important points of knightly conduct. She elaborates the social, moral, ethical, political, and religious prescriptions to guide her sons into adulthood (84–87). Mélusine's advice constitutes a portrait of a noble ideal: she talks of the whole man, his obligations as a knight and as a governor, and practical wisdom and knightly ethos are intimately intertwined. In this world the knight must satisfy both God and humanity.

Mélusine repeatedly admonishes her sons not to become objects of public shame or ridicule. This advice is important in a family whose impulse to act rashly when feeling shamed causes much unhappiness to all of its members. But Mélusine also speaks against false pride, maintaining that practical wisdom is not unbecoming to a knight. She counsels that even in cases of just vengeance, it may often be preferable to accept reasonable amends [prenez amende raisonnable] than to extract retribution at all costs. Justice should never countermand reason. Mélusine's magical powers are mentioned once, and then only in passing. Upon her sons' departure, she gives them a pair of rings:

> Enfans, veez cy deux anneaulx que je vous donne, dont les pierres ont une mesme vertu. Sachiez que tant que vous userez de loyauté, sans penser ne faire tricherie, ne mauvaitié, et que vous les ayez sur vous,

> vous ne serez desconfiz par armes... ne sort, ne enchantement d'art de magique, ne de poisons... ne vous pourra nuire. (84)[33]

She had given such rings to Remond when he returned to the court of Poitiers after the count's death; she does so again when he rides to the king of Bretagne. The rings appear one last time, at her sorrowful parting. Handing them to Remond, she tells him that he and his heirs will not be defeated in battle or in combat if they fight for a good cause (259). The rings are never used as intended. Instead, their presence signifies the magical link between Mélusine and her family, even after she disappears.

Magic marks the life and "death" of Mélusine and her family, but it does not save them from themselves. It provokes conflicts between the bonds of loyalty to a cherished person and the compulsion to act, either without reflection, as when Elinas rushed to see his newborn daughters, or in response to an overpowering suspicion that a breach of honor has occurred, as with Remond's intrusion into his wife's space. These opposing notions of loyalty and the urge to act govern much of the action in this romance. Elinas's and Remond's transgressions of the interdicts, Mélusine's counsel to her sisters that they kill their father, and Gieffroy's murder of his brother Fromond and his fellow monks at Mallieres are examples of such conflicting dispositions. In all three instances, the female protagonists are unable to neutralize the conflicts or to diffuse the urge to transgress; they are thus betrayed in spite of their magical powers. These actions take place with a maddening and saddening inevitability that is indicative of how tightly the women and the men are tied to established modes of behavior, locked into a fixed pattern of responses. The conte de Foretz provokes his brother Remond where he is most vulnerable: his jealousy of his wife's disappearance and his fear of losing face before the court. Similarly, Remond responds immediately and unreflectively; he acts before he thinks, for he is bound by the pattern of responses dictated by his roles as man, husband, knight, and ruler.

At other times the actions are not as clearly motivated. Conte Aimery de Poitiers's death is one such case. When he beholds the portent in the evening sky, the count speaks as if he knows that Remond will kill him. The count's words seem to signal not only that he forgives his nephew for what he is about to do, but also that he knows about Mélusine's intervention on Remond's behalf. The narrative ambiguity resists any definitive elucidation, although critics have attempted various explanations.[34] Jean d'Arras makes it clear that Remond kills his uncle in an effort to save him, yet this account does not entirely dismiss the possibility of Conte Aimery's prescience:

> Par Dieu, dist ly contes, tu le [what I know] sauras. Et saiches de certain que je vouldroye que Dieux ne li mondes ne t'en demandast rien, et l'adventure te deust avenir de moy mesmes, car je suiz desormais vieulx, et si ay des hoirs assez pour tenir mes seignouries, car je t'aime tant que je vouldroie que si haulte honneur feust eslue pour toy. (20–21)[35]

If one could accept that Conte Aimery has some foreknowledge, it might be easier to understand why Remond never really does penance for his uncle's murder. The aura of sanctity that surrounds Remond at the very end of his life renders moot the question of his guilt. If the stars did not merely predict but also compel, Remond's actions would have been beyond his control, and his sin—conforming to our judgment—would be one of impulse, not of deliberation. This distinction plays an important role in the narrative: when a crime is premeditated (as it is in the intrigue directed against Hervy at the court of the king of Bretagne or in the conte de Foretz's gossip), vengeance, albeit belated, is thorough and total. Although Remond pleads for mercy for his late father's adversaries, the king orders them hanged without further discussion. No "amende raisonnable" exists here; mercy and pragmatism give way to a more archaic system of justice, as archaic as that which is evident in Mélusine's prophylactic command to kill Horrible, her youngest son.

After being duly instructed in the rules of knightly conduct, Mélusine's sons Guion and Uriens serve with great distinction both in battle and at foreign courts. For the most part, they follow her advice and are rewarded with land, wealth, fame, and noble wives, who bear them their needed heirs. The conflicts they help to solve are the usual fare of romance: a land-hungry widowed king threatens a fatherless heiress; a sultan desires not only the land but also the daughter of a Christian king; a king dies in battle, leaving his young daughter unprotected and his vassals bereft of their lord. The land that in this way comes under the Lusignan family's control is so immense that it covers much of Europe. Along with increases in wealth, influence, and territorial power for the sons, tensions rise at home, articulated by the narrator's apostrophes and comments directed to his audience. The text rehearses an intense fear of an impending catastrophe that no one will be able to avert.

Because of these narrative asides, and following the intertwining of magic and history, the reader cannot help but know that disaster has been brewing for a long while. The course of events has been given its direction far back in time, long before the narrative begins: Presine's meeting with Elinas, his marriage, his trespass at Mataquas's prompting, his daughters' vengeance, and Hervy's unwitting murder of the king's nephew are all events that determine with inexorable precision the unfolding of the narrative. The plot's structure is controlled by what appears to be a predetermined doubling and tripling of events that propel the action forward to a point beyond which it cannot be altered or stopped: the actions and reactions of Presine and Mélusine and of Elinas and Remond, the meetings at the mysterious fountain in the woods, the interdicts, the characters' loss of control at crucial junctures in the narrative, the couples' separations, the wife's disappearance. As a result, Mélusine's misfortune overtakes her and her family in a circuitous and yet poignant way.

Instructing her sons in the rules of knightly conduct, Mélusine never mentions that taking monastic vows might also be an acceptable calling for a nobleman. Her son Fromond decides to take this very path to salvation. At first glance this choice appears completely normal. It is quite appropriate to the mentality of the actors and to the Christian tone of much of the narrative, a fitting gesture of atonement for the deed that his father, Remond, had never acknowledged except to his wife. But this first glance proves to be deceptive: Gieffroy—whose violent temper is alluded to repeatedly and whose mark, the great boar's tooth, has given him the epithet "au grant dent"—epitomizes the fact that in this situation, family order and normalcy are always only surface phenomena, continually subject to profound disturbances when provoked from the outside.[36] While Fromond takes his vows with his parents' blessings, Gieffroy misconstrues his brother's decision to be an act of public shame, more specifically, his own shame: Gieffroy will not have it said that he has a monk for a brother [ne il me sera ja reprouvé qu j'aye moine a frere] (251). He burns down the monastery, killing all monks and—in a flash—regrets his misdeed. In his murderous temper and in his immediate regret, he resembles his mother as well as his father. Paralleling his father's story, his trespass is followed by his remorse and eventual forgiveness. Mélusine, Remond, and Gieffroy give in to their feelings so completely because in each instance their shame is a matter of public knowledge. Seated before the entire court, the conte de Foretz had earlier addressed his brother Remond:

> Beau frere, la commune renommee du peuple court partout que vostre femme vous fait deshonneur et que tous les samedis elle est en fait de fornicacion avec un autre.... Et les autres dient et maintiennent que c'est un esprit fae, qui le samedy fait sa penance. (241)[37]

The "commune renommee du peuple" is correct, as the reader knows; Mélusine may indeed be an "esprit fae." However, by now the narrative has established the reader's sympathy for Mélusine so firmly that this fact becomes secondary to the fear that Remond will break his promise. He cannot live with the gossip about his wife's absences and the implicit aspersion on his honor. The conflict of loyalties is especially weighty for Remond: it sets his reputation as knight and lord against his promise to his wife, to whom he owes this position in the first place. His momentary lapse reflects his helplessness in the face of the attack on his public reputation. It suggests as well the most traditional vulnerability of the husband of a beautiful woman whose secrets seemingly remove her from spousal control. His power over her originates in the fact that she does indeed have a terrible secret, and this contributes as much to the ambivalence of the tale as does her penance for the secret.

It is important to note that Remond regrets his action at the very moment when he sees his wife, half woman, half serpent or fish, playing in a marble tub. With her scaly tail she beats the water in cascades all the way to the ceiling, lending a beguiling playfulness to this potentially strange and threatening image.[38] Remond is not afraid, as one might expect. Rather, he is immediately relieved of his jealousy and overwhelmed by remorse. Clearly, he is more distressed at public murmurings about an unfaithful wife than about the suspicion that she might be a strange and frightful creature from another world. The narrative has reached the stage where the balance between knowing and not knowing becomes precarious, where the equilibrium between history and salvation is about to be disturbed. Although despondent to the point of illness, Remond keeps quiet. Mélusine knows his secret; but as long as he keeps his, she will keep hers. Her gesture of sexual closeness puts his tormented conscience at ease:

40   *Defining Dominion*

> Quant Remond l'[Mélusine] ouy venir, si fist semblant de dormir. Et celle se despoille et se couche toute nue delez lui ... et ... cuide qu'elle ne sache rien de ce fait. Mais pour neant le cuide, car elle scet bien tout. (243–44)[39]

Remond's momentary loss of self-control—this brief denial of love and trust, which is first hidden and then, as a hapless response to the fratricide, enunciated in a public accusation—transforms father and son. Moreover, it destroys the parents' marriage and Mélusine's longed-for salvation. Ultimately, it leads as well to the demise of the conte de Foretz. The count jumps to his death from his castle's tower, driven by his desperate attempt to escape the avenging violence of Gieffroy after he realizes that the count's remarks had started this unhappy chain of events. Justice is meted out in a direct and archaic manner. The gravity of the offense justifies extreme measures before order can return to the realm.

All conflicts resolved, the impulse to act is directed toward beneficent results: the deeds of Mélusine's remaining sons in the service of beleaguered fellow knights and defenseless women celebrate their valor and their extraordinary heritage. The lengthy reports on the wars of acquisition in which Mélusine's sons are engaged function as more than narrative fillers or mere entertainment. The care devoted to narrative coherence and to the colorful world of pan-European exploits legitimates Mélusine's suffering. Even after she plunges into the darkness of the sublunary sphere, she lives on in the orderly government of her sons, in their deeds and in those of their children. They will die a Christian death.

Gieffroy, however, remains outside this marital and dynastic utopia; he does not take a wife. Still, while most people fear him and try to maneuver around his violent temper, he also earns affection. It is said that the sultan of Barbarie shows unusual devotion to his former enemy: "Et estoit le soudant moult en amourez de Gieffroy, et lui tenoit tousjours compaignie, et lui offroit tousjours tout le plaisir qu'il pourroit faire. Et Gieffroy l'en mercia" [And the sultan was very taken with Gieffroy, and he always kept him company, and he offered him all the pleasures he could think of. And Gieffroy thanked him] (237). No further comment is offered, no explanation given. Nor has this brief episode any further narrative consequence; it simply makes Gieffroy a more human actor.

The same can be said of Mélusine's sister Mélior, who toward the end of the romance reappears in the adventure "de Chastel de l'Espervier" (302). Only a male descendant of her lineage can successfully complete a certain test: once he watches a hawk for three nights and three days without sleeping, he can ask a favor of the lady. Echoing the motif of the interdict, he can ask for anything except for the lady herself: "demandez pas son corps, car cellui ne povez vous avoir" [do not ask for her body, for that you cannot have] (303). The accustomed reward—which in the traditional adventure is frequently the lady—is not granted; the old rules are suspended and the knight will fail. The hapless knight is Guion d'Armenie, Mélusine's grandson and Mélior's grandnephew. After three sleepless nights, he does not want gold or silver, only the beautiful stranger for his wife [pour moilliers] (305). Mélior must now tell the ill-fated king what the reader has known all along:

> Povre fol, n'es tu pas descendu de la lignie du roy Guion, qui fu filz Melusigne, ma seur, et je suis ta tante, et tu es si prez de mon lignaige, posé que je me voulzisse assentir a toy avoir, que l'eglise ne s'i vouldroit pas accorder. (305)[40]

The misfortune of Mélior—who is descended from the family of Faye Morgana (who in an incestuous union with her brother, Arthur, had conceived Mordred, murderer of his father and spoiler of his kingdom)—concludes the story of her family's sexual taboos and transgressions. Waiting for her savior, Mélior also represents her own and her family's future. Matrilineal energies accompany the family history into the present; they are evident in Mélusine's periodic cries, and they are recorded both on Presine's tablet and on the walls of the room where the proud king of Armenie keeps watch three nights running:

> Le roy y entre et regarde par my la chambre, et y voit grant foison de chevaliers pains, armez de leurs cottes d'armes toutes armoiees de leurs armes. Et estoient dessoubz leurs noms escripz, et de quel lignaige et de quelle region ilz estoient. (304)[41]

Guion d'Armenie should have known that he was reading the history of his own family when he contemplated the images enacting this history on the walls of Mélior's castle. Had Mélusine's grandson been more open to what he saw before his eyes and less to what he felt in his desiring heart, he might have understood that the narrative coherence of the frieze vouched for the narrative truth of the Lusignan history. His naive passion for the body of the lady of Esprevier destroys his chance to play the part of the hero instead of the fool. The beating he receives from unseen hands makes him feel the magic energies of his adventure in a decidedly inglorious, unchivalric manner.

The carefully constructed narrative of this family's history and its explicitly paratactic structure authenticate, so the author repeatedly assures us, its claims to verisimilitude. Nevertheless, the apparent control that the characters seem to exercise over actions and events barely disguises the chaos that is always imminent. Narrative tensions hover on the verge of eruption because these characters always remain dangerously close to losing control. The often faulty judgment of the leading male characters and their inability to keep their promises represent dangers for the women but also for the future of the entire family. From the outset the clearly patterned narrative puts the reader into the privileged position of knowing what is about to happen. Most importantly, the reader knows Mélusine's secret and knows what Mélusine does not even tell her husband until the die has been cast:

> Et toutesfoiz je vueil bien que vous sachiez qui je sui ne qui fu mon pere, afin que vous ne reprouvez pas a mes enfans qu'ilz soient filz de mauvaise mere, ne de serpente, ne de faee, car je suiz fille au roy Elinas d'Albanie et a la royne Presine. (259–60)[42]

Such narrative transparency is characteristic of Jean d'Arras's claim to historical veracity; he never tires of reassuring his reader that he watches diligently over the truthfulness of his tale: "Et ne vous vueille desplaire se je vous ay ceste adventure amenteue,[43] car c'est pour raison de l'istoire de quoy je pense a traictier, de quoy j'ay dessus parlé" [And I do not want to displease you if I tell you this tale, for it is for reasons of history that I want to treat that of which I spoke above] (14). Historical veracity does not allow embellishments; history must be told as it unfolds. Within the framework of the magical-theological worldview that governs the past and guides the present, the truthfulness and veracity of this history cannot be questioned. World history and salvation history authenticate this story. Readers have to fit this information into their own mental universes. The narrator does his best not to violate the implicit contract to tell a "true" story about a family whose castles, churches, and descendants are still present in his world. Portents, giants, interdicts, and magical knowledge of events to come are all part of this universe, which, though chaotic, still has to submit to the laws of God and history. Insofar as this worldview admits to magical forces being active in the cosmos, it affords the author a more elastic concept of truth and a more ambiguous understanding of guilt and punishment, of living and dying. Within the framework of this tale's experiential realism, the reader accepts the events as true because the narrator's belief in a macro-microcosmic harmony cannot be doubted. The magic that makes the women of Mélusine's family exceptional and that allows Conte Aimery a moment's foreknowledge just before his death are part of the same world; magical beings and family history have not yet reached the state of hostile separation that will make Mélusine a satanic creature more than a century later.

It is clear why Mélusine accepts and forgives Remond's betrayal, just as her mother had accepted and forgiven Elinas's trespass: Mélusine and Presine must leave the world of the chronicle, of secular history, because such exceptional women cannot, in the end, be integrated into medieval or early modern historical contexts. They have access to a magical world that remains closed to the male actors, but they are also bound by, and tied to, this privilege. Women like Mélusine, her mother, and sisters would threaten the accustomed order were they to remain active in this world, for they show that they can and will exercise justice as independently and as deftly as any man. The Lusignan women do triumph over death, if by death one means forgetting. Their history becomes part of universal history. They introduce the exceptional, the magical into the family chronicle, which will accompany the Lusignan house until the end of time.

The wheels of this history turn slowly. Not until the loss of his wife does Remond have a chance to do penance for his trespass, and—in spite of the accident's ambiguity—perhaps for the death of his lord Aimery also. Hervy's betrayal is not avenged until the next generation has grown to adulthood. The men remain, for the most part, the activists in history. The women participate in this history because they have power over words, over language. They predict events (Presine, Mélusine, and Mélior); they transmit information (Presine's tablet); they tell about the future by making visible the events of the past (the frieze in Mélior's chamber); and, finally, they mourn their family's and society's impending losses (Mélusine's ritual wailing can be heard when a family member is near death, and her spirit moves around the tower of the Lusignan castle). These women articulate history and convey it into the future.

Seen in this light, the question of whether a fairy can be the founding mother of a Christian noble house becomes insignificant. Although the action remains driven by mortal males, the Christian cosmos is nonetheless filled with such creatures, which affect human lives. Memory remains in the safekeeping of the women, whose tale the author tells. Ultimately, history will complete its course and its resolution in the salvation of both the fairy women and their mortal spouses and descendants. At that point, magical and human history will converge into sacred history, and absolution will be granted for all transgressions.

3

Magic and the Science of Man and Woman: Theophrastus Bombastus von Hohenheim, called Paracelsus

Never truly forgotten after her banishment to the never-never-land of the nondead, Mélusine continued to appear in narrative and nonnarrative texts for centuries.[1] Her magical nature had given her the aura of the unusual, the strange, the ominous. While she was denied a Christian death, her gesture of forgiveness toward her husband and the humility and loving tenderness that she showed toward her family reassured the reader that her wish to find peace would be granted in due time. The magical universe in whose sublunary vaults she awaited the end of time remained the object of much speculation and observation in the ensuing centuries.

The natural philosopher and physician Theophrastus Bombastus von Hohenheim, known as Paracelsus (1493–1541), who was one of the sixteenth century's most relentless explorers of the cosmos, mentioned Mélusine repeatedly. Because of his popular little essay "Liber de nymphis," he became a sort of champion of the humanity of such a creature.[2] He identified her as an elemental spirit. Of the four elements—fire, air, earth, and water—she inhabits the watery depth. Paracelsus defined a water spirit as one who, while lacking a soul, was capable of love and worthy of marriage with a mortal man. Seeking to understand creatures like Mélusine became a cipher for the nobility of scientific inquiry:

> Seliger ist es, die Nymphen zu beschreiben, als die Orden zu beschreiben; seliger ist, den Ursprung der Riesen zu beschreiben, dann die Hofzucht; seliger ist Melusina zu beschreiben, denn die Reuterei und Artillerie; seliger, die Bergleutel unter der Erde zu beschreiben, denn Fechten und den Frauen dienen. (LN, 464)[3]

In other words, it was more worthwhile to engage in the study of the magical sciences than in any other pursuit, with the possible exception of theology.[4] Paracelsus's God lived in a house of many rooms. Along with many of his contemporaries, Paracelsus believed in the existence of elemental spirits ("Geister") who populated the sublunar sphere and who had a fixed and useful place in his triadic universe. Paracelsus and his scholarly cohorts found support for this view in writings on magic and natural philosophy that went as far back as Aristotle. They were his disciples as well as detractors in the more than thousand years that separated them from antiquity.

No contradiction marred Paracelsus's vision of a universe that was unique, and whose macrocosmic unity and harmony enclosed as a microcosm God's favored creation: humankind. Historiography, philosophy, and magic guaranteed the experiential realism of humans' place in this universe since they had begun to commit their knowledge to writing. Even if there were still secrets in the human experience of the cosmos and of the divine, God would see to it that these secrets would soon be revealed. Paracelsus's philosophical and theological optimism provided him with a vision of the universe that in all its magical wonder was representable and available to human understanding. The magus was the one to whom the whole of nature and the universe would ultimately be known. Magic as *philosophia adepta* transmitted knowledge of all that was found in heaven and earth, and the adept recognized "was die natur durch ire krefte tut, da ist natürliche magie (*magia naturalis*) was die himmlischen krefte in uns tun und durch [Gottes Einwirkung], ist die himlische magia [aus dem Licht des Heiligen Geistes]."[5]

Thus, Paracelsus is known as a passionate observer and commentator of nature and the universe, seen and unseen, and as a tireless defender of the use and exploration of white, licit magic.[6] Like the philosophers of antiquity and the theologians of the Middle Ages, he viewed the world as an ordered cosmos in which the microcosm, humanity, stood in a homological relationship to the universal macrocosm.[7] All around humankind the world was alive in semiotic correspondences between and among the elemental, astral, and divine universes; man and woman were part of the whole signifying cosmos. Theirs was a uniquely privileged position: poised at the center of the universe, they participated in all of its complex workings. As noted in the previous chapter, man and woman had been created in God's image, and for them alone Christ had died (PS, 326). For this reason humanity was rated even higher than the angels: "so that humankind be saved and brought to Heaven—God did that [had his son crucified]. Humankind, therefore, is God's favorite creation" (PS, 326). Earth's sole reason for existence was to bear fruit and to house humankind (VP, 209). God had created humans last because he wished for a creature to rule his creation after Lucifer rose against him in arrogance, forfeiting his place in Heaven. But man and woman succumbed to temptation: the first couple transgressed against the only prohibition that God articulated when he placed them in the Garden: they were not to eat the fruit of the Tree of Knowledge; they fell from grace because they wanted to know.

After Adam and Eve were driven from paradise, God wished that humans would explore his creation. To this end he created the sciences and, above all, magic, the science that represents the inquiry into the unknown and that expressly transgresses the limits that keep humans from conquering what eludes their understanding. Paracelsus's view of the universe is an amalgam of those of many of his predecessors. He did, however, differ from them in one major way: he went the furthest in the attempt to mold a magical, esoteric cosmos to the real world of human experience:

Er läßt uns... suchen, die Erde durchwandern und vielerlei erfahren. Und wenn wir es alles erfahren haben, sollen wir, was gut ist, behalten.... Nun sind alle Künste vollkommen in den Geistern, sie seien gut oder böse; aus ihnen muß es an uns kommen. (MI, 270, 273)[8]

The divinity of his universe does not stand in the way of the human imperative to uncover its secrets. His self-assured search and his independent interpretations of what he read, saw, and learned from tradition not only confused and amused but also startled his public. His contemporaries recognized the exceptional in him, comparing him to Luther and Dürer.[9] During the debate over the real power of witches, his name was used by representatives of both camps, by Weyer as well as by Bodin.

Magic, humankind's apparent ability "to accomplish more in its life than its talents seem to permit," was to reward its search with knowledge and wisdom.[10] However, along with the promise, magic always carried with it the threat of destruction; in knowing the forbidden, one risked damnation. Paracelsus never tired of assuring his readers that licit magic—while not appropriate for all practitioners—was a godsend and a God-willed exercise in human intellectual pursuit:

[Magica] ist eben das, daß sie die himmlische Kraft in das medium bring[t].... Das medium ist das centrum; das centrum ist der Mensch. So kann durch den Menschen die himmlische Macht in den Menschen gebracht werden. (PS, 146)[11]

To know the mysteries of nature, "so that we know and see with our own eyes," was part of the privileged relationship enjoyed by the Creator and his creature (AR, 339). As microcosm, humanity carried all creation within itself, for it had been given dominion over all that had been created. Not until the exile from paradise, however, did humanity accept this inheritance and with it the challenge to rule and govern, to experience and to understand the world. Humanity's role as governor of the universe defined its existence. But it also served as a metaphor for its will to know, and as such it was an expression of its hubris. Those bent upon pushing the limits of knowledge and power further—the scholars, discoverers, and conquerors of the sixteenth century—shared the belief in the legitimacy of their quest to know and to possess what they gazed upon either with their own eyes or through the mediation of letters, books, and pictures: "Je mehr deine Füße dich in fremde Länder tragen um so erfahrener sind deine Augen, je mehr haben die Ohren gehört" [The more your feet carry you into foreign lands, the more experienced your eyes will become, the more your ears will hear] (PS, 291).

Paracelsus shared with his predecessors Ficino and Giovanni Pico the belief that humans' wish to know made them the very special and beloved children of God, who had offered them the world.[12] The relentless exploration of the unknown and humans' unwillingness—or inability—to accept limits are considered the hallmarks of their nobility, a nobility based on intellectual and artistic accomplishments, not on blood ties or familial distinction. The determination of nobility was a favorite topic of humanistic speculation. Pierre Charron's tract *De la sagesse* (1601) can be considered exemplary. Quoting Seneca, he asks: "Who is a nobleman? A mind that strives naturally toward virtue, and such a mind can come from all social ranks and rise to attain happiness."[13] In the context of such conviction, it is not surprising that Paracelsus declared physicians as the most divinely favored of men, occupying a position that compelled them to be "truthful and honorable," not subject to moral turpitude, as "a hangman, or a liar" might be (PA, 568).[14] Scientific magic could only be practiced by physicians, magi, if they were virtuous and served their patients and God honestly and devoutly. The medical arts rested on four columns that represented the three areas of knowledge—philosophy, astronomy, and alchemy—to which was added ethics and morality, *virtus* (PA, 496). Physicians needed to be pure (*rein, keusch*) and devout (*gläubig*).[15] This combination of intellectual, spiritual, and moral character was meant to ensure that their service to humankind and God be rendered in the right spirit and that their work be blessed (PA, 496, 572). Only in this way could magic perform both its epistemological and its hermeneutic function, which was always one of prophetic mediation among God, humankind, and nature as well as among people as part of the body politic.[16] Faith in the divinity of the medical arts kept the physician safe from satanic delusion. Interestingly, Weyer, who was in complete agreement with this tenet, prescribed that the "bewitched" woman should be instructed in the articles of faith and encouraged to attend church frequently.

Almost a generation before Paracelsus, Ficino and Giovanni Pico had praised divine wisdom as the ineffable power, source of human intellect and foundation of licit, divine magic. Paracelsus reinforced this conviction, insisting on the divinity of humankind's intellect and desire to know. Practicing *scientia magica,* men sought an approach to God: by attempting to understand the secrets of the universe, they strove to heal the rift between themselves and their Creator, between body and soul. To help articulate this union, Paracelsus developed the model of an existential triad that united in the living person the elemental, spiritual (astral), and divine bodies. Death meant the separation of these three bodies, the time when the divine soul would join its Creator. It was the task of the adept, such as Paracelsus, to explore in the service of God this triadic, closed universe and to make the cosmos, humanity's privileged space, accessible to the elect.

Even in its most benign form, *scientia magica*—meaning licit or white magic—always represented the institutionalized, scientific transgression of boundaries, those linguistic and ritual articulations of the limits imposed on humanity.[17] Magical knowledge was believed to lead its practitioner to self-knowledge and to the understanding of humanity's place in the universe: "propter te factus est mundus."[18] However, magical knowledge also threatened damnation if attained by the wrong people; for Paracelsus that meant women, Jews, gypsies, or the charlatan physician.[19] Paracelsus returned repeatedly in his writings to the exclusive, noble nature of magic in an attempt to justify his scientific methods. He sharply ridiculed his detractors, emphasizing the divinity of his art and of his suffering:

> Aber ihr könnt wohl mit den Juden, alldieweil ihr in der Arznei jüdisch handelt, sprechen, ich sei ein Verführer des Volkes, ich habe den Teufel, ich sei besessen, ich sei aus der Nigromantie belehrt worden, ich sei ein magus; diese Dinge all sprachen die Juden auch zu Christus. Ich bin so viel, daß ihr mir nicht die Riemen vom Schuh auflösen könnt. (PA, 521)[20]

He rejected the accusation of being a "Lutherus," i.e., a radical reformer. He insisted instead that Luther would mind his own affairs while he, Paracelsus, would take care of what concerned him: "ich will das mein selbst verantworten" (PA, 496). He spurned those who persisted in thinking that only other people could gain access to the true healing arts; the "Other" was shown to be a figment of the imagination of each people's and group's fearful and distorted view across the fence into the stranger's yard: "Ihr sollt euch...nit verwundern, denn Verwundern kommt aus einem Unwissen und Unverstand" [Do not be amazed, because amazement comes from ignorance and stupidity] (VP, 180). For Paracelsus, such ignorance only lined the pockets of the charlatans. It led to deficient medical practices and, ultimately, straight to hell (BA, 8, 9).

The consequences of the unending struggle between white magic, the divine science, and black magic, the satanic affliction, is seen in all its contradictory force when viewed together with two other publications of roughly the same period: Giovanni Pico's *Oration on the Dignity of Man* (1484) and the *Malleus Maleficarum* (1486).[21] However different and contradictory their views on magic, these tracts did agree on one point, namely, that the greatest danger as well as the single most powerful sign of humankind's special status was its free will. Only free will drove men and women to seek knowledge, be it of good or of evil. Paracelsus concurred; he agreed that free will was at once humankind's greatest gift and its most precious divine burden.[22]

Paracelsus's perception of the world as divided into macrocosm and microcosm was based on the pneumatic principle of Stoic and Neoplatonic metaphysics, that is, on the concept of a uniform, planned universe, a universal sympathy that united all creation and in turn lent each part its existential meaning.[23] In a world full of hidden connections, natural and "unnatural" occurrences were potent signs of arcane knowledge that it was humankind's task to discover. For Paracelsus, knowledge was never forbidden, only veiled, not yet accessible to the immature human mind. Paracelsus returned to this theme again and again, and with special insistence in his *Philosophia sagax* (1537–38).[24] Of the two paths leading to wisdom—the eternal and the human—one emanated directly from the Godhead; the other came from nature (42). Again Paracelsus identified himself as different from his colleagues:

Ich schreib christlich und bin kein Heide, ein Deutscher, nicht ein Welscher, ein interpres, nit ein sophist.... [Ich bin] kein Zauberer, kein Heid, kein Zigeuner.... hab ich doch die Gab und Gnad des selbigen Geistes, der vom Vater... ausgeht. (PS, 44, 46)[25]

He read the pages of the book of nature, where throughout all of creation one can find "letters that signify what humankind is" (65). Nature's arcana are meant to teach humans, and if they refused to read and to learn from the pages of her book, they were "blind with seeing eyes" (LME, 449). Wisdom's only adversary was the person who would not admit to the truth before his or her eyes: "wisdom has no enemy but the liar" (PS, 305).

While wisdom attracted man, it did, on the whole, elude woman. She shared with man the privilege that she was not created directly out of cosmic chaos but only after the creation of the universe was completed. In his attempt to exculpate woman from satanic involvements, Weyer made much of the notion that women had smaller brains, which limited the female intellectual faculty to such a degree that independent and rational action became impossible. Paracelsus's opinion was less dichotomous: the male, as the first to have been created, carried within him all things created before him; formed from the *limus terrae*,[26] according to the laws of divine magic, he was the son of all the world:

So also ist der Mensch die kleine Welt, das ist, der Mensch hat alle Eigenschaft der Welt in ihm, darum ist er der microcosmus. Darum ist der das fünfte Wesen der Elemente und des Gestirns oder Firmaments in der obern sphaera und im untern globul. So ist die große Welt ein Vater der kleinen Welt. (PS, 70)[27]

Woman was formed from the rib of this small world, man. She was similar to him because she, too, had to be considered elect. She had been created in God's image, albeit after man. This special status separated man and woman from the angels, as from the elemental spirits, neither of the two could claim the same nearness to God or such favored creation (PS, 69, 70, 77).

Man was not born once but thrice: in the realms of the earth, the stars, and God. To this triple birth man owed his elemental, astral, and spiritual (immortal) body. Since only he who was of God could recognize God, man's essence as a child of the divine became his most valued possession and his highest reward. This gift prevented man from being innately and totally corrupt and corruptible; God would not permit the corruption of his creation (BG, 62). By definition, woman was made of man's matter; she shared with him this divine nature. She bore the generations of children who would lead humankind back to God.[28] Owing to the privilege of their creation, humans had to fulfill two tasks on earth: they had to enhance human knowledge; and they had to procreate. Mélusine's building and birthing fits right into this activist image of life on earth, the preparation of humankind for salvation, a salvation she would have been able to achieve, had she died Remond's wife:

Mit der Melusina ist ein trefflich Aufmerken zu haben, denn sie ist nit dermaßen, wie sie von den Theologen angesehen worden ist, gewesen, sondern war eine nympha; aber das ist wahr: besessen mit dem bösen Geist, den sie, wenn sie bis zum End bei ihrem Herrn geblieben wäre, von sich gebracht hätte. (LN, 489)[29]

In community with each other, man and woman obeyed God's laws. They shared this world with the spirits of the elements and the *monstra*. The spirits derived their origin from the four elements; the *monstra* issued forth from illicit sexual intercourse. The *inanimata, Nymphen, Gigantes, Lemures, Gnomis, Vulcani,* and *Umbragines* were born of divine and elemental sperm but with no soul, since they lacked the *quinta essentia,* which was the privilege of those created in God's image (PS, 138). When the spirits died, they left behind no trace. Sixteenth-century experience confirmed this belief. Spirits were not of the same flesh as Adam; therefore they could be considered to be related or comparable to the "new people" recently found across the sea (PS, 138).[30] These "new" people surely could not be issue of Adam's flesh; neither could they be related physically to humanity. Instead they had to be of a different Adam, of a different creation.[31]

In the sixteenth century, the century of the new natural science, the Europeans found a radically different world and people across the sea. They responded with great awe to the unimagined diversity of flora and fauna. And some scholars theorized that, as Paracelsus suggested, they may have found a different race that had issued forth from Noah after the flood.[32]

At a time when discussion about the Americas was becoming increasingly less benign and when whole populations had already been eradicated, Paracelsus articulated a neutral, scientific point of view concerning the discoveries.[33] He did not express great wonder at the "new" creatures; he conceived the world as a book whose pages are continually being turned to reveal new facts, new signs. This belief removed limits to knowledge; it allowed for interest and fascination but precluded superstitious and fearful wonder as well as the notion of an inaccessible, distant, unreachable Other.[34] Knowledge could be found in the context of the familiar as well as on distant shores. In much the same way as exploration of the magical arts took place, the assimilation of the unfamiliar required simply that one "see," knowingly and without fear, that one arrange the "new" within known reality. The inquiring gaze had to be kept free of confusion and fear; it had to construct new categories to aid comprehension.

In changing times wisdom and art also change, and the true physician, like the true artist or scholar, finds the truth appropriate to a given historical and cultural context (VP, 240). Like the *monstra* of broadsheet fame, the natives from across the sea had a purpose, and—God's works were wonderful—they had a rightful place in creation. Like the elemental spirits and the *monstra,* they served as omens of events to come; they announced God's anger at his creation. They articulated his wish to warn humans of the consequences of their actions and of Judgment Day, when his plan for the world would be fulfilled, when all knowledge would have been acquired and revealed (LN, 492, 497). Paracelsus's conviction that all knowledge was ultimately historical, and as such predetermined to be revealed in time, allowed him to accept without difficulty the notion that there were regions on this earth where people lived unusually long lives, knew different phenomena, and had different beliefs (VL, 482).[35]

Writing in the 1530s, Paracelsus did not appear to be directly influenced by the polemics of the *Malleus Maleficarum*. Still, since he was deeply interested in magic and in human nature, he wrote much about woman's special nature.[36] His ruminations lacked a clear and coherent vision of the physiological, psychological, social, or political disposition of the female. Woman appeared as the third creation, most often in her role as part of the human couple. By the mid-thirties, under the influence of Reformation writings on marriage, the wedded couple had become the smallest, most important building block of human society and the most significant metaphor for the ordering structures of human life. As such it occupied much of Paracelsus's thought.

Since magic and human and divine nature were inseparably linked in all that Paracelsus said about life on earth and about man's favored place in the universe, he sought to explain woman's nature in this context. Paracelsus stressed the fact that women were both similar and very different from men in their rational, physical, and pathological natures. Despite his early modern misogynist notions, he tried to construct a greater equality for women than was the norm among his contemporaries, even concerning the exercise of female free will and responsibility. He did not, on the whole, condemn women for their "inferior bodies" and "weaker morals," and his writings for the most part lack the strident and accusatory tone that characterizes the *Malleus* and similar texts. This difference is especially noticeable when Paracelsus constructed scientific, rational, accessible explanations for even the most complicated occult realities, such as the appearance of spirits, the nature and activities of witches, and other magical phenomena. Wishing to rid these phenomena not of their magical but of their superhuman and nonhuman aura, he endeavored to demystify them, to make them not less wondrous but more recognizable and comprehensible.

This demystification in turn affected his view of woman. Man was part of the greater world, the macrocosm, outside of which he could not exist; woman was of man and could not exist without him (PS, 77). This version of theological truth had significant consequences: it compelled Paracelsus to formulate an exceptionally positive attitude toward marriage, and, conversely, it forced him to assume a negative stance on celibate life, be it male or female.[37] Although not a declared Protestant, he was in this respect in total accord with his contemporary Luther: marriage was necessary to accommodate humanity's sexual and procreative needs.[38] Man and woman belonged together, and when the right man was joined with the woman predestined to be his wife, they would be tied to each other in steadfast love and devotion (OP, 107). Paracelsus's high regard for marriage[39] led him to condemn virginity as an inappropriate mental state and life-style, dangerously separatist for males as well as for females.[40] In the event that a person was born a eunuch or had been "castrated in the service of the Lord [i.e., had become celibate]," this man or woman was never to marry or have a child because such a child would displease God, having been born outside of his will and order (PS, 260). Illegitimacy, signaling sexual activity outside of the bonds of matrimony, emerged as a powerful metaphor for deviation and anomaly. A "child of a whore," a *Bankert,* not only meant a bastard but came to mean all ill-founded thinking in general, all ill-formed things in nature. Conversely, all that was "ehelich," or within marriage, was by its very nature perfect in the eyes of God, who had created a complete and an incomplete wisdom and art. The complete knowledge is still legitimate (*ehelich*), because it derives from God; all others are imperfect and therefore bastard (*Bankert*). That is, those who only have an incomplete understanding of God's wisdom are illegitimate (*unehelich*) in their art and wisdom. True wisdom and true art were "eheliche Weisheit und Kunst"; anything else was pretend art, sham wisdom (LF, 15).

In his medical tracts as well as in his writings on philosophy and magic, Paracelsus meticulously described the weaknesses and illnesses of male and female physiology and psychology. His wide-ranging comments on the physical and spiritual nature of humankind show clearly how his thinking on the *scientia magica* permeated his scientific and religious views. The arcana of procreation appear as a mixture of physiology, philosophy, and magic; they reveal the effects of visible and invisible cosmic forces on men and women. Paracelsus was convinced that human procreation—like the whole of creation—was part of a sensible and reasonable, albeit not yet fully revealed, physiological and psychological system.

On the basis of his procreative theories, Paracelsus constructed a pattern of social behavior: the woman carried her child in the uterus, the matrix, "the smallest world," as he called it. He compared the woman's role in procreation to the planting of a field; her conception is described as the blossoming of a flower, which in due time will bear fruit.[41] Father and mother carried within them the senses (firmament = father) and the blood (elements = mother) that helped to form the child (PS, 79). If the matrix—the woman, called "mother" in contemporary English medical texts[42]—was spoiled, the children would also be spoiled; and if the seed (i.e., the male) was defective, so would the fruit, the child, be defective. The spiritual and physical well-being of the child was thus the responsibility of both parents (OP, 170–71). A virtuous life and restraint in sexual intercourse on the part of both parents protected the fetus's development.

In the female body were gathered all the elements of the greater and smaller world, which she passed on to her children. The child resided in the woman's body like a fish in water or a bird in the air; it was one with her and yet separate from her. This separation of womb and fetus enabled the woman to bear male children without endangering them. Her sex would not influence the character of the unborn male child; her feminine nature would not lessen his manliness. This separation also offered a reasonable explanation for Christ, who was of woman born.[43] Different formative actions in the body guaranteed sexual difference: *in utero* male and female children were nourished differently; they took their food from the womb according to their specific needs. As the one who gave birth, the woman was closer to the world, to nature, than was man; she nourished the children as the world nourished the people inhabiting it. Despite their functional, structural, and spiritual differences, however, man and woman were physically similar: "Drum ist er ihm gleich in der Gestalt, denn sein Bild muß er empfangen" [Therefore it (the female body) is similar in status to it (the male body), for it must receive God's image] (OP, 149).[44] As small and smallest worlds, man and woman were enclosed by skin so that flesh and blood would not intermingle with the greater world, the macrocosm, and be destroyed by it (OP, 134–35). This differentiation between the small and smallest worlds enabled Paracelsus to view each sex's special position in creation both positively and negatively. Thus, while the woman's bearing of children was valued, specifically female diseases that demanded special treatment were isolated as problems. The same was true for her male counterpart (OP, 135, 149). Men and women needed, respectively, *männische* and *frauische* medicine.

Due to her mental and moral fragility, woman was especially prone to sin, melancholy, sadness, and temptation—what Paracelsus called the "invisible illnesses."[45] Weakness of the spirit tended to erode her ability to resist enchantment and made her susceptible to satanic subterfuge. How differently Paracelsus treated this phenomenon comes more clearly into focus when we remember that Weyer built a whole apologia of femininity based on the female susceptibility to melancholy. Bodin, however, reversed the argument by claiming that men, not women, tended more toward melancholy because their humors were cold and dry.[46] By leaving aside the humoral pathology, which governed medical theory and practice into the seventeenth century (and which is not the subject of this study), and replacing it with his theory of all life (*Entientheorie*), Paracelsus was able to free himself from the straitjacket of Galenic medicine and explore a type of medicine that considered the whole person, i.e., where body, soul, and spirit influenced human health. The controversy between Weyer and Bodin that so stirred late-sixteenth-century demonologists would have found no partisan opinion in his works.

Paracelsus recommended that women's medical treatment be different than that of men (OP, 13, 138). Unlike his mate, man was incapable of direct intervention in his offspring's development (MI, 221, 223).[47] The woman imposed her thoughts and desires on the unborn child: "what the body sees and desires during pregnancy will also come forth in the child" (MI, 223, 228; BG, 55). The *imaginatio* was guided by strong magnetic powers. It drew into the matrix what the eye perceived; in this way it was believed to resemble the imagination of a painter who reproduces what he first sees with his inner eye.[48] If during conception the womb insufficiently attracted the man's or the woman's seed, the child resulting from this union would be born malformed. It would either lack body parts or have too many of them; if twins were born, they would fail to separate completely (BG, 50).[49] The child's sex was determined by the partner who produced the stronger seed and whose seed reached the matrix first. The child inherited the infirmities of the more passionate partner, the one more active in the sexual encounter (BG, 44). If neither sex dominated, a *hermaphroditus* resulted, who "obwohl er beider Gestalt hat, hat er aber nit beider Eigenschaft,... [ist] weder der Frau vollkommen gleich noch vollkommen dem Mann—und also ein Mißgewächs aus der Irrung der Natur" [Although it ha[s] the appearance of both partners, it does not, however, have properties of both..., [is] neither the total likeness of the woman nor of the man, that is, it [is] a malformation, an error of nature] (BG, 48).

Paracelsus constructed a scientific as well as a moral explanatory model for such errors. Unnatural creatures, such as hermaphrodites or *monstra,* could be read as signs of divine or satanic interference. They could also be considered indicators of a disorderly nature and moral misconduct because aberrant sexual behavior led to wrongly deposited sperm, another cause of freak births (BG, 50). In extreme cases—if an animal's seed entered the woman's womb or if the human seed was ingested by animals—the result was the birth of a monster, which people in their ignorance considered something wondrous. The "sodomites" and those who "let sperm fall into their mouths" were possible bearers of monsters (LH, 436, 437). Their errant ways prevented the natural development of the seed in the matrix; they hindered the growth of a well-formed body, which was necessary if spirit and soul were to be received, if a true human person was to be formed. "Natural" sexual intercourse—natural in terms of position, state of mind, and sanctioning through marriage—was essential for the unity of body, spirit, and soul; man and woman were held equally accountable for their sexual transgressions. Such phenomena could not be ascribed to Satan, for he could not act without God's sanction, and what the "coarse intellect [did] not understand [was] not necessarily the Devil's doing" (MI, 270). Paracelsus, Weyer, and, as the following chapter will demonstrate, also Bodin agreed with most of their contemporaries when they denied direct and independent satanic agency.

Man and woman were made for each other; like the elemental and stellar bodies, like body and soul, they were united until death. Each had the right to one spouse only. Every man and every woman had one specific partner assigned at birth:

> So wißt nun hierauf, daß ein jegliches Maidlein "eigen" und vergeben ist schon im Mutterleib, und so auch jeglicher Knab "eigen" und seinem Weib im Mutterleib verheiratet ist; das ist die göttliche Vorsehung. (LNA, 83)[50]

This statement sustained the divine interdict against both adultery and polygamy. Paracelsus's postulate of conjugal predestination explicitly forbids the coveting of another's wife or husband. He took Lutheran marital emphasis a step further: if a man took any but the preordained woman for his wife, he made this woman a whore, just as if he had engaged in adultery (LNA, 86). Divorce was seen as sinful except in the case of the wife's adultery (LME, 87). Should she remarry, a woman likewise was considered to commit adultery, for marital vows could not be dissolved—a wife was bound to her husband even beyond death. Paracelsus went so far as to insist that marriages with elemental spirits, such as Mélusine's to her mortal husband, were meant to last forever, even if the spirit disappeared. Clearly, he accepted the notion of a world where spirits and human beings intermingled, and he was not frightened by this prospect. A theological, moral command, the "forever" of the marital commitment, became a social interdict that was valid even in unions with spirits: "He who breaks up his marriage and goes astray is condemned by God regardless of who he may be, learned or not, a man of the cloth or a layman" (VA, 370). Whoever has the good fortune to find the predestined partner should live with him or her in harmony and piety. This means, among other things, that neither partner should express unseemly lust for the other. Conception based on lust was judged a sin: "Der in Gottesfurcht gebiert, gebiert einen reinen Menschen; der in Lust gebiert, gebiert einen Weltmenschen" [Who bears children in the fear of God bears pure human beings; who conceives in lust bears a child wise in the ways of the world] (VH, 232).

In spite of his strong rationalist and scientific thinking and his often positive view of woman, Paracelsus shared with his contemporaries the belief that women were more strongly dominated by their sexuality than men. Since women were not by nature designed to lead a chaste life, and since they were meant to wed and to bear children, Paracelsus never tired of counseling that they should be married as soon as they reach physical maturity. Indeed, unbridled female sexuality was a most dangerous trait. Sexual indifference, on the other hand, was judged to be similarly perverse. Paracelsus scorned women "Wenn sie sich von Männern wenden und ihrer gar nichts achten; der Buhlerei, veneris vergessen, die Samstag, Freitag, Donnerstag sonderlich feiern... den Mann fliehen... sich verbergen, allein sein... selten kochen... allein liegen, sich versperren... [Männer] nicht ansehen" [When they turn from men and do not pay attention to them; forgetting about love-making... fleeing men... hiding, wanting to be alone,... not wanting to cook... lying alone, shutting themselves in, refusing [men's] advances... not looking men in the eye, lying alone, refusing a man" (DS, 446–47). These marginalizing, asocial behaviors were interpreted as expressions of aberrant sexuality. They were potent indices of satanic dependence. Since an appropriately modest sexuality could be practiced only within the bounds of matrimony and thus in support of the body politic, excessive sexual appetite and apparent sexual indifference were condemned equally, as much for their antisocial impulses as for their implicit self-indulgence.

Owing much to his championing of marriage and procreation, Paracelsus directed his most virulent criticism toward women who abandoned themselves to sexual fantasies "that they complete[d] by themselves" (MI, 235). But, ever the scientist, he stated that, besides being a moral abomination, such practice led to the production of an infertile sperm. The latter could not produce children but rather spawned incubi, succubi, and monstra, whose reality Paracelsus accepted. He wanted, however, to remove the terror implicit in such creatures. Although monsters and night ghosts might seem terrifying to the ignorant, they were merely the inevitable result of abnormal, immoral sexuality, i.e., "against the order of nature" (MI, 236). Male and female witches engaged in such practice, as did old women, "die der Fruchtbarkeit entwachsen und über den natürlichen Lauf hinaus sind, daß sie sich selbst anreizen und unkeusch gefunden werden, und mit sich selbst dermaßen spekulieren" [who could not bear children any more, and who excited themselves and became unchaste, and (imagined) by themselves] (MI, 238).

Since the Fall, Paracelsus argued, men and women were subject to the elements and to natural change: they ate, they voided, they matured, they aged, and they died. To live, "man ate himself": certain foods nourished specific body parts. Each food contained the mystical quintessence of its energies, as did each medicine.[51] It was essential that physicians understand such powers in order to engage their own magical faculties. What was no longer useful to the body was voided in the form of excrement, urine, sweat, and tears. Woman underwent monthly menstruations, the *menstruum*, and after childbirth she produced milk. No food was as pure as the latter, no poison as deadly as the former, "ein Exkrement der in die matrix laufenden Dinge, welche darin sterben und was dann ausgeworfen wird" [An excrement of things collecting in the matrix, which die there and (are) expelled] (OP, 153). The menses cleansed the matrix and prepared it for conception. Paracelsus scorned doctors who equated the *menstruum* with mother's milk.[52] The former was a poison that some "Devil's whores" used for brewing deadly tinctures, the latter a most subtle food, the purest distillate of what a woman consumed. Between conception, birth, and cessation of lactation, nature did not produce its poison (*menstruum*); the woman's physical cycle was stilled, as God stilled the course of the sun for the benefit of his servant Joshua. The reproductive cycle assumed the dimension of a cosmic drama, and woman's role in it was seen as part of a subtle but no less divine magic.

Paracelsus's detailed discussion on the nature of *menstruum* predates Ambroise Paré's study on monsters and marvels (1585) by several decades. He rehearsed this fact of female physiology in the context of his theology and anthropology of human conception. Paré quoted Jewish and classical sources in support of his theory that "it is a filthy brutish thing to have dealings with a woman while she is purging herself [is menstruating]."[53]

Although Paracelsus believed in the existence of witches, his interest in them was that of a scholar, not that of an inquisitor. He knew that faith could move mountains; it could therefore also affect people, who could be prayed to death and who could become lame as a result of prayer. In this way natural illness was transformed into something unnatural (MI, 201). Paracelsus's interest in scientific magic and his fundamentally positive view of man and woman as created in the image of God prevailed over theories that conceded too much authority and activism to Satan. In his only work devoted exclusively to the nature of women as witches, the incomplete *Fragmentum de libri de sagis et earum operibus,* Paracelsus identified as their "midwife" not Satan but rather evil planetary spirits, the ascendants, who attended the birth of each child.[54] While these spirits were powerless during the child's early years, when the child grew to maturity, they incited it to do those things that the ascendants had in themselves, such as thievery (DS, 443). Paracelsus believed that if an appropriate education did not protect the child against its evil influence, the ascendant would, in the end, be victorious over the child's better nature: "So erwachsen auch die Hexen in der Geburt; wenn der Geist...nit ausgetrieben wird...wurzelt es in der Hexe so lange, bis er sie unterrichtet" [In such a way, witches are created already at birth, and if the spirit...is not driven out...it will be rooted in the witch until such a time...that (the Devil) instructs her] (DS, 443). Witches could prophesy even without having been instructed in the magical arts. If an adult was jealous, envious, and hateful, he or she would fall to the ascendant, to Satan. But Satan was never the initiator of human depravity; rather he was the beneficiary of human weakness. When the planetary spirits averted woman from marital, i.e., male, love, they soon yielded to "unnatural behavior" and "shameful generation" (DS, 456–58). Education played the same role in the life of the child as earnest striving did in the life of the adult:

Auf dieses merkt, daß alle Ding, die wir im Alter gebrauchen sollen, von Jugend auf in uns erzogen werden müssen, und das Erziehen

> bringt und macht in uns einen Felsen. Denn was die Gewohnheit von Jugend auf in uns einbildet, das ist ein Fels, auf den die Natur baut. (DS, 444)[55]

Because witches' lives were ruled by envy and hatred, the ascendant diverted them easily from the path of virtue to that of speculation, fantasy, and the intense pursuit of others in order to do them harm ("hitziges Nachtrachten"). The human mind was especially vulnerable at night when plagued by spirits, *Hexengeister*. In their ignorance, people thought that witches learned their arts from Satan; yet he could not teach anything but what was in nature, however hidden. A properly raised and educated person, male or female, who in due time married the right partner and became a virtuous member of the Christian community, would be immune to satanic deception and open to God's guidance to knowledge.

Paracelsus's view of magic permitted him to project a world where humankind lived rational, healthy, devout lives and still pursued knowledge to its ultimate limits. His projection, however, is not coherent; it lacks the systematic clarity that would have made it palatable to a wider public. For all its seemingly arcane cogitation, its realism is both rational and visionary in the attempt to meld the spiritual with the practical, to join theology with science. Paracelsus's name appears frequently in sixteenth-century writings; he is praised, criticized, and even ridiculed, but few of the commentators cast doubt upon his basic understanding of the universe. The lack of systematic coherence in Paracelsus's deliberations should not obscure the fact that he is singular in his attempt to create a language and a context in which things known and things feared can be considered together as objects of inquiry. He is one of the few writers during the first half of the sixteenth century who tried to dispel fear while insisting on the natural and God-willed origin of all strange and frightening phenomena. The naturalistic and libertine skepticism that so disturbed the second half of the century had not yet found many followers. On the basis of a system of scientific magic with debts to ancient, medieval, and contemporary scientific models, Paracelsus moved toward an anthropology that allowed him to strengthen people's self-confident insistence on their humanity while deepening ties to a divine and benevolent intellect. Paracelsus's God was a reformed but still a Catholic God, a physician as well as a theologian.

Paracelsus believed, as did Bodin several decades later, that the medical arts and the attitude toward the divine and toward human morality were determined by history and geography. Jews, Saracens, and Turks related differently than Europeans to the ineffable. However, changing times brought changes in healing and worship practices. Lack of reason, Paracelsus contended, did not lead Germany's ancestors into error, rather error was caused by lack of experience (VP, 231, 382). In Adam's time, he commented, brother and sister could marry each other, or a man could keep many wives, practices threatened with severe punishment in the world he knew. The future might, Paracelsus postulated, bring even greater changes, or it might lead humankind back to what had been: "Drum so ist es nichts, die Dinge für ewig in gleicher Fassung vorzulegen, denn was kann der Mensch Ewiges auf Erden machen oder aufrichten?... Die Dinge gehen aus der Zeit, und niemand ist über der Zeit, sondern unter ihr" (LI, 337).[56] The skepticism toward human experience and history detectable in these reflections explains, in part, the peculiar oscillation in Paracelsus's thought, the impossibility of organizing his writings into a system of logical deductions or theological totality. The magic underlying this system is *archive* and *episteme*, unchanging and constantly in flux, at the same time. This linguistic and philosophical opacity explains the controversy that his writings initiated and that was to last for centuries. It also explains the continued fascination with his writings during the centuries following his death. As the ensuing chapters will demonstrate, discussions on the nature of magic will be filled with innumerable intertextual echoes.

4

Magic and Gender: The Struggle for Control in the Witchcraft Tracts of Kramer, Weyer, and Bodin

Paracelsus vigorously defended his work on magic, medicine, the cosmos, and man and woman's role in it against all those who accused him of heretical thinking. The stridency and occasional defensiveness of his rhetoric notwithstanding, Paracelsus's writings did not show the shrill and combative tone that marked the discourse on magic in Kramer's *Malleus Maleficarum* and that was to sharpen considerably in the second half of the sixteenth century and survive well into the seventeenth century. Significantly, while Ringoltingen's German prose adaptation of *Mélusine* continued to sell well and enjoyed considerable favor with the reading public, scholars who wrote on scientific magic found it increasingly unacceptable that the fairy Mélusine should be presented as a valiant Christian woman. Their knowledge and experience confirmed that the universe was inhabited by creatures like Mélusine. But they felt that such women had moved closer to the demons, who, in the course of a long cultural metamorphosis, had become Satan's minions.[1] The steps along the way led from the syncretism of ancient religions and the mysteries of the Old and New Testaments to the demonisms of medieval heresies and, finally, to the fusion of heresy and witchcraft in the theological and juridical debates and reforms of the late fifteenth century.[2] By no means the first, but by all accounts the most comprehensive, effective, and far-reaching consolidation of magic's relationship to witchcraft and heresy, Kramer's *Malleus Maleficarum* gave the starting signal to a discourse on witchcraft and women that gathered momentum in the late fifteenth and early sixteenth centuries and realized its full destructive potential between the years 1580 and 1630.[3] The discourse on witchcraft grew more intense and more belligerent, in part because of Weyer's attempt to steer the discussion in a new direction. As it turned out, his "defense" not only fanned the flames but also helped the *Malleus* gain renewed attention and notoriety after it had fallen into relative obscurity during the first half of the sixteenth century.

In vain we raise the question about the "reality" of witchcraft in the minds of the accused, the accusers, and the authorities who sat in judgment. Nature and the divine constituted "experience" and "knowledge" in the minds of scholars and peoples of antiquity, the Middle Ages, and the early modern period. They moved from presupposition to certainty on the basis of their readings and interpretations of authoritative texts from Greek and Roman antiquity, the Bible, and the church fathers. They observed that lay people, who for the most part could not read or write, harbored beliefs in invisible forces. They sought, moreover, to find where the support for such beliefs might originate, what kinds of natural or supernatural occurrences or forces might support witchcraft. On the basis of their learning, philosophers and theologians populated the universe with demons and angels who mediated human experience with super- and subhuman worlds. Consequently, Mélusine was thought to have lived a human life, not only because of the evidence of buildings attributed to her that could still be admired, or by her sons' epic conquests, but because science, religion, and popular beliefs testified to her existence.

The cultural semiotics of magic led to the semiotics of witchcraft. Its phenomenology was established in the context of experiential realism, which bases knowledge on the existence of the real world; recognizes that reality, such as the Christian religion, places constraints on satanic powers; believes in the reality of divine truth and grace beyond the internal coherence of things; and is committed to a stable knowledge of the world and the universe. Furthermore, the familiarity with magic, either learned or popular, and the knowledge that magic could be exercised by women were integrated into a "principle of attachment," meaning that an unfamiliar action or fact was attached to a familiar one. What at first glance appeared incommensurable seemed less so when supported by the learned authorities of past and present and by everyday experience, which increasingly became the subject of public accusations and trials.[4] Factors such as the ability—indeed the inescapable compulsion—of early modern people to think magical thoughts and to practice and fear witchcraft placed magical discourse at the center of sixteenth-century intellectual debates. Society's earnest and committed attention to all magical phenomena, such as those seen in Paracelsus's cosmology and theology, was striking. Magic figured alongside and interacted with the discourses on discovery and religious dissidence.[5] In fact, as this chapter will illustrate, Bodin, for one, frequently combined his witchcraft condemnations with sharp indictments of contemporary religious strife and the increasing confessional fragmentation.

Weyer and Bodin commented extensively on Paracelsus's work. Weyer repeatedly directed critical comments against Paracelsus's supporters, accusing them first of using, then of distorting, the tenets of Weyer's teacher, Agrippa, and the learned abbot of Sponheim, Trithemius, in their effort to prove that Paracelsus was the superior thinker.[6] Paracelsus not only believed in the reality of creatures like Mélusine; his epistemology provided the needed proof for her existence. But a Lutheran skeptic such as Weyer saw a good deal of self-serving argumentation in the tale; he identified political ambition as the source for such mythical creations.[7]

Less of a skeptic than their adversary Weyer—and, although of profound learning, not scientists—Bodin and Fischart accepted the reality of *Mörfinnen* in Germany or *fées* in France with little difficulty. Adding one of his not infrequent comments to and about Bodin's text, Fischart, writing in support of Bodin's acceptance of such beliefs, cited Paracelsus, who "[did] not want to call such water spirits ghosts (*Gespenst*)." While not mentioning Mélusine by name, Fischart noted that in the woods surrounding Lusignan, such female creatures were said to have had sex (*Bulschafft*) with mortal men (67). The casual impreciseness of this comment signals that Fischart assumed a general familiarity with the tales of sexual contact between spirits and mortals. Mélusine had become a cipher for such contacts.[8]

Frequent references in their writings confirm Weyer's and Bodin's familiarity with Paracelsus's opinions on magic and spirits as well as with his texts on alchemical medicine. Paracelsus had explored the inner and outer spaces of the cosmos; he had theorized about their mutual influences; he had probed the mental and physical dimensions of being; he had affirmed repeatedly and insistently that humans must recognize their existential and epistemological limits so that they might surmount them. By mid-century his writings had gained a considerable audience and had begun to cause scientific and spiritual controversies that were not to end for some time to come.[9]

Paracelsus had praised magic as the science capable of opening the mind and liberating the adept to pursue a knowledge believed to be the unique privilege of human election. Kramer (Institoris) (*Malleus Maleficarum* [1486]), Weyer (*De praestigiis daemonum* [1563]), and Bodin (*La démonomanie des sorciers* [1580])[10] engaged the reader in a theological, medical, and juridical debate on magic and witchcraft that was much less speculative than Paracelsus's thinking. For that reason their work enjoyed a much broader, much less specialized reception. The three voluminous tracts were well known and often quoted during the authors' lifetimes and later.[11] Though they were learned and endeavored to provide the legal and philosophical weapons in a war of killing words against an inarticulate and frequently illiterate enemy, Kramer, Weyer, and Bodin polemicized and inflamed the witchcraft debate. Helped along by social and religious upheavals, their participation fostered a struggle between man and Satan, a struggle whose expiatory burden was borne primarily by women. According to current consensus, women comprised 75 to 90 percent of the victims.[12] But these sixteenth-century writers also legitimated the inquiry into the phenomenon of witchcraft as a science with philosophical, medical, and legal implications.

The close intertextual relationship between the *Malleus Maleficarum,* the *De praestigiis daemonum,* and the *Démonomanie des sorciers* is so conspicuous that these texts can be identified as a trilogy.[13] Together they constitute *the* paradigm of the early modern discourse on witchcraft and satanic magic. In his study of the witch persecution in Bavaria, Wolfgang Behringer has shown that, beginning with the trials at Rottenburg/Sonthofen (1586/87), the court proceedings were based on the *Malleus* as well as on Fischart's translation of the *Démonomanie.* Calling the witches' sabbath a *Hexenreichstag* (Vorred, 109), Fischart from the start emphasized the pervasiveness as well as the social and political threat of this crime.[14] Fischart's empathy with Bodin's opinion is obvious. His frequent insertions and additions—signaled here by the notation "Fischart/Bodin"—broadened Bodin's perspective to include Germany, whose witches were growing in number.[15] Witchcraft, which had survived somewhat submerged through the centuries, surged to the surface with violent force, reaching its climax in the last third of the sixteenth and the first quarter of the seventeenth centuries.

The influence of these three tracts on the debate for or against witchcraft remains undisputed. Critics have, however, left aside the fact that these texts also reproduced—to a larger degree in Bodin's and Weyer's works than in Kramer's—extensive learning and much engaged, if not engaging, authorial self-representation.[16] The informational and instructional intent of these witch tracts—compendia of early modern scholarly knowledge, considerable passion, and obvious misogyny—went far beyond the persecution and/or defense of women identified as witches. Written in the tradition of learned discourse, these texts display a collection of authoritative testimonies on a number of pertinent issues extending from the nature of the universe to questions of early modern judicial and medical practice. They include comments about the culture of the natives in the New World, the perils of the religious strife in Europe, and inquiry into the ways that history and geography might have affected the experience of magic and the habits and numbers of witches. Each tract bears its own specific emphasis: Kramer highlighted theological and inquisitorial concerns; Weyer placed medical and psychological phenomena into the foreground; and Bodin, the most universally educated of the three, tended to emphasize juridical issues.[17] Bodin's virulent attacks and Weyer's psychomedical apologia were placed within the larger context of early modern learned culture in order to signal the pervasiveness of the threat. These writers, especially Bodin, show clear awareness of the incongruity implicit in the pursuit of an illiterate, often poor, and—by all social and political reasoning—insignificant female. Addressing the apparent contradiction in their proposals to punish a crime whose tenets made logical reasoning difficult, they pointed out that the witch knew her secrets not from reading books but strictly from following Satan's direct instruction. Most sorcerers or male witches—such as Dr. Faustus—by contrast, gained their knowledge from books. Knowing without reading, which was thought to be characteristic of witches, was tantamount to knowing beyond authoritative control and orthodox hermeneutics.[18] The struggle over access to knowledge—the prohibition of texts designated as unsuitable to an uninitiated reading public—was always a struggle for control over woman and was part of her persecution as witch.

Each of the three authors had a clear professional profile that was determined by his training in all the most popular and prestigious disciplines: theology, medicine, and law. In the course of his disquisition, each author also found himself forced to enter—and he did so with the appropriate apologies and disclaimers—into areas of knowledge beyond his personal expertise.[19] Trespassing onto another's professional domain put one in real danger of being disqualified and consequently excluded from the dispute altogether.

In his *Vorwarnung* to the translation of the *Démonomanie,* Fischart remarked on Bodin's penchant for adding pleasing and gracious materials so that his reader might find something "daß jhm muntet vnd schmecket" [that he could savor]. Weyer and Bodin appreciated in equal measure the heuristic value of a good story. Aside from the considerable learning employed to instruct and persuade readers—and no doubt to frighten them into rejecting witchcraft and/or denouncing witches—the tracts contain a surprising number of entertaining tales.[20] Many a story about magic and possession, sexual practices and moral failings, the psychology and physiology of women and men, the silliness of the clergy and the stupidity of scholars, are included and frequently repeated to heighten reading pleasure.

Kramer, less a teller of tales than a preacher of reproof and retribution, quoted a wide array of church authorities, thereby keeping his use of exempla to the minimum needed to stress the seriousness of his message and to make it geographically explicit.[21] Weyer and Bodin, however, assembled an impressively varied collection of tales, which they gathered from authoritative texts of the past, from contemporary reports of magistrates, jurists, and exorcists, as well as from stories people told in the marketplace. Clearly, they knew the taste of their audience and wanted to accommodate it. Weyer put it best:

> Now, lest I sicken the delicate reader with too lengthy a catalogue of statements detailing the wondrously varied and monstrous enterprises of demons, and lest, on the other hand, I appear to have failed those of stronger stomach, who seek out and welcome a variety of such spices, I shall simply indicate the chief passages in the ancient authors. (65)

Nonetheless, he more often than not told, rather than simply referenced, these tales, wishing to avoid boring those "with stronger stomachs."

Kramer, self-proclaimed expert on the witchcraft phenomenon—and in this role, a harbinger of conflicts to come—had the authority for his inquisitorial endeavors bestowed upon him and his coinquisitor, Jakob Sprenger—both Dominican monks—by a papal bull. Pope Innocent VIII commissioned both men through an order known by its initial words, "Summis desiderantes affectibus," issued on December 12, 1484, in Rome. Ernst Pitz has shown that the production of such an order did not necessarily mean that the pope's directive was in any way a personal mandate to Kramer and Sprenger. But the document conferred papal authority and sanction on them as they went in search of those men and women in upper Germany whom they suspected of satanic interests and preoccupations, i.e., of being a threat to Christendom and to the whole of society.[22]

The *Malleus* was written in a hurry. It was intended more to provide advice and justification for immediate action than to entertain and educate a public with literary or intellectual pretensions. It wanted to convince a not yet truly receptive readership of the presence of witches in their midst. For the benefit of this audience, the author of the *Malleus* defined a crime and prescribed a procedure for prosecution as well.

> [Es ist] kurtz wegen der Zusammenziehung sehr vieler Autoren ins Kurtze.... Daher es nicht für unser Werck, sondern vielmehr für derjenigen geachtet wird, aus deren Worten fast alles und jedes zusammengetragen ist.... So überlassen wir die Übersehung des Werkes unsern Gesellen, die Vollziehung aber denen, welchen das strengste Gericht obliget, deswegen, weil sie zur Rache der Bösen ... gesetzt sind von Gott. (Apologia, xlvi)[23]

The text is divided into three parts, each of which is in turn arranged into numerous and often repetitive categories. According to its author, the work was "old and new": "old" because of its content; and "new" because of the way the content was arranged (xlv). The cast of characters is small: the witch (sometimes male, most often female),[24] the inquisitor, and Satan. The detailed, frequently cumbersome structure contrasts sharply with the simplicity of the stated theme: how to identify, try, and judge the most elusive, perpetually growing, dangerous crime, witchcraft, and how to capture and control its principal agent, woman:

> Da es unsere Hauptabsicht in diesem Werke ist, uns Inquisitoren der Länder von Oberdeutschland der Inquisition der Hexen, soweit es mit Gott geschehen kann, zu entledigen, indem wir sie ihren Richtern zur Bestrafung überlassen. (Pt. 3, 7)[25]

Kramer insisted that the reality of this threat was not to be doubted. He based his arguments and his actions on the church's pronouncement—and therefore irrefutable truth—that the world was filled with legions of witches and that their number was growing. These witches not only endangered themselves by forsaking the salvation of their souls; they imperiled the world because "mit Hilfe von Dämonen, kraft ihres mit diesen geschlossenen Paktes, mit der Zulassung Gottes wirkliche Hexenkünste vollbringen zu können" [with the help of demons, and because of their pact with them, and with God's tolerance, (they could) practice real witchcraft] (Pt. 1, 10).

The confusing and repetitive chapters are as much the result of the work's hasty production as of Kramer's attempt to provide preachers with a guide to, and commentary on, the witch phenomenon.[26] Preaching on witchcraft inevitably meant preaching on the depravity of women, whose weakness of body and spirit always put them in grave danger of falling into superstitious practices and satanic subterfuge. A woman's sin was judged more bitter than death, which destroyed only the body; witchcraft had the potential to destroy the soul. Kramer defined authoritatively and for all times the nature of the witch as one who by her own free will entered into a pact with the Devil, becoming his demon lover. She could move about while her body stayed behind, practiced cannibalism—especially on children—and injured people, animals, and crops through her magical arts. Kramer branded midwives as especially dangerous: "Hexenhebammen" either killed babies at birth or pledged unbaptized newborns to the Devil (Pt. 1, 92). Woman's very name, "femina"—from "fe-minus"—indicated her status as the lesser creature, the one with "little faith." Kramer believed that female weakness also signified perverse and dangerous strength: a woman's extraordinary affect and passions, her lust for pleasures of the body, and her attraction to the forbidden all made it impossible to control her through reason alone:

> Alles geschieht aus fleischlicher Begierde, die bei ihnen unersättlich ist.... "Dreierlei ist unersättlich und das vierte, das niemals spricht: es ist genug, nämlich die Öffnung der Gebärmutter." Darum haben sie auch mit den Dämonen zu schaffen, um ihre Begierden zu stillen. (Pt. 1, 106)[27]

Although she is the undisputed protagonist of Kramer's handbook, woman does not speak on her own behalf, nor is she spoken to; she is only spoken about. Neither Weyer, who of the three writers was the most benevolent toward her "lesser" nature, nor the legalistic Bodin ever allowed her to come forth from the text and face her audience. She was, however, an extremely active object of their attention. Through demonic agency she changed people's hearts; inflamed men or women with unseemly, destructive, rest-robbing passions; obstructed the powers of procreation; removed the sexual organs in males; induced abortion or early birth; and sacrificed children to the Devil.[28] The three tracts never tire of affirming that woman, witch or not, required above all society's firm, constant, and total control. Yet one could never be sure that she would not find a way to circumvent even the most rigorous surveillance.

The woman-turned-witch was relentless in her assault on human order. She was to blame for the terror of the man who looked down at his body only to find a smooth surface where his penis had been. Kramer firmly believed that the witch, in collusion with the Devil, did in fact make the penis disappear (Pt. 1, 137). The dread of being sexually vulnerable to witchcraft, to satanically induced castration, was intensified by the image of the disgendered male, whose sexual organs may have been pulled inside his body, making him appear female. Medieval and early modern physiology distinguished male from female less by the physiological difference of their sexual organs than by their location. What in males had been placed outside of the body—the penis and scrotum—was in the female positioned inside—the vagina and uterus. Insufficient body heat was believed to have prevented protrusion of these body parts, this biological inversion, when the baby was growing in the mother's womb. In this context, a missing penis did not merely signal impotence but the even more terrifying prospect of having been changed into a woman.[29] Far from portraying a rare occurrence, Kramer's report made this affliction a common and public event: "was feststeht nachdem, was sehr viele Leute gesehen und gehört; auch nach dem öffentlichen Gerede, daß durch das Sehen und Betasten die Wahrheit bezüglich jenes Gliedes bekannt wurde" (Pt. 1, 138).[30] The fact that such a change was not real, and only appeared to be so because of demonic trickery, did not comfort the afflicted. Nor did it diminish the gravity of the crime directed against the institution of matrimony, since it affected procreation.

Early modern demonologues were convinced that the Devil and the witch both envied and detested the married state because God had blessed its institution. The pursuit and punishment of the witch implied the protection of marriage, whose stabilizing and disciplining force was the subject of much debate in the sixteenth century.[31] Although the witch could not really prevent conception in marriage, she could, with the help of demons and with God's sanction, make conception difficult by causing impotence or infertility, by inducing a stillbirth, by diverting the attention of marital partners away from each other, or by killing children as a sacrifice to Satan (Pt. 1, 127). These actions not only damaged marriage in its role as the most important agency for the control of social and moral behavior; they also threatened the whole of the body politic.[32] Just as significantly, witches could slow the approach of Judgment Day, thereby affecting the course of sacred history:

Denn der Teufel weiß, daß [vor der Taufe ermordete Kinder nicht in den Himmel kommen]. Daher wird auch das jüngste Gericht länger hinausgeschoben [werden], je langsamer sich die Zahl der Auserwählten ergänzt: ist sie voll, so wird die Welt aufgehoben werden. (Pt. 2, 138)[33]

Early modern discourse on heresy and witchcraft subjugated and diminished especially the older, poorer woman; but it also unintentionally enhanced her status. Legal practice and jurisprudence became progressively bureaucratized with regard to the definition of the crime and the pursuit of the supposed female perpetrator. For centuries woman had been identified as the lesser creation.[34] Still, her sin was judged to be so grave precisely because she knowingly and actively entered into her pact and denied the efficacy of the sacraments, that is, she exercised her free will (Pt. 1, 178, 196). The witch instinctively knew how to do harm and how to control certain powers in nature (Bodin, Vorred, 97). Her sin outweighed the trespass of the fallen angels because she sinned in full awareness of the consequences; having been baptized, she actively scorned the state of grace. Her sin was condemned as a direct and willful affront to God, the Creator and Redeemer (Pt. 1, 202).

The weight of this predisposition to commit the most heinous acts made Weyer's attempt at pathologizing such crimes difficult. He needed to find a way around this supposed female activism. In his effort to protect woman, he diminished her responsibility and reduced her obvious willfulness and her potential, albeit negative, strength. His persistence in characterizing the woman, the typical suspect of witchcraft, as old, decrepit, melancholic, and mad considerably limited her ability to exercise free will. Weyer was not alone in this diffident attitude toward humankind's self-determination. Adding a personal comment to Bodin's text, Fischart tempered the French jurist's positive assessment of humankind's freedom to act. He criticized Bodin's source, the Jewish philosopher Moses Maimonides, as overly self-confident, and he expressed doubts about humankind's ability to practice reasonable judgment after the Fall.[35]

In the course of increasing juridical formalism, an unexpected and ironic revaluation of woman nevertheless took place: the inquisitors relentlessly insisted that woman was—as God's creature—responsible for her own acts, that she had been granted and could exercise free will. Neither Kramer nor his successors reduced this responsibility to a metaphor, a mere cipher for her damnation. The Devil is prevented by God's power from exerting direct influence on the freedom of human beings to decide their fates. But man and, especially, woman are weak, easily influenced by satanic tricks; such weakness leads them to abandon the path to salvation.[36] This newly highlighted understanding brought unintended consequences. In cases of heresy and witchcraft, early modern court proceedings authorized the woman and those who shared her precarious existence—the child,[37] the dishonored, those convicted of false testimony—to bear true witness. Even if of ill repute and known to be a witch, a woman could and—aided by the increase in the number of trials on heresy and witchcraft in the early modern period—did testify as a fully recognized person under the law. Chapter 3 of the *Malleus,* "the criminal code" of the inquest, specifies that these individuals could not testify for the defendant, only for the prosecution:

Merke, daß Exkommunizierte, ebenso Teilhaber und Genossen des Verbrechens, ebenso Infame und Verbrecher, Sklaven gegen ihre Herren zur Verhandlung und zum Zeugnis in jedweder Glaubenssache zugelassen werden; ebenso wie Ketzer gegen Ketzer zum Zeugnis zugelassen wird, so auch Hexer gegen Hexer, jedoch nur mangels anderer Beweise und immer gegen und nicht für. (Pt. 3, 42)[38]

When, in the course of punishing a *crimen exceptum,*[39] help was needed to prosecute the heretic or the witch, female testimony and that of dishonorable persons ("Meineidige und Ehrlose") were validated by the fact that such testimony provided the evidence ("Indizien") needed to induce a voluntary confession and to assure successful prosecution.

Consistent with inquisitorial law, Kramer insisted that the prosecution required two women to testify in place of one man. A century later, while still mentioning the two-for-one rule, Bodin added the claim that in the case of witchcraft, one witness sufficed. He based his opinion on changes in canon and imperial law:

> Aber die Römischen Keyser vnnd Juristen / als sie wargenommen / daß / wofern dise Vberzeugungen nicht platz finden solten / der grösser theil Mißhandlungen vnnd Verbrechen vngestrafft hiengehen würden.... So ist derwegen zu vnserm vorhaben gäntzlich erheischlich / den Weiberen dißfalls Glauben zu zustellen / Vnbetracht / ob sie schon / wie vnsere Doctores sprechen / würcklich mit der That ahn Ehren verleumbdet / oder ... geschmächt oder Ignominiosae weren / gleich wie ein Ehren verwegen unzüchtig Weib deßgleichen sein mag. (214)[40]

Such developments were coupled with other changes concerning the inquisitorial procedures against witches, notably the secrecy of testimony; the greater weight placed on circumstantial evidence, such as facial expression or nervousness; the permission to use undercover informers; and the instituting of a carefully prepared system of interrogation. These alterations in the law underscore an inconsistency. They reflect the growing inability of the victims to escape once they were caught in the net of the inquisition. But they also suggest that the procedures were organized in such a way that the failure to observe prohibitions against the unauthorized use of torture and excessive cruelty could be, and often were, punished.[41] In addition, the demands for total accuracy and exhaustive detail when transcribing the interrogations ensured that "the notary [wrote] not only all the answers of the accused but also all his comments, gestures, and everything he said under torture, including all his sighs, cries, laments, and tears."[42] The inquisitors became well versed in the interpretation of verbal and nonverbal signs.

Researchers commonly acknowledge—and I have pointed to this fact repeatedly in the course of my analysis—that after the first violent outbreak of witch persecution between the years 1486 and 1520, a relative calm, what Behringer called a *Latenzphase*,[43] set in; from then until the middle of the sixteenth century, the *Malleus* all but disappeared from printing programs.[44] During the fifties the debate heated up again, so much so that Weyer felt compelled to enter the discussion. The *De praestigiis daemonum* was published in 1563, the year the Council of Trent came to an end. From this time forward, the debates about witchcraft grew in intensity, as did the persecutions: the fires were lit with terrifying frequency in southwestern Germany, in Lorraine, and in parts of France.[45]

For many years court physician in the service of the duke of Cleve, Weyer shared with his contemporaries a belief in the efficacy of Satan and his minions, the precariousness of the human spirit, the vulnerability of women, and the salutary impact of knowledge and information. His work begins with a position statement:

> Intending to explain the illusions and spells of demons, I shall begin with their principal cause—the Devil—and his wiles, aims, and power.... I totally reject the maxims of Aristotle and the Peripatetics... that demons do not exist in reality.... They suffer an infinitely more severe punishment for their fall, and await a heavier punishment in the future, than does humankind for its transgression. (*De praestigiis daemonum*, 3–5)

Weyer's and Bodin's world looked a bit different from Sprenger's: the reform movements had changed the religious landscape, and the conquest of the New World had broadened the geographical, cultural, and political horizon. These changes are fully present in Weyer's and Bodin's works, but they are incorporated without any identifiable impact on their traditional and conservative view of the divine universe. In this universe the new people of the Americas were not—as Paracelsus, Cardano, and Giordano Bruno had believed—a totally different, pre-Adamic race; they were heathens whose adoration of idols and practice of human sacrifice confirmed, consistent with common assumptions, that demons existed everywhere in the world (20). Weyer and Bodin/Fischart drew supporting evidence from the travel report of the Catholic priest André Thevet, who early in the century had been sent to convert the Brazilians, and from Girolamo Benzoni's *Histories of the Indies,* translated from Italian into Latin (1578) and French (1579) by his compatriot Urbain Chauveton (Urbanus Calvetus).[46] Thevet had reported that the Europeans considered the god Agnan (or Aygnan) to be the most prominent and the most feared of the various deities revered by the natives. Agnan, whose home was in the woods, was said to change his shape and to afflict his people cruelly (Weyer, 77).[47] The similarity to Satan was undeniable, especially since these new people were said to be cannibals.

On the basis of such readings, Weyer concluded that the belief in spirits was universal: they were adored in equal measure by the natives of faraway Canada and Guinea. He had heard that the priests and seers of the native peoples approached their demons only after they had abstained from sexual contact with their wives for twelve days. This practice was not unlike the cleansing rituals that prescribed sexual abstinence to the European magus prior to his practicing magic.[48] As part of the ritual, the American magus was said to rest on a bed prepared for this purpose by a maiden twelve years of age—the age customarily associated in early modern physiology with puberty. Recounting his experience with a similar ritual practice, Christopher Columbus reported that before searching for gold, the natives spent twenty days fasting; during this time of cleansing and self-control, they also practiced sexual abstinence. Christian and pagan ritual thus accorded with each other and gained a new and acceptable effectiveness for Columbus; he attached desired Christian results to unfamiliar ritual. In this way he resolved the incommensurability between Christian and pagan beliefs. The experiential realism of the conqueror—his knowledge that certain behaviors had specific consequences—enabled him to deal with the native people as if he understood their actions. Fitting all that he discovered into what he already knew, he incorporated the American experience into the European model.[49]

The travel literature circulating widely at this time provided Weyer and his contemporaries with information on the natives' use of herbs such as tobacco and of potions to induce trances and visions (Weyer, 230). Weyer distinguished between benevolent medicine, such as herbal remedies, and noxious herbs ingested to induce a state of prophetic trance. Judging by his comments, Weyer did not doubt the veracity of the reports he read. He believed them to be as "true" as the tales from ancient texts that he cited to illustrate his message. Old or new, visions resulting from smoking or ingesting strange herbs were, to Weyer's mind, satanic delusions—fewer in number in his day than in the past, but of the same origin. Throughout *De praestigiis daemonum,* Weyer held firm to his conviction that devilish acts, regardless of where they were committed, or by whom, were illusions. He repeatedly criticized and contradicted Kramer's contention that a demon could have sexual intercourse with a man [as a succubus] and then swiftly transport the seed to the woman with whom he lies as her incubus (249). He rejected this notion for reasons of physics—no demon could move fast enough to stop the seed from growing cold and dying—and for those of logic—

the human race would have long since become a "mother of monsters" (250). Weyer employed tales from antiquity as well as from contemporary sources to illustrate his points and entertain the reader, confirming the efficacy of storytelling as a didactic tool.

Woman, the main protagonist of the struggle between Satan and humankind in Kramer's *Malleus* and in many of the late-sixteenth-century treatises on witchcraft, played a more differentiated and psychologically subtle role in Weyer's work. Indeed, as Midelfort points out, toward the end of the sixteenth century, jurists felt increasingly compelled to call on physicians to assist in determining whether an accused woman was truly melancholic or simply possessed.[50] Two types of the possessed female emerge from this learned exposition, which was also a dispute with scholarly predecessors. One finds the young, often unmarried woman or girl who, when healed of her affliction, will live happily ever after. And one reads of the demented, lascivious, melancholic old woman. Implicit in these two types are the traditional female dichotomies: young/old, pretty/ugly, fertile/barren; and, by implication, productive/useless. Both female types are potentially and dangerously sexual.

In the case of the young woman, Weyer reflected the reformatory emphasis on marriage and family, insisting and confirming by his examples that she could and must be saved, i.e., tamed, in marriage. He tells of one such young woman, for whom possession ended when she forcibly began a life elsewhere. The brutality of her situation can be read between the lines: after the young woman entered a convent because of an unhappy love affair, she showed all the signs of satanic possession, infecting her fellow nuns with the same affliction. She was arrested and taken away. While imprisoned, she twice became pregnant by her guard, whose offspring she bore, and "she lived out the rest of her life free from any suspicion of witchcraft" (306). In another instance a young woman—again unhappy in love—was tempted by a demon. She resisted, whereupon he tortured her with frequent fantasies. Ultimately, however, she was saved in marriage and enjoyed splendid health forever after. The message could not be simpler: for the Protestant Weyer, marriage was the only real, if not entirely reliable, protection against possession.

No such haven existed for the older woman. In the early modern imagination, the elderly female was foolish, depraved, and prone to scandalous sexual promiscuity. Social historians describe many of the victims of the persecutions as older women, more often than not living in a closed rural society, lacking education, typically employed in some kind of menial labor.[51] In book 3 Weyer proceeds to define witches in traditional terms. He prefers to call her *lamia:*

> I use the term *lamia* for a woman who, by virtue of a deceptive or imaginary pact that she has entered into with the demon, supposedly perpetrates all kinds of evil-doing, whether by thought or by curse or by glance or by the use of some ludicrous object unsuited for this purpose. For example, she can ignite the air with strange bolts of lightning or shatter it with terrifying claps of thunder, beat [down upon the earth] with a damaging profusion of unexpected hail, rouse storms, ravage the fertile crops in the field or transfer them elsewhere, stir up unnatural diseases for men and beasts and then heal them again, travel great distances abroad within a few hours, dance with demons, hold banquets, play the role of succubus or have intercourse with demons, change herself and others into beasts, and display a thousand monstrous mockeries. (166)

The woman who could effect all this was "dulled by old age, or inconstant by reason of her sex, or unsteady because of her weak-mindedness, or in despair because of a disease of the mind" (174). Kramer had offered the etymology of *fe-minus* to define female nature; Weyer quotes Augustine and Lactantius, who took *mulier* to come from *mollities,* which Gratian understood to mean "softness of the spirit" on account of her frailty, weakness, and infirmity (182). Weyer called her decrepit, of corrupt imagination, raving, poor, mentally unstable, and wanton. The women's oft-claimed intercourse with the Devil was purely imaginary, though still despicable because it resulted from self-stimulation, "helped by their imaginings" (231).[52]

To the young woman, danger came less from the demon than from her inexperience. It misdirected her thoughts toward impure sexual visions and tempted her to practice "lascivious rubbing," which could potentially cause defloration, thereby destroying the sign of virginity necessary for the marriage contract (235). There was no doubt in Weyer's mind—for he responded as a physician and as a devout Lutheran—that masturbation and its potential consequences could expose the young woman to spiritual danger.[53] Social censure directed against sexual behavior deemed aberrant was a greater threat to her than satanic possession. Weyer was adamant about this issue; clearly he preferred to punish sexual misconduct than to persecute for witchcraft. To underscore this point, he categorically denounced what he described as the "sexual mingling of witches among themselves," or lesbianism. Fearing potential harm if he were to report such "odious" examples from his own time and town, he safely selected an example from the past of another culture.[54] In the African city of Fez, there lived a group of women said to claim "great familiarity with demons." However, instead of consorting with demons, these women, called *Sahacat* or, in Latin, *fricatrices* (the etymological link to *fricere* [to rub] is no accident), had sexual relations among themselves "in damnable fashion" (249). They were even said to have seduced women who came to seek their counsel. Worse yet, they turned these women's affections away from their husbands. Obscuring established social/sexual identities in married women, such morally unacceptable and illicit sexual activity constituted a serious threat to social order. It therefore had to be punished, "with sticks" or even at the stake.

While he spurned this "unnatural" passion, Weyer acknowledged that on occasion women acted like men, not for sexual pleasure but for reasons of greed or self-defense. In such cases ridicule rather than harsh punishment was the recommended response. In spite of his stern criticism, Weyer insisted that carnal relations with demons were not necessarily to be equated with the impulse of women who turned to each other for sexual gratification. Rather, women had this dangerous and maddening inclination to "take great delight in filthy lust and would perform it [the sexual act] upon themselves rather than in conjunction with men if this were at all possible" (254). Far from blaming satanic delusion for such behavior or for the rare change of a woman into man, Weyer, as a scholar and physician, considered such occurrences to be natural. Women's physiology was constructed in such a way that they could become men. Of course, the same physiology militated against this metamorphosis occurring in the other direction. Having extensively studied the past and present medical literature, Weyer was sufficiently familiar with the similarity of male and female sexual organs, with what Thomas Laqueur calls the "one-sex" model, to describe this potential transformation in clinical detail (345). He believed that changes from male to female—but not in the reverse—were rare and that they had nothing to do with possession or witchcraft: "Although women are feminine in actuality, I would call them masculine in potentiality—it follows necessarily that the order of change proceeds only from the female sex to the male" (346).

The entertainment as well as the instructional value of Weyer's message is irrefutable. Compared with Paracelsus's scientific writings, which are often linguistically difficult, the *De praestigiis* is an accessible and enjoyable work. One notes, moreover, that Weyer's earnestly urgent attempt to break the vicious cycle of the witchcraft debate informed his writing. His sincerity in this regard is striking, as is his pleasure in telling stories of the danger of demonic temptation. Weyer mentions a collection published in Paris in 1580 entitled *Unusual Stories from Around the World* as his source for some of the tales (352). This book, also known under the title *Historia festive figmenta: foemella daemonica (Unusual stories about possessed women)*, was merely one among any number of tracts on the subject, signaling the great popularity of the topic, not just among the learned public.[55] Judging from the production and the rapid increase in publication and circulation of learned tracts on witchcraft, it is clear that the reception of such texts was widespread and included members of all social classes among its readers/listeners.

Weyer's place is assured in the pantheon of those who fought against the persecution of women called witches. Just why he and others who shared his skepticism were not more effective in their opposition against the terror, or at least in turning the discussion in a less frightful direction at this early stage of the persecutions, has remained largely unexplained. In part the reasons must be sought in the fact that his opponents were extremely vocal and reflected the majority opinion, learned or popular.[56] An additional reason might be that many demonologists on both sides of the argument, including notables such as Weyer, Delrio, Johann Gödelmann, Scultetus, and Friedrich Spee, never doubted the existence of witches and their susceptibility to satanic temptation. In spite of their disagreements, they did concede that the most important prosecutorial tool—irrefutable proof—was impossible to secure.[57] As the debate became more virulent and violent, anyone who agreed with Weyer's theses risked imprisonment, banishment, or, worse, the stake. Dissimulation, the formulation of opinions in such a way that one could not be accused of colluding with the enemy, therefore became a conscious tactic.[58]

The growing inquisitorial chill affecting the debate about witchcraft did not prevent Weyer's work from being widely circulated. Several editions (six in the original Latin, and numerous translations—four into German [one by Weyer himself], plus two into French) appeared during his lifetime (van Nahl, *Zauberglaube und Hexenwahn*, 66). He amended the last Latin edition (1583) with a sixth book, which was in part an effort to respond to Bodin, whose broad attack on the *De praestigiis* had appeared in 1580. Bodin's work was widely read and translated equally quickly. It contributed significantly to Weyer's marginalization and to the decidedly reactionary, legalistic, and bureaucratic turn taken by the witchcraft debate. In spite of sharp attacks that employed all the weapons of theological and sociological polemics, the main thrust of Bodin's relentless critique was a challenge to Weyer's professional competence: Bodin accused Weyer of having argued in favor of changing the legal procedures in witch trials without credentials, i.e., without the authority of a conferred legal degree. Similar attacks came from theologians, who denied Weyer the right to speak on issues such as heresy and witchcraft. Thus the struggle for and against women as witches was fought as much over scholarly turf as over the issue of the woman herself.[59]

In a lengthy preface, Bodin specifies the reasons for writing his tract. It is meant as an answer to Weyer, "so sich für ein beschürmer der Hexen außgibt" [who calls himself protector of witches] (71). His title already draws attention to the seriousness of his message in contrast to, in Fischart's terms, the mild approach that characterized Weyer's treatment of the topic (Vorred, 3). Throughout the text this epithet or ones similar to it are used when Weyer is mentioned.[60] Bodin begins *in medias res*— with the story of Johanna Hartwilerin, a witch from the area of Compiègne who testified that her mother had pledged her to Satan at the age of twelve, the age when girls became "mannbar" (marriageable) (Vorred, 1).[61] Following this dedication, she became Satan's consort for many years, remaining with him even while married. Her mother had been burned as a witch in Senlis, confirming the belief of theologians, jurists, and the common people that witchcraft was passed on from generation to generation, especially from mother to daughter. Mother and daughter had both been known for frequent and suspicious moves from one community to another: "Namen, Ort vnd wonung offt zu ändern / dadurch jhre händel heimlich vnd hehl zuhalten" [Name, town and residence often changed / (with the help of which she tried) to keep her doings secret and hidden] (Vorred, 2). Against the demand of the people (*das Volk*), who wanted to burn Johanna immediately for fear that she might cause more harm, the judge insisted on a "gebürlich verfahren" [due process]. He secured all necessary information to ensure a fair trial. When the time came to pronounce judgment, the jurors imposed the death sentence but could not agree on the method of execution. In the end, she was burned alive:

> jhre abschewliche Laster vnd Mordstück / auch die straffen von Göttlichen vnnd Menschlichen Gesatzen dergleichen Vbelthätigen aufferlegt / vnd sonderlich den gemeinen brauch der Christenheit / welcher von alters her inn disem Königreich vblich. (Vorred, 2)[62]

Starting his treatise with a case of such notoriety—he mentions Johanna Hartwilerin repeatedly in his text—Bodin set the tone and stated the theme of his lengthy disquisition: the witch was a woman, often given at birth to Satan, with whom she would have intercourse even while married. Though the practice of witchcraft was very old—its lengthy history is reviewed carefully and in detail—Bodin wanted to impress upon his readers that witchcraft was a contemporary phenomenon and a grave danger to Christendom. He insisted that wise judges and magistrates had to ensure that the laws be observed and justice done, even if overzealous and terrified common folk called for immediate execution.

Weighing the social, political, religious, and judicial impact of witchcraft differently, Bodin and Weyer were also at odds over what they considered possible, comprehensible, natural, supernatural, human, divine, and demonic.[63] Both accepted that proof of witchcraft was found as much in the persistence of its history as in the expanse of its geography, its presence around the globe:

> Darauß [aus Geschichten über Hexen] alsdann bescheinen soll / wie eigentlich dergleichen Historien / so sich auch bei vnderschiedenen Völckern / vnd zu weit vnterschiedlichen zeiten begeben / allezeit zusamen treffen vnd stimmen / vnd solches auß der Zauberer vnnd Hexenhändel vnd bekantnussen selber. (Vorred, 11)[64]

People like Weyer, who tried to excuse or save these witches and who believed their existence to be a matter of fiction (*Fabelwerck*), were considered a menace to the country and an affront to God.[65] Whereas Weyer had interpreted the conquest of the New World as evidence of the possibility of superstition existing anywhere on earth—the woman-turned-witch was merely one such example—Fischart, in an extended aside upon the Bodin text, took the "satanic" practices of the foreign people to be confirmation that demons did exist at all times the world over. Fischart articulates an opinion that Bodin shared: that nature offered innumerable examples of the strangest occurrences and things. Long before Columbus arrived in America, the natives had practiced religious ceremonies that induced possessions and strange visions (*wunderding*) (17).

The historicity of witchcraft as well as the existence of Satan and his minions in the New World since time began was confirmation as much of this truth as of its contemporary satanic manifestations. Commenting on Jean de Léry's description of the siege of Sancerre (1573), Fischart reviewed the horror of the Wars of Religion: there was, he argued, no reason to feel superior to the American cannibals.[66] The experience at home was every bit as horrendous. His description seems to conjure the witches' sabbath:

... sie jhre wehrlose Mit Christen vnd Landsleut zu Leon ermördt / vnd in den Fluß Saone geworffen / sie widerum herauß gezogen / auffgeschnitten / das Schmaltz heraußgenommen.... Auch / die Lebern vnnd Hertzen / sampt andern stucken Menschliches Leibs gefressen.... Wann nuhn nach ob abgezogenem Gesatz / die / so Menschenfleisch fressen den Todt sollen verwirckt haben / warumb procediert man dann nicht gegen diesen Hunden gleich so wol als wider die Todtenfressenden Hechssen / demnach sie ein nie erhörte Vnmenschlichkeit vnder Christenleuten ohne schew haben eingeführet. (239)[67]

Like the experience of total disorder that was implicit in cannibalism at home, human sin in general and witchcraft—its most nefarious expression—in particular affected human, natural, and sacred history.[68] No place on earth could escape its scourge; the northern European countries were plagued as much as the "occidentalischen Newen Insulen... Innmassen der Bischoff von Upsal Olaus Magnus / vnnd die Indischen Historien solches bezeugen" [the occidental new islands... as the bishop of Uppsala Olaus Magnus / and the Indian histories bear witness] (147).[69] Across the ocean among the indigenous people could be found "vil Frawenklöster / welche von verschnittenen entmandten Leuten / so auch Nasen vnd Meuler abgehauwene hatten / sehr fleißsig verwart wurden" [many nunneries / that are very diligently cared for by eunuchs /whose noses and lips have been cut off]. In the margins Fischart noted:

"Nunnenklöster in Indien" (18). Like the children of Rome, who were said to have carried a phallic symbol around the neck to ward off "allerley gespenst" [all kinds of spirits], these natives carried images of "Pederastia oder Buberonigkeit" [pederasty and buggery] for the same purpose (178).[70] The conquering Spaniards interpreted the natives' imagined proclivity toward sodomy and other "unnatural and shameful" acts as a justification first to subjugate and then to exterminate them. Bodin seemed convinced that the American natives were ruled by Satan, who had taught them their rituals a long time before "welches dann nicht fremd noch neu ist" [which is neither strange nor new] (18). Where there were "entmandte Leute" [castrated people], there also had to be demon worshippers, i.e., witches.[71] Bodin found confirmation for his deduction in Benzoni's *Historien von den Occidentalischen Inseln;* there it was said that the heathen god Concote slept with the natives' wives. To a European observer or reader, this information could only mean that these gods were devils and that the native women practiced the same kind of witchcraft as the women at home (131). In this way, the unfamiliar was easily familiarized; learning and logic provided the tools that helped reduce a potentially terrifying new people to the status of barely human. Experience at home created expectations that served as so many mental categories for knowing the new reality and for motivating the actions necessary to affirm the superiority of Europeans over the new worlds opening up before their eyes.[72] Thus for Bodin and for many of his contemporaries, the suppression of witches was as much a problem of instituting political and social order as it was of punishing perceived transgressions. Those who tolerated witchcraft, demon worship, unruly women, and disorderly communities endangered the kingdom and its people as well as their individual souls.

In the last chapters of their tracts, the three writers discussed at great length and careful detail the legal implications of their works. The legist Fischart even went a step beyond the theoretical, appending to his translation several pages of meticulously explicit inquisitorial questions as an aid to his colleagues on the bench. Their differing approaches to the witchcraft issue notwithstanding, Kramer, Weyer, Bodin, and Fischart were similarly struggling to construct unassailable judicial proofs and legally correct trial procedures in response to the ever increasing doubts about whether or not an admission of guilt, "the queen of proofs" needed for a just sentence, was attainable or even of any value if extracted under the threat of torture.

For Kramer and Bodin/Fischart, this meant tightening and clarifying the rules of prosecution and courtroom procedures. Weyer wanted to change the presuppositions and keep the women out of the courtroom altogether. He maintained that a woman stood accused whether she spoke or whether she remained silent. Indeed, women often lost consciousness, and after recovering told of having traveled great distances. In a celebrated case, Johanna Hartwilerin admitted to such an experience before she was burned (289). Bodin and Fischart saw in such confessions an admission of truth.

More than a translator, Fischart made Bodin's tract accessible to German audiences; as a commentator, he entered into the dispute with Weyer on Bodin's side, and ultimately he contributed to strengthening the authority of the *Malleus*. In 1582, a year after the publication of the Bodin translation, Fischart's two-volume edition of several witch tracts appeared in Frankfurt, a sign that his work was appreciated.[73] As before, he corrected, added marginalia, and chapter headings; in short, he made these texts, especially the *Malleus,* accessible to a broader audience. Fischart had become an expert on the literature, and his editing and translation reflected his own thinking. His work on this later edition confirms what his many marginal comments and efforts at a clearer organization of the Bodin tract indicated: he shared with Bodin the belief that witchcraft presented a grave danger for all of Europe, and that the strict enforcement of laws was needed to vanquish the enemy. Neither Bodin nor Fischart seemed discomfited by the apparent contradiction between this conviction and their other writings. Witchcraft was a crime against public order; even if Bodin was, as many of his contemporaries seemed to believe, a "Judaizer" and/or a skeptic, he shared with them the belief that religion—and the fear of witches was only its darkest side—was needed to keep order among the people. Witches embodied the essence of disorderliness, for they subverted the order of sexual and procreative practices, family structure, and the divine institution of the state.

The works of Kramer, Weyer, and Bodin/Fischart were to have a long history. All three texts appear frequently in the citations and references of the literature on witchcraft written in the following decades. It is not surprising that Lancre, witchcraft expert at the Parliament of Bordeaux, frequently cited Bodin, reserving special approval for his judicial acuity and political understanding of the witchcraft phenomenon. Lancre's writings confirm that as the years wore on, the witchcraft debate gained judicial precision and deadly force.

5

Magic and the Margins: Pierre de Lancre

The French magistrate Pierre de Lancre lived and worked in Bordeaux, the city of his birth, around the turn of the century. Like Bodin, he was one of the immensely learned lawyers who, toward the last third of the sixteenth century, gave a destructive twist to the witchcraft dispute. There were other sources, but Bodin's influence on Lancre is pronounced; in turn, both writers were frequently read and widely quoted.[1] They shared the conviction that a stern judicial approach was primary in any attempt to control the practice of satanic magic.

But the task was far from easy. At times Lancre seemed overwhelmed by the inescapable realization that in all parts of the world, however remote, there were men, women, and children who had been seduced by Satan. Whatever other cultural differences separated these victims, they were always considered a danger to themselves and a threat to their communities as a result of their contact with the Devil. The personal and the communal thus came together in the practice of magic and witchcraft. While Lancre rejected the idea that demons could procreate with human women, he accepted, as did many of his predecessors and contemporaries, the likelihood that witches transported semen through the air at great speed in an effort to produce children with and for the Devil. With Paracelsus, Bodin, and Fischart, he shared the belief that spirits (fairies) occasionally came to live with people. He tells the story of the Swan Knight (who appears modernized as a soldier) and of King Roger's fairy lover (who bears the king a son). In both cases the partners had transgressed against an interdict forbidding the question about who they were and from whence they had come. The question was asked, and the fairy lovers disappeared (*Tableav*, 230–31). Two hundred years after Jean d'Arras had created his enduring memorial for Mélusine, she and her cohorts thus still lived real lives in history and in the minds of learned men, who felt threatened by witches in their midst.

The trilogy on demonology and witchcraft produced by Kramer, Weyer, and Bodin constituted the basis for most of the ensuing discussions on magic and sorcery. In fact, any discussions and declarations for or against their stated positions constituted a disclosure of one's sympathies in this dispute. As magistrate at the Parliament of Bordeaux, specialist in demonology, lawyer of great learning and nationalist passion, and leader in the fight against the practice of black magic and witchcraft in the Labourt region of France, Lancre knew these classics well. He shared the "realist" view initiated by the *Malleus*.[2] He was almost in total agreement with the tenets of Bodin and Kramer, despite the fact that he repeatedly named Sprenger as the author of the *Malleus*. Lancre was entirely convinced of woman's inclination toward witchcraft and of the universal threat to the individual, the community, and the state caused by this proclivity. He felt especially convinced that such practices threatened political and economic stability in the French border regions, especially since the French religious wars had made it imperative to secure France and its territories. The presumed instability of the Basque people, their distance from the French national center, Paris, and the fact that the Basques had become part of France only a century before are three reasons that explain the difficulty of rallying the Labourt population firmly behind the cause of French national interest. It was not until 1747 that the borders between Spain and France were drawn definitively, thereby putting an end to the peculiarly free and exempt status of this people between two rivaling European powers.[3]

Lancre's frequent comments on the antisocial and antinationalist behavior of the Basque people make it clear that the witch prosecutions had not only religious but political motives as well. These prosecutions clearly formed part of the French move toward the absolutist state. We note that, alongside their tracts on demonology, Bodin and Lancre also produced lengthy tomes on the order and ideals of the state and on the nature of princely government. Thus demonology was less an odd deviation in the thinking of otherwise reasonable men than it was an extension of their ideals concerning the role of authority in society.[4]

Born in 1553 or 1556, Lancre studied in Toulouse and Turin. In 1583 he joined the Bordeaux parliament as a magistrate. In 1609 King Henry IV of France appointed him head of a commission to investigate the activities of witches in the Labourt, the Basque region of France. Situated in the extreme southwest corner of France, which bordered on Spain and Navarra, the Labourt had approximately thirty thousand inhabitants. According to Lancre, most of these people engaged in active satanic associations and practices. During the course of a visit that lasted until December 5, 1609, Lancre by his own account led investigations against forty-six suspected witches, among them twelve priests, and thirty-five informants. His report notes that three priests and eight witches were actually burned. In 1612 the Spanish inquisitor Salazar, who was occupied with the same problem on the Spanish side of the border, reported eighty persons burned as witches in the Labourt.[5] During that year Lancre published a report on his extraordinary four-month stay in the Labourt, the *Tableav de l'inconstance des mavvais anges et demons, ov il est amplement traicté des sorciers et de la sorcelerie*, the *Tableav* for short.[6] Lancre based his book on the original trial records. Since these records were destroyed during the eighteenth century, Lancre's report has to this day assumed the authority of an authentic witness to the persecutions.

Lancre's orthodoxy in all witchcraft matters has been frequently and unfavorably compared with Michel de Montaigne's more tolerant and skeptical stance concerning the reality or mere plausibility of witches and the sabbath.[7] Isa Dardano Basso characterizes Lancre as a second-rate player, a negative assessment dictated more by her response to Lancre's rigidity in witch persecutions than by the scope of his learning or his ability to record what he had observed.[8] Julio Caro Baroja is more realistic when he comments that "much has been said about Pierre de Lancre, not all of it sensible; but it can be said that he is the last systematic author on this subject who possessed judicial authority and himself carried out violent repression."[9]

Closely scrutinizing the Labourt, which to him was a foreign culture, Lancre produced a report that went beyond the established parameters on witchcraft indictments and warnings. The reasons for this departure are twofold: Lancre's account is clearly more politically motivated than comparable tracts of the period; and his authorial posture, that of a man encountering a strange culture and an unfamiliar people, has much in common with contemporary reports of travels to the New World.[10] Descriptions of exotica from across the ocean supplied Lancre with a rhetoric that familiarized the unfamiliar, the rhetoric needed to articulate the combination of strangeness and fear that marked his encounter with the Labourdins. His descriptions of the religious, demonological, and judicial aspects of the magic/witchcraft phenomenon were guided by the investigative gaze of a bureaucrat with strong anthropological interests. His depictions of the Labourdins and their unfamiliar language and customs oscillate between amazement at their strange behavior, on the one hand, and on the other, authoritative pronouncements about people who were, like him, subjects of the king of France and bound by monarchic law.

Lancre was a product of elite French culture—he was raised and educated at the court and the university—and his social and economic distance from the people whose deliverance from satanic magic was entrusted to him could not have been greater. He found to his utter amazement that these people, not unlike the natives of the New World, adored Satan and his demons and practiced rituals that would have been as incomprehensible to him as those of faraway peoples, had it not been for his previous knowledge of demons and witches. Worse yet, since Christian missionaries had been successful in spreading God's word among the natives, Satan and his demons had been forced to leave their hiding places in the Americas and to return to Europe, specifically to the Labourt, in large numbers. Lancre cites travelers who had seen them flying across the sky:

> voyageurs venant querir des vins en cette ville de Bordeaux, nus ont asseuré auoir veu en leur voyage de grandes troupes de Demons en forme d'hommes espouuantables passer en France. Qui fait que le nombre des Sorciers est si grande en ce pays de Labourt. (40)[11]

It had been reported from overseas that the natives sought access to their demon-divinities by inhaling the smoke of a plant they called *cohoba:* "ayant ainsi demeuré quelque temps en extase, se leuent tout esperdus et affolez contant merueilles de leurs faux Dieux qu'ils appellent Cemis, tout ainsi que font nos Sorcieres qui reuiennent du Sabbat" [Having remained a certain time in an ecstatic state, they rise all lost and crazed, telling marvels about their false gods that they call Cemis, just like our witches when they return from the sabbath] (38).[12] From what Lancre could observe, the Labourdins practiced similar customs. They smoked tobacco, which seemed to put them into a trance; when they awoke, they reported having flown across the sea to distant shores in the company of many of their friends and having delighted in strange and wonderful experiences. Lancre believed in the reality of such transports. But he also saw the poverty of the people who smoked those weeds, and he offered yet another, more sober explanation for such indulgence. He noted that the herbal smoke quieted hunger pangs and that the imagined travel to distant and happier shores might merely have been a fanciful escape from the misery and poverty of daily life.[13]

In spite of Dardano Basso's negative judgment, writers on the subject of magic and witchcraft acknowledge that Lancre's work was "well known and popular," "a celebrated work which has always been easily available," and that he demonstrated an "inexhaustible erudition."[14] More than twenty years ago de Certeau noted that travel literature needed to be viewed in the same context as demonology. In his attempt to broaden the range of critical access to Lancre's work, Jean Céard has heeded this advice and analyzed the witch of the *Tableau* as the "inside other," comparing her to the New World native, whom he labels the "outside other."[15]

Sent to "clean up" the Labourt, Lancre did not succeed entirely in accomplishing his mission. Still, he attended to his obligations with all the severity and thoroughness befitting a man of his religious and juridical orthodoxy, so much so that, according to the archbishop of Bayonne, Lancre neglected to exercise due process of the law: "the affair came to the notice of the parliament, which [in the wake of the increasing number of prosecutions] suspended the commission of the judge, giving orders that he was to return home."[16] The archbishop, Bernard d'Eschaux, strongly opposed the measures undertaken by Lancre against the alleged witch menace among the Labourdins, and he appealed to the king and the Parliament of Bordeaux to intervene against what seemed to him to be entirely too fanatic a witch hunter. Lancre's comments offer a different reading of the events. He felt sure of episcopal support when he observed: "le sieur de Bayonne qui est Euesque diocesain des lieux, qui s'est tousiours monstré autant affectionné à exterminer ceste peste du genre humain, comme il a d'interest, estant bon Pasteur, de deliurer sa bergerie et la purger de cette abomination" [the lord of Bayonne, who is the bishop of this diocese, has always shown himself to be as serious about exterminating this human plague as he is interested, as a good shepherd, in delivering his flock and purging it of this abomination] (405). Clearly, the archbishop's actions and Lancre's assumptions on this issue diverged. The former might have supported the magistrate in the beginning; his interest in a pacified Labourt was as great as that of the king's magistrate. But when the archbishop realized that the consequence of Lancre's crusade was a mounting witch panic among the people, he moved quickly to have Lancre removed. The people had to be calmed before whole villages faced extinction.

The archbishop's concern was not without foundation. In his study of the inquisition in the Basque region of Spain, Henningsen concludes from inquisitorial records that the Spanish witch craze had been imported from the French Labourt, and that the hysteria had decidedly political overtones. Initially, the nobility of the region had petitioned the parliament for help against the witch menace.[17] It appeared that the persecutions had started after a local aristocrat, the French comte d'Urtubie, had seized "certain old women on his own authority.... Those mentioned in the account [those found belonging to the witches' sect] were enemies and opponents of the lord of Urtubie."[18] The cause-effect relationship between the witch craze in the French and Spanish Labourt appears in a different light when one considers that Lancre may have been an unwitting agent of local hegemonic interests, as he was the upholder of Catholic orthodoxy and royal order. While stationed in the Labourt, he stayed at the home of the comte d'Urtubie, whom, along with the comte d'Amo, he described as "promoteurs de la commission contre les sorciers" [promoters of the commission against witches] (141). Rightly or wrongly, it appears that Lancre felt supported and justified in his mission by the highest secular authorities.

Contemplating his experiences months later, Lancre not only committed to writing a wealth of impressions about the Labourt, its people, and their customs; he also conceived his book as an explanation of, and an apologia for, his relentless—and, judging by the many appeals to the French crown made against him—questionable legal practices exercised in governing the prosecutions of the Labourt witches and their priestly coconspirators. Lancre came to the Labourt firmly convinced of the reality of witches and of their real transport to the sabbath. It seems that he left the area just as certain of these phenomena. In spite of his remarkably keen ethnographic eye, his tract remains to the very last line a fierce indictment of all those whom he considered lenient or in any way skeptical about witchcraft accusations. Given such zeal, it is not surprising that Lancre respected Bodin and often quoted him.

The experiential realism of Lancre's report combines the physical proximity of the observer to the object of his interest with the distance of the prosecutor. It unites his horror at a people misguided by devilish proclivities with his sense of social order and government agency. His work thus evidences both the rapture of the male onlooker and the fanaticism of one committed to the eradication of sin. In spite of the skepticism articulated throughout the century by many educated men in Italy, Spain, France, and Germany, the coherent depiction of the magical world—real witches dancing at a real sabbath and representing a real threat to the community—controlled Lancre's gaze and that of likeminded men as they attempted to identify the members of the witches' sect. The discursive virulence of his language, which so shocks contemporary readers, was to a large extent prompted by the passionate and, by all appearances, intra-European dispute about the reality of the witch phenomenon. The violence of this debate dominated Lancre's thoughts and actions as he struggled for mastery over the strange behavior of the Labourdins and over the chaos that such behavior represented.[19] Nowhere does he even hint that he understood his mission to be a measure of support for one faction over another in a local political dispute. As his dedication sympathetically suggests, his administrative and judicial enthusiasm, his religious orthodoxy, and his absolutist sympathies focused his attention on a problem that transcended all local concerns:

> außi estes-vous [Monseigneur de Sillery, Chancelier de France] le premier et le souuerain chef de toutes les compagnies soueraines de ce Royaume, que faictes mouuoir tous les ressorts de *ce sacré horloge de la Iustice,* et qui guidez en toute droicture *le charriot du soleil de la France* par tous les lieux de ses venerables Parlements. (Dedication, iii)[20]

The sun-drawn chariot of a mythical France held a king, a new Apollo, whose divine healing powers had long been part of the royal mythos.[21] It appears that Lancre understood his mission to be to bring light into this dark corner of the realm and as part of the French monarchy's inexorable move toward absolute power. Pacifying and purging the Labourt of satanic elements also meant the clarification of the disputes over the borderlands that had occupied Spain and France for some time. The elaborate title-statement celebrates the French monarchy as unique and destined to lead Europe: *Tableav de l'inconstance.... en laquelle on voit, combien l'exercice de la iustice en France, est plus iuridiquement traictē, et auec de plus belles formes qu'en tous autres empires, royaumes, republiques et estats* [the Tableau of the inconstancy.... in which one sees how justice in France is handled with greater judicial dexterity and in more pleasing ways than in any other empire, kingdom, republic, or state]. The royal councilor at the Bordeaux parliament translated this charge into a political agenda of royal self-presentation of the highest order. Witch hunting was eventually subsumed under the myth of the supremacy of French royal power. Lancre was convinced that his objective had to be cast in the context of the sacred power of the state, which transcended even the church's authority:

> la raison en est prinse de ce que les Heretiques troublent l'estat, dans lequel est l'Eglise, et non l'Estat dans l'Eglise ... et que les Iuges d'Eglise ... n'ont autre coërction que le glaiue spirituel. (516)[22]

The superior authority of the state over the church was especially important in matters of witchcraft, an even more heinous crime than heresy. Heretics congregated together and endangered only each other; they tried to remain hidden. Witchcraft, on the other hand, constituted an aggression against all living souls, and therefore its practitioners affected the whole public good (517). Referring the reader to his 1607 tract on the inconstancy of all nations, Lancre further underscored his belief that only under the rule of a just king would and could France be victorious in the struggle against Satan's assault (Dedication).[23] The echo of the religious wars is inescapable. Lancre enumerated four dictates that impelled him to action: first, the need to convince all doubters of the reality of the witch menace; second, his belief that witchcraft was heresy and apostasy but was even more dangerous to state and church than either of these crimes; third, the depositions of enumerable witnesses about the real bodily transport of witches to the sabbath, which must effectively silence the doubts of even the "plus durs, stupides, aueugles, et hebetez" [most stubborn, stupid, blind, and dazed] of his colleagues; and finally, confirmation once again of the accuracy of those who wrote on the subject before him (Advertissemens).

Given less to telling tales for the entertainment and instruction of his audience than were Weyer and Bodin, Lancre kept close to the facts as he understood them, producing a document that "develop[ed] a factual science, without exceeding the limits of experience."[24] The truth that he observed went beyond mere theoretical coherence. His commitment to the existence of a stable knowledge of his world, to the macro/microcosmic relationship of humankind to God, allowed him to fit what he saw—a people who seemingly turned from God and abandoned themselves to Satan—into the grid of established knowledge. His observations were assimilated, without any contradiction, into the existing framework of his thoughts: God had charged him to lead this people back to the order and benevolence of French royal power.

Lancre pledged to apply a firm hand of discipline and control to what he judged to be the disintegration of social structures that threatened the Labourt.[25] His report "jostled for [the] discursive space"[26] that he needed to recognize the threat without being overwhelmed by a still-unfamiliar culture. He strove to cultivate a posture of sober assessment, to analyze with detached authority how the familiar joined with the unfamiliar in a new epistemological space, where the judgment of a people's involvement with Satan meant judgment over life and death.

Furthermore, the *Tableav* emerged as a document of justification for Lancre's actions in the witchcraft convictions of three Labourdin priests who had been found guilty of celebrating Black Masses and leading their parishioners in the sabbath rituals. Lancre's reflections on the judicial and theological quandary of clerics who, along with the people in their care, had contracted and cavorted with Satan color this tract with the underlying and distressing apprehension of impending chaos. The ominous persistence of such remarks points to Lancre's difficulties in adjudicating conflicts that called into question the privileged status of churchmen. Must the authority of the church be upheld even in the face of the moral and ethical failings of some of its members? And does this imperative supersede the dictate to punish those who had fallen away from the faith, forsaking their duty to vanquish Satan? Lancre's answer is an unequivocal yes to punishment, no matter what the position of the accused. But he pleads for secret proceedings, defending his position by referring to the faithful who, upon hearing about such trials, might lose their spiritual direction and abandon themselves to faith-killing doubt.

The stated mission of his travel to the Labourt and the actual identification and punishment of practitioners of the black arts presented Lancre with a number of difficult challenges. These were realized in the form of conflicts that extended beyond the judicial realm to the theological question of priestly authority. In the process of clarifying his actions to himself and to his readers, he argues as a layperson with the conviction of a seventeenth-century jurist in the service of the crown, defending the superiority of the state over the church in matters of national religious interest.

Several years after his stay in the Labourt, he returned to this topic in the *Livre des princes, contenant plusieurs notables discours pour l'instruction des Roys, Empereurs et Monarques (1617)*. This volume explicates the political and nationalist imperatives of the emerging absolutist state, issues to which he alluded in the *Tableav*. Written between the *Tableav* and his last work, *L'incredvlité et mescreance dv sortilege plainment convaincue* (1620), the *Livre des princes,* with its emphasis on the ordering power of the state and the importance of marriage and the family, synthesizes all of Lancre's work into a coherent political and social program. Comparing the practice of witchcraft to life at court, he found that they shared a love and need for secrets, dissimulation, and theatrics, understood to mean make-believe or an alternate reality. "Je sçay bien," he says in the *Livre des princes,* "que les plus fins et les plus corrompus sont les meilleurs et les plus parfaits Courtisans" [I know that the finest and most corrupted are the best and the most perfect courtiers].[27] In this respect, too, he resembled Bodin, whose *Démonomanie* predated the *Six Books of the Republic* and his final, consummate work, the *Colloquium Heptaplomeres*. Witchcraft and magic emerged as political obstacles in the path of social order and absolutist rule. The elimination of alleged witches and the establishment of external security and the protection of domestic calm could, in this context, be considered as a single thought—they are indispensable to the wielding of political power. The humanist-turned-witch-hunter was not, it turns out, a psychological aberration but the consequence of a cosmological and theological belief-system that had been brought in line with political imperatives.

Lancre was convinced of Satan's efficacy and the ubiquity of demonic power; unlike many of his contemporaries, however, he vigorously denied the divinity, legitimacy, or even the usefulness of scientific magic. His position was not a reflection of the fact that he did not believe in magic's revelatory power or that he denied its status as a privileged form of knowing. Rather, he spurned *scientia magica* because he was convinced that its dangerous closeness to diabolical practice made it too perilous an investigative tool. While he praised Sprenger, Paulo Grillando,[28] and Bodin for their efforts in stemming the tide of satanism as well as for their erudition, his pronouncements on Giovanni Pico, Agrippa, Trithemius, and Weyer were uniformly negative. He did not share the humanist view of nature as a great and inexhaustible collection of curiosities presided over by God, the *Magus supremus*. Nor did he wish to follow the scientific imperative that called upon man, the divine creation, to explore the universe, as Paracelsus had done throughout his life. Besides condemning the practice of magic as suspicious at best and diabolical at worst, Lancre was convinced that magic's authority and epistemological value had diminished steadily as it was successively handed down by generations of the adept. In the golden days of the past, magicians were philosophers. Practitioners of magic in Lancre's day, however, hailed from among the unlettered and poor laity and served less esoteric and honorable ambitions than had their forebears (410).[29]

The conflict that arose between the purpose of Lancre's book and its ultimate effect was revealed from the start in an act of involuntary irony. Then as now, the attentive reader is caught in the conflict between the epigraph of the title page, "Maleficos non patieries viuere" [Witches must not be allowed to live], and the theme of the dedicatory sonnet. In this sonnet, le seigneur d'Espaignet, Lancre's cochair on the commission, commented on the role of writing when committing deeds to memory. Clearly intending to flatter Lancre politely, Espaignet referred to Lancre's 1607 book on the inconstancy of all worldly things and of all nations and then asked:

> Pour te monstrer constant a tretter l'Inconstance,
> Lancre, tu nous fais veoir les changements divers
> Des bizarres Demons hostes de l'Vniuers,
> Par ce second tableau que tu peins a la France:
> Mais quoy? ne vois tu pas combien peu de Constance
> On te donra, voyant sur le bord des Enfers
> Les vmbres voltiger de ce peuple peruers,
> Duquel tes iugements ont faict iuste vengeance.
> Et maintenant tu fais par vn contraire sort,
> Que l'immortalité succede a cette mort,
> Ta plume leur donnant vne immortele vie:
> Et pour vn second mal; tu feras naistre ainsi
> Mille et mille Sorciers des cendres de ceux cy,
> Qui pour reuiure auront de mesme mort enuie.[30]

Espaignet's praise reveals the same distance between cause and effect that I identified above as one of the inadvertent consequences of Weyer's tract. Intended to defeat the menace of witchcraft by addressing it openly and refuting it in detail, the widely read *De praestigiis daemonum* intensified, not lessened, the persecution in the period following its publication. Wanting to produce a document that constituted a warning to future generations, during his four-month stay in the Labourt, Lancre immortalized the men and women he had come to prosecute. Not unlike Weyer, although for different reasons, he had given them a voice. Meticulously recording the names, relationships, and ages of the accused, he assured them a permanent place in the social history of the Labourt and the witch prosecutions.

While this insight into the possible reaction of future audiences did not deter him, Lancre did express fear that his openness in reporting on the depositions of witnesses and his attention to specific details might be misconstrued as putting dangerous suggestions into the minds of the uninitiated. Hoping to lessen the danger of misunderstanding, he outlined the thoughts that had led him to tell nothing but the unadorned truth. He would only report what he himself had seen and what credible witnesses had related: "c'est pourquoy ie suis resolu... [de] me contenter du simple recit des depositions des tesmoins, et confessions des accusez: lesquelles ont tant d'estrangeté en soy, qu'elles ne lairront [sic] pas de contenter le Lecteur, bien que ie les laisse en leur naïfueté" [Therefore I have decided... to be content with the simple account of the depositions of the witnesses and confessions of the accused: which themselves seem so strange that they will not fail to satisfy the reader, although I am leaving them in their naive form] (Advertissemens). Not unlike the travel reports from the New World, the experiential reality of witches and the sabbath were affirmed by truthful witnesses or eyewitness reports. Lancre provided such assurances for the reader: "i'en pourroy alleguer vne infinité d'autres exemples qui nous sont passez deuant les yeux" [I could cite an infinite number of additional examples that have passed before our eyes] (108). Testifying to a witch's ability to go to the sabbath even while imprisoned, he wrote reassuringly that "elle allois presque toutes les nuicts au sabbat; ie pous asseurer qu'elle n'auoir ny onguent ny graisse" [She went practically every night to the sabbath; I can assure you that she had neither ointment nor salve in her possession] (114)— that is, she had no recourse to visible magical means of transportation. The danger to human souls and to the state could only be held in check if all the facts were known. The greatest possible frankness was thus required in the descriptions of all the abominations recorded during the inquests. Only the most detailed and disciplined reports could counteract the noxious diversity, liberty, and inconstancy of Satan and the witches. The enmity that arose among theological beliefs, judicial discipline, the state's need for law and order, and the Labourdins' passion for disguises "pour se faire mescongnoistre" [to make themselves unrecognizable] was seen as emblematic of the conflicting values colliding in the mind of the magistrate—and of the measures he took in his attempt to force them into harmony. While the modes by which Satan and his minions perpetrated their deeds had to remain untold—hidden from human view by divine intent—Lancre vowed to open to public scrutiny all records of the effects of such satanic manipulations.

The commission was to work quickly; by royal decree, the problem had to be solved in four months because it was of such urgency (Advertissemens). The violent clash of cultures in this remote province of France was profound and multifaceted. The two Frenchmen and the Basque women faced each other unable to bridge the chasm of ignorance, prejudice, and nonunderstanding that separated learned and popular, high from low culture. The educated government official from Bordeaux had been ordered by the king to establish order on the basis of evidence that, as it turned out, had less to do with witches than with local jealousies and battles for border control. Such conflicts are evident in the text's very first pages. Between the biblical motto and Espaignet's sonnet is interposed the prefatory statement. It names Henry IV as the originator of the commission and dedicates the book to monseigneur de Sillery:

> le seul païs de Labourt qui n'est qu'vn recoing de la Guyenne, [en] fourniroit parauanture plus que tout le reste de la France: le nombre de Sorciers y estant si grand, que Satan est demeuré maistre absolu.... Les Officiers de la Iustice se trouuent quasi foibles en ce lieu là. (Dedication)[31]

It appears that those appointed to uphold order in this remote corner of France, the judges and the priests, had proven unreliable for this task because of their familial ties with the people entrusted to their care. Lancre delineated the extraordinary character of his mission, and he emphatically insisted on his independence from local—that is, Bayonne or Bordeaux—authority: "le Roy... decerna commission à vn President et vn Conseiller de la Cour de Parlement de Bourdeaux.... ce pour leur [the witches in the Labourt] faire et parfaire le procez souuerainement, non obstant oppositions ou appellations quelconques" [the King... decreed a commission to a president and a counselor of the Bordeaux parliament.... This was meant to grant them due process, no matter what the opposition or rank] (Advertissemens). As it turned out, the whole undertaking proved very difficult due to the pervasive and much lamented inconstancy of the players, who made reliance on any help other than God's an illusion, and the conflicts over governmental authority. The archbishop clearly remained suspicious of Lancre's order to investigate trespasses that were in his, the archbishop's, purview. Judicial and administrative actions were perpetually threatened by the potential inability of the magistrates to separate what was real from what was imagined and to identify who was truly capable of cooperating with them and withstanding Satan's trickery.

Once at his destination, Lancre encountered a rebelliously free people whose culture and language were so foreign to him that the only discourse available to capture the flavor of this otherness was that of the New World discoveries:

> Les Indiens, comme il appert par les lettres escrites de ce pays là, adorent et les Dieux du ciel, comme ils disent et les Diables, mais ils font les images des Diables de plumes ex tremement diverses en couleur: sans doute c'est pour signifier leur *inconstance et mutabilité* marquee par les plumes et par la diversité des couleurs. (16)[32]

Comparisons to the natives of the New World and other peoples at the periphery of the known world abound in this text.[33] The strangeness of the people across the ocean and the fascination radiating from the Labourdin women are captured in the dehumanizing, devaluing, and potentially destructive discourse of the satanic Other:

> Et comme les Indiens en l'isle Espagnolle prenant la fumée d'vne certaine herbe appellee Cohoba, ont l'esprit troublé, et mettant les mains entre deux genoux et la teste baissée, ayant ainsi demeuré quelque temps en extase, se leuent tout esperdus et affolez contant merueilles de leurs faux Dieux qu'ils appellent Cemis, tout ainsi que font nos Sorcieres qui reuiennent du Sabbat. (38)[34]

Keenly aware of a potential communications gap and under pressure to assert his authority in the region, Lancre repeatedly stressed the linguistic and cultural superiority of all things French. Explaining the reasons for his decision to write in French rather than in Latin, he opined that French suffers less than Latin from a potential rhetorical opacity.

Moreover, French does not hide meaning under the veil of linguistic pomposity and dissimulation, as do the Spanish and Basque languages. In particular, he wished to avoid the practice of writers who, in their attempts to limit their audience to the learned and to exclude women from their readership, hide the truth behind the obscurity of Latin. Lancre judged the latter attempt vain: "lesquelles [women] neantmoins en [of secret knowledge] sçauent plus que nous ne leur en sçaurion iamais aprendre" [nevertheless, they know more about [these secrets] than we would ever be able to teach them] (Advertissemens). Concern about women's access to magical arcana of the satanic kind without the benefit of formal learning was frequently expressed by writers on witchcraft. Bodin's reservations about female inquisitiveness and consequent ability to learn about magic without having to open a book expressed a general male consensus, as did the common conviction that witches would not be deterred by national borders or differences in language. Aside from a few varieties in matters of transport—Italian witches preferred riding billy goats; German witches tended more toward broomsticks; and the French counterparts employed flying ointments—the sabbath experience seemed to be similar the world over (121). Consequently, anxiety about border crossings and the danger of contamination was considerable.

While Lancre attempted to rid the French Labourt of witches, the Spanish Inquisition was busy fighting the same enemy on the other side of the border. In his investigations Lancre found the needed reaffirmation not only of the reality of witches and their sabbath meetings but also of the fact that almost all the Labourdins were members of this sect. Clerics on the Spanish side, most of them in the service of the inquisition, reacted quite differently to the results of their inquests. Antonio Venegas de Fugueroa, the bishop of Pamplona, along with several of his investigators, reached the conclusion, formulated most concisely by Salazar de Frías, that "there were neither witches nor bewitched until they were talked and written about," which means until the prosecutions had started in the French Labourt.[35] On the basis of intense investigations by the Spanish Inquisition and subsequent careful evaluation of the evidence, Venegas and Salazar concluded that the craze was the result of panic conveyed into Spain and Navarra from France. The panic had started in December 1608, after the first reputed witch, twenty-one-year-old Maria de Ximildegui, had returned to her childhood home after working three years as a servant in the Labourt. Accused by the French authorities of practicing witchcraft, she had been granted absolution.

But soon after returning to her native Spain, she admitted attendance at local sabbaths, identifying neighbors who had allegedly joined her.[36]

During their respective investigations and prosecutions, Lancre and the Spanish inquisitors occasionally communicated about the witch menace and about their efforts at fighting it. They exchanged names of accused men and women in an attempt to stem the growing tide of Labourdins fleeing to Spain to escape the grip of Lancre's commission: "Ils s'en fuïoïent à nostre arriuee par carauannes et par mer et par terre, la basse / et haute Nauarre, et la frontiere d'Espagne, s'en remplissoient d'heure à heure" [upon our arrival they fled in caravans by sea and by land; lower and upper regions of Navarra, and the Spanish border areas were filled from one hour to the next] (40).

Leaving aside the skepticism of some members of the Spanish Inquisition, it seems clear that, like Lancre, the majority of the inquisitors remained convinced of the reality of witches and their physical presence at the sabbath. They pursued the presumed perpetrators with comparable vigor. Still, not unlike the witchcraft disputes elsewhere in Europe, especially in midcentury Italy, the Labourdin prosecutions indicate that a skeptic such as Salazar and a zealot such as Lancre—men of great learning and trained in the schools of Catholic orthodoxy—could reflect on the same phenomenon at the same time and come not only to very different but to mutually exclusive conclusions about its efficacy. This discrepancy reaffirms what has already been observed in the debate between Weyer and Bodin: even if the reality of Satan's power remained undisputed by both men, belief in the reality of witch activities and ideas on how to deal with presumed misdeeds were, even among the members of the inquisition, anything but monolithic.[37]

The bishop of Pamplona's active and unwavering support of Salazar's skepticism and scrupulous adherence to the rules of evidence prompted an official change in the regulations concerning the acceptance and use of evidence in 1614. Henceforth, inquisitors were to emphasize confession and forgiveness rather than conviction. Suspicion of witchcraft no longer automatically led to the confiscation of the victim's property, an action that effectively removed greed as a possible impetus for denunciations.[38]

The inquisitors' insights, rational and humane as they appeared, and eventually—given the virtual disappearance of witch burnings in Spain—proved to be, were not guided entirely by spiritual enlightenment. The inquests began incurring expenses that grew disproportionately large, too large to continue. Furthermore, the growing wave of prosecutions and panic led to overcrowded prisons and life-threatening disease among the inmates, killing several of the accused witches before they could be convicted. Others who had already been convicted died before they were to be executed; these were punished in effigy.

The Spanish witch-hunts of the early seventeenth century came to a climax in the auto-da-fé at Logroño (November 7–8, 1610). According to contemporary witnesses, this event was a spectacle of judicial authority and ritual formalism of awesome proportions.[39] It comes as no surprise that Lancre devoted an entire chapter of his tract to the detailed report of this event, once more underscoring what had been stated on the title page: justice was handled differently in Spain than in France. Commenting that "detant que leur forme de Iustice est toute autre que la nostre," he concludes that on this occasion sentencing had been much too lenient: "on vsa de beaucoup de misericorde enuers les dictes personnes, considerant beaucoup plusleur repentance que l'énormité de leurs fautes" [given that their kind of justice is completely different from ours... one exercised much charity toward these persons, weighing much more heavily their repentance than the enormity of their sins] (387).

Such criticism notwithstanding, Lancre appeared overwhelmed by the auto-da-fé. He was greatly moved by the solemnity of the procession. The gravity of the crimes, whose judgments were read aloud; the torches lighting the place of assembly; the musicians, the robes, and the flames of the stakes; and the great multitude of people assembled to watch all caused him much emotion (382–98). Again he found himself at odds with the Spanish inquisitor Salazar, who, in retrospect, judged the Logroño auto-da-fé to have been what we today would call a public-relations fiasco. The people on both sides of the border had been incited into great religious and prosecuting fervor. Accusations became so pervasive that the more rational leadership was forced to curb the prosecutions. Judicial skepticism and economic necessity combined to initiate efforts at calming the panic of the populace and to check as well the zeal of the provincial officials. One of the first measures to this end was the prohibition of what Lancre had found so impressive, the public recitation of witch sentences and/or of admissions of guilt and statements of repentance. The practice of reading recantations and making accusations and retractions part of sermons that were delivered in the vernacular had contributed significantly to the spread of witch panics.[40] In the *Malleus*

Kramer had been the first to include such pronouncements into the inquisitorial rules:

> die vorgenannte Abschwörung aber finde in der Umgangsprache statt, damit sie von allen verstanden werde.... [Am] Sonntag soll der Prediger in Bezug auf die vorzunehmende Abschwörung und den zu vernehmenden Urteilsspruch... eine allgemeine Predigt halten. [Danach wird vom Notar] das verlesen, bezüglich dessen der, welcher abschwören soll, überführt ist. (Pt. 3, 139, 142)[41]

At the Logroño auto-da-fé, not only the sentences but also the prologues to the judgments were read publicly, with some of the lengthier ones taking considerable time. In fact, the sentences of Marie de Iureteguia, Ieanne de Telecha, and Marie Zozaya amounted to descriptions of the sabbath that did not omit even the smallest of details (388, 389). Marie Zozaya's conviction filled forty folio pages and took at least two hours to read: "having listened to so many ghastly monstrosities for the space of two whole days... we all returned home crossing ourselves all the while."[42] During the proceedings, onlookers took notes, and broadsheets on the incredible witch stories went into circulation almost immediately. The officials of the inquisition realized that they were in danger of losing control over the inquisitorial process; several among them agreed that it had to stop. Salazar's revised instructions adopted by the Supreme Council in 1614 stated: "[the] public discussion of the witch question has produced very undesirable consequences.... The Tribunal is therefore to issue an order imposing silence on these discussions."[43] This order indicates that the inquisitors had made the connection between public pronouncements on the witch craze and its perpetuation. This resulted in the attempt to limit further public discussion so that the panic could be calmed. Lancre completely rejected such a procedure. By then he had returned to Bordeaux and published his treatise. France was to experience many more episodes of witch burnings and possessions.[44]

In spite of Lancre's bias, his book must be considered one of the most compelling reports of the period to describe Europe's encounter with the witch as, to adopt Céard's phrase, "the inside other." Characterized by great linguistic and cultural diversity, the Labourt was, according to Lancre, a perfect playground for Satan and an exceptionally fitting meeting place for the witches' sabbath. The remoteness of the mountain villages and towns allowed the witches to travel through the regions with great speed. And after fear had been transported across the French/Spanish border by those who fled from Lancre's prosecution, inquisitorial practice helped the craze to flourish and spread.

Lancre's eagerness to prosecute was seriously hampered by his inability to speak Basque. In his effort to alleviate this problem, he hired a translator/interpreter. Though Lancre did not name this person, Henningsen was able to identify him as the French cleric Lorenzo de Hualde, who had grown up in the Labourt. A young priest eager to advance his career, Hualde was intimately involved with the political ambitions of the comte d'Urtubie, who had installed Hualde as parish priest in his domain on the Spanish side of the border. Hualde had cast an ambitious glance on an appointment as inquisitor, a wish that came to fruition several years after he had finished his work with Lancre. A firm believer in the reality of witches and the sabbath, Hualde proved to be an intractable opponent to the moderate and skeptical faction of the inquisition, notably to Salazar. While Lancre may have been unaware of Hualde's clerical ambitions, he did know about his translator's friendship with Urtubie; Spanish documents mention Lancre being a guest in his house during the investigations.[45] Still, Lancre did not express anything that might signal complicity in Urtubie's or Hualde's plans.

Lancre's alleged negligence in matters of due process of the law seemed to have been entirely the result of his unrelenting fear that if it were not stopped, the witch menace might engulf the whole of France. Repeatedly his writings communicate serious and troubling doubts about his ability to uncover the truth in inquests where all information was filtered through a translator/interpreter. His awareness of the potential danger for the process is obvious:

> de mesmes les Interpretes lesquels sont encores Iuges plus importans et necessaires, pouuant tromper ou pour le moins eluder... tournans les mots basques comme bon leur semble. (401)[46]

Lancre had been told that the Basque language was sometimes more efficient in expressing truth than French and sometimes less so. Translation thus seemed to preclude complete accuracy: "outre que toutes langues perdent de leur beauté et de leur grace au change" [besides that, all languages lose their beauty and their grace in translation] (404). Lancre acknowledged that the translator estoit fidele, prompt, clair, bien entendu en la langue, et homme entier et de bonne reputation, et d'vne profession qui s'approche plus de la saincteté que toute autre. Aussi on compare les Interpretes aux Anges et aux saincts, qui rendent fidelement à Dieu toutes les prieres des mortels. (403)[47]

Nevertheless, Lancre was troubled, to the point of constant anxiety, by the possibility that a translator might alter the message of the accused in a number of ways, intentionally or unintentionally. An interpreter could either translate the words incorrectly, or he could distort them for reasons of ignorance or through a desire to take sides in the dispute. Translators, Lancre believed, must be "vrays Echos, qui demeurent en perpetuel silence si on ne parle...estant necessitez de parler si on parle, et ne varier mesme en rien les paroles qu'on leur dict" [true echoes that remain perpetually silent if no one speaks...since it is necessary for them to speak only if someone is talking, and they should never vary even a little bit the words spoken to them] (408).

The persistent threat to linguistic and epistemological transparency, the risk that distortions would be brought to the text by unreliable translator-go-betweens or court witnesses, were increased substantially by the special nature of witch inquests. The uncertainty and inconstancy of Satan and his associates continually disturbed and discredited the judicial process.[48] Lancre's persistent return to the question of whether language was capable of representing truth in a world fraught with uncertainty underscores the fear implicit in his writing that discursive imprecision, and the opacity potentially present in all utterances, could and did encourage the intellectual skepticism that led to judicial leniency. The latter is the object of his explicit denunciation:

> on leuera l'erreur de plusieurs qui nient les principes du Sortilege, croians que ce n'est que prestige, songe, et illusion: et ferons voir clairement que le doubte, et l'impunité ou douceur que nos peres et les Cours de Parlements y ont apporté iusqu'icy, ont nourry et main-tenu la faulse croyance et engendré la multiplicité (Advertissemens).[49]

Multiplicité and *inconstance* characterized Satan and his minions, as they did the Labourdins, especially the women, who proved to be a source of perpetual frustration but also of intense interest to Lancre. With uncommon visual acuity, he turned his almost impressionist gaze to the beauty and the strange ways of the people he had come to discipline, observing them with an equal measure of reluctance and fascination.

He structured his descriptions carefully, in an almost painterly fashion: first, he pictured the region's history, geography, and economy; then he turned to the physical characteristics of the people; and finally he commented on their social interactions. Progressing from the general to the particular, from nature to culture, he constructed a model meant to advance him and his reader toward an understanding of the nature and behavior of the Labourdins, and of the measures he had taken to bring them under the control of the French authorities. In the process he provided an answer to the question he had come to explore, namely, why this people was so entirely susceptible to satanic seduction.[50]

The answer is found in part in the geographic disadvantages of this rough, ungentle country. Caught between arid mountains and the wild and boundless sea, surviving mostly on millet and fish, the Labourdins appeared to Lancre a people of few ambitions and an undistinguished history. They existed in a land whose contours seemed to lose all definition between the sea and the mountains. Given neither to building great edifices nor to founding large towns, they made their living by the sea, settled under the high sky of their mountainous land, dressed mostly in floating toile, which made their attire appear colorful and airy, seemingly floating around them. The infertile earth allowed little farming; witches destroyed what few crops had been planted. The Labourdins showed no gentleness and seemed indifferent to social graces and to human affections; Lancre judged them "rustiques, rudes, et mal policez" [rustic, crude, and poorly policed] (31). High winds and thunderstorms kept the skies in a state of constant agitation and the sea in perpetual motion, visible in the endless ebb and flow and the storm-tossed churning of the waves. Unable or unwilling to farm or work at crafts or trades, the Labourdins entrusted their entire fortunes to the water. They were led "sur les flots qui les agitent nuict et iour: qui faict que leur commerce, leur conversation et leur foy est du tout maritime" [on the waves that toss them day and night: which means that their commerce, their conversations, and their faith are entirely determined by the sea] (31). A passionate love for the sea, to which they surrendered their men and themselves with confidence and careless abandon, fashioned their lives and their character, "legers et volages qu'ils sont" [so light and unsteady are they] (32).

Under the magistrate's inquiring and curious gaze, the image of a poor but free and proud people of distinct customs underwent an interpretive change. Unlike these people, who lived, loved, and died by the sea, whose lives were dependent on the water, he perceived the sea as a metaphor of uncertainty and anxiety: "la mer est vn chemin sans chemin" [the ocean is a path with no direction] (32). To him the water was the archetypal image of lawlessness, sin, and despair, "vn vray et temeraire desespoir" [a true and reckless despair] (32). Elsewhere in the text, the world is seen as a theater, expressing the same horrifying experience of uncertainty and irreality: "le monde est vn theatre ou le Diable ioue vne infinité de diuers et dissemblables personnages" [the world is a stage where the Devil plays the role of an infinite number of diverse and dissimilar persons] (13).

But Basque geography, real or metaphoric, was by no means all that captured Lancre's attention. Caught up in his voyeuristic pleasures, he was unable to escape the mental seduction of the people's almost pagan sense of freedom, which he registered with a mixture of amazement and dread. The dichotomy between these "pauures gens souffreteux et incommodez" [poor suffering and burdened people] and their apparent haughtiness; between their unwillingness to bend to the discipline of work and the arrogance with which they made titles out of their tiny landholdings—calling each other "dame" and "sieur" and affecting an air of proud nobility—astonished Lancre. Their insouciance toward all social conventions as he knew them likewise unnerved him (45). In his eyes, they affected nobility where they had only poverty, freedom where there was satanic enslavement. He could not tolerate this undoing of his world.

Lancre's perceptive description was by no means class-blind. He made little secret of the fact that the otherness so captivating to him was exhibited only by the women of the lower classes. The manners of the Basque aristocracy, male and female, were familiar to him; since they spent much time in the company of their French equals and were educated at French schools, their language and their comportment conformed to the rules of French courtliness. What he observed in the Labourt was vastly different. He spoke with wonder of the "menu peuple" [small people], of the women's carelessly free way of life. He was struck by the specialness of their beauty, whose crowning glory, quite literally, was the unique quality of their hair. Giving voice to visual impressions, he described with the intensity of a lover's praise the women's tresses falling over their shoulders and seductively covering their faces, making their eyes shine with extraordinary brilliance:

> leurs cheveux voletant sur les espaules, et accompagnant les yeux de quelque façon, qu'elles semblent beaucoup plus belles en cette naiueté.... Elles sont dans cette belle cheuelure, tellement à leur auantage, et si fortement armees que le soleil iettant ses rayons sur cette touffe de cheveux comme dans vne nuee, l'esclat en est aussi violent et forme d'aussi brillans esclairs qu'il fait dans le ciel, lors qu'on voit naistre Iris, d'où vient leur fascination des yeux, aussi dangereuse en amour qu'en sortilege, bien que parmy elles porter la perruque entiere soit la marque de virginité. (42)[51]

This beauty was deceptive. Lancre knew that hair was always a potential tool of bewitchment; one of the first and most profoundly intimidating gestures in most witch interrogations was the shearing of head and body hair.[52] He had read that Kramer and Bodin urged judges to avoid looking into the eyes of a suspected witch for fear that she might inspire leniency merely by the power of her gaze.[53] The closeness of erotic love and satanic seduction was as obvious to him as it was to his compatriot Jacques Ferrand, who wrote about this affinity in his *Treatise on Love Sickness* (1610, 1623). Ferrand had described love's affliction in clinical detail, calling it "erotic melancholy," "amor hereos," or, in its more specifically feminine manifestation, "uterine fury," whose emotional intensity was transmitted through the eyes, and whose human or satanic compulsions had all the characteristics of a disease that was easily contracted but difficult to cure.

Living in their counterparadise, the Labourdins, true children of a Basque Eve, grew only one fruit in any quantity, the apple. With this fruit of transgression, they seduced the children of Adam: "elles mordent si volontiers cette pomme de transgression, qui fist outrepasser le commendement de Dieu, et franchir la prohibition à nostre premier pere" [they ate with abandon this fruit of transgression, which caused the trespass against God's commandment and ignore the prohibition made to our first father] (43). Small wonder, then, that living in the inhospitable mountains and swimming with lascivious abandon in the inconstant and dangerous sea, these "filles et ieunes pescheurs" [girls and young fishermen] lent their ears as willingly to the seductions of men as to those of Satan (43). In the grottos by the ocean and on the high, inaccessible mountains, they found ready hideaways for their sexual pleasures. Lancre watched them returning from their diversions and observed how they regaled each other with what he presumed to be tales of their exploits, for they were laughing and dancing about in careless abandon. As the outsider, the learned city dweller, he was convinced that it made little difference to the obvious amusement and gaiety of these women and girls whether they told about their erotic exploits at some village feast or at the witches' sabbath.

It seemed to matter even less to the priests in whose care the souls of these women had been entrusted. Negligent yet arrogant servants of the church, the priests seemed to join the sabbath celebrations of their flock as readily as if they were leading them in Sunday mass.[54] Contrary to the accepted practice, which allowed only males to handle the implements of worship or approach the altar and view the elevation of the host, the *benedictes,* as the women were called, carried the chalice and ornaments during mass and generally attended to the ritual needs of church services and, by implication, of the church servants (44). Their intimacy with priests was as remarkable as their persecution as witches was inevitable: "on leur en permet la veue à l'eleuation ou on leur donne licence de tirer le voile et le rideau, et leur a-t-on aussi concedé les responses" [they were permitted to view the elevation of the host, or one gave them permission to draw the veil or the curtain, and one also conceded that they do the responses] (60).[55] Lancre's suspicions became convictions: witchcraft in the Labourt was not only a family but also a community affair; there was no haven for the innocent, not even the church, and no person was secure, not even the smallest child. Lancre was convinced that of the thirty thousand Labourdins, the majority, if not all, had sworn allegiance to Satan.

The Labourdin life-style clearly favored this dangerous inclination. Families were left without male protection and control during the six months of every year that the men spent at sea, fishing off the coast of Newfoundland and the New World. Only women, children, and old and infirm men remained behind. They formed, or so it appeared to the magistrate, a kind of countersociety. Given their easy association with Satan, their seeming disinclination to work inside or outside of the home, and the lack of male control and protection, they had become accustomed to a life-style that struck Lancre as a seductive carnival of perpetual movement and search for pleasure. Behind the harsh reality of everyday life—the poverty and the familial separations—Lancre suspected a counterreality that was inaccessible to him but real nonetheless. Central to this reality was the sabbath as a giant, ongoing party celebrated not only at night but during the day, not on faraway mountaintops but in the towns and even in the homes of the witches:

> vne si grande pompe et magnificence, où il fait aborder en vn moment tant de personnes, de toutes qualitez, et parroistre tant de variété de choses nouuelles, et ce auec vn si grand esclat, que la plus part de Sorciers allant esdictes assemblees, croyent aller en quelque Paradis terrestre. (37)[56]

But that was not all. The long absences of the men gave rise to much disaffection and even hatred among those remaining behind in the villages. During their semiannual presence in the community, the men appeared prone to violence, murder, and vengeance; they were motivated more readily by dislike, even hatred, than by forgiveness (41). They valued their reputations (*fidelité*) as their greatest goods; nothing else seemed to matter to them, and the apparent emotional isolation of men and women led to disinterest and coldness in personal contacts: "ils [the men] n'ayment aussi guïres leurs femmes,... ils ne leur touchent guïres au coeur" [they hardly love their wives at all,... they barely touch their hearts] (38). The nobility, raised "à la française," had escaped such ill effects and showed no such rudeness. They were not subject to the precarious existence at the margins, not threatened by hunger and want. Although they were occasionally mentioned as sabbath participants, they rarely appeared in the ranks of the accused and even less frequently in those of the convicted. In the Labourt, as elsewhere, witchcraft was a poor people's, indeed a poor women's domain.

In the *Tableav* one image returns time and again, an image as alluring to the magistrate as it is to us today: the vision of liberty, freedom, and lack of control that characterized the life of these "half-year" wives in the eyes of the magistrate and in the minds of his readers. While husbands, lovers, sons, and fathers were at sea, wives and sweethearts, free of disciplining work, unencumbered by male control, and lacking any object on which to focus their affection or with which to satisfy their passions, turned to Satan and their demon lovers. To him they dedicated the children born during the absence of their human fathers. In this satanic company, the women seemed to be engaged in a perpetual feast.

This ambiance of natural beauty and presumed personal freedom produced changes in the conception of the witch that were to define her image through the twentieth century. She became younger. Pledged to Satan as a child by the mother, nurse, or other relative, a woman participated fully in the sabbath by the age of twelve or thereabouts (sometimes not until twenty or twenty-two) after undergoing the ritual of satanic copulation and/or the anal kiss. Her apparent autonomy, the absence of parental or conjugal control in all domestic matters, her closeness to nature, to the sea, and to the mountains, all gave the woman a devilish lightness that made her a fitting companion for demons, with whom she flew about "inconstante et vagabonde" [unfaithful and a vagabond] (19).

The sabbath, conjured before Lancre's mental eye in the women's coached depositions, was not without its playfulness. Many described their experiences as happy and carefree. They talked about—and Lancre never tired of insisting on the consistency among the many testimonies he heard—how much they loved to dance day and night: "non la dance reposee et graue, ains decoupee et turbulente.... Et dancent auec le mesme tabourin qu'ils ont accoustumé de dancer au Sabbat" [not resting or calm, always in motion and turbulent.... And they dance to the tune of the same tambourine that they use when they dance at the Sabbath] (41). They recounted their happiness when they made love with total disregard of the sex, age, or familial closeness of their partners. Lancre felt only revulsion at these descriptions; he found the dancing repulsive—both the real activity that he witnessed and the activity that he heard described; it was incompatible with any kind of order, which he knew to be the foundation of society. He compared the sabbath to the dance called the spider dance, the *tarantale* or *tarantism,* a dance of possession and healing practiced in Apulia, in southeastern Italy, and around Naples.[57] The only difference was that in the Labourt the dance brought no healing, only possession and the loss of the dancers' souls.

Lancre had been an eyewitness to such dances. Before his mission had consigned him to the Labourt, Lancre had traveled extensively. He had observed women whose dancing reminded him of the Basque witches, that is, dancing

> à la Bohemienne, car aussi les Bohemes coureurs sont à demy Diables: je dy ces longs poils sans patrie, qui ne sont ny Aegyptiens, ny du

Royaume de Boheme, ains ils naissent par tout en chemin faisant et passant païs, et dans les champs, et soubs les arbres, et font des danses et bastelages à demy comme au sabbat. Aussi sont ils frequens au païs de Labourt, pour l'aisance du passage de Navarre et de l'Espagne. (208)[58]

The difficulty of containing these marginal people surfaces again.

In Italy Lancre must have heard about or seen the spider dance because he describes the dancers as persons "qui estoient teintes d'vn venin qui faisoit fair mille et mille sauts" [who were tainted by a poison that made them jump a thousand jumps] (17). This dance is old; it may even go back to pre-Christian possession rites.[59] But the healing dance of Apulia was to Lancre just another demonic ritual, not unlike those practiced among the peoples of faraway Japan or of the islands of the New World. Lancre was convinced that the history of dance, like the history of magic, had evolved from the beneficial to the satanic. What had been dances performed in honor of God or to encourage warriors before battle had become a ritual "impudique pour atterrer des femmes... et encore plus salement et vilainement en les Sabbats" [shameless for seducing women... and even more disgusting and more crudely at the sabbaths] (202). In his mind this was yet another case of cultural disintegration, of which inquisitorial permissiveness was the most horrifying.[60] His comments on the threateningly sensual dance that had been introduced into France from across the border from Spain, the *sarabande* or *chicono,* suggest his outrage: "c'est la dance la plus lubrique et la plus effrontee qui se puisse voir" [it is the most lascivious and offensive dance one can see] (203). He associates the dance's violence, animation, passion, and obvious licentiousness with the sabbath dances, which he had never seen except in his mind:

> Car l'homme et la femme passant et repassant plusieurs fois à certains pas mesurez l'vn prés de l'autre, on diroit que chaque membre et petite partie du corps cherche et prend sa mesure pour se ioindre et s'associer l'vn a l'autre en temps et lieu. (203)[61]

Typical for the inverted world of the sabbath, some participants even dance back to back—"et à certaine cadance ils se choquent et frapent impudement cul contre cul" [at a certain beat they bump each other and shamelessly grind backside against backside]—or they do as the gypsies, half devils in Lancre's mind, and dance in the round a kind of *gaillarde* for two persons (209).

Bodin described a similar dance, the *Newen Gaillartische[n] Volta,* which had come from Italy to France:

> da man einander im Welschen Dantz an Schämigen Orten fasset / vnnd wie ein getribener Topff herumbher haspelt vnnd wirbelt... dz solcher Wirbeldantz voller schandtlicher Vnflätiger Gebärden vnd Vnzüchtiger Bewegung ist... daß vnzahlig vil Mord vnnd Mißgeburten darauß enstehen. (111)[62]

Citing Bodin with approval, Lancre agreed that this cultural exchange was endangering customs in France, even if, or maybe because, such dancing now adopted by the French and called "à la Françoise" had found its devotees at court. During a visit by the Italian prince Pietro de' Medici, the dance had been the cause of much amusement; the prince was apparently unaware of his compatriots' passion for dances that Lancre feared endangered the soul (205).

The Basque people were indeed as foreign to Lancre as any of the peoples across the ocean or in the far corners of Europe.[63] When he did not condemn their sensuality and their lust for life, he scrutinized them as if they were children. His reaction was not unlike the early discoverers, who had similar reactions to the New World natives. Columbus's letters to the Spanish sovereigns and Las Casas's defense of the natives made equally effective use of the image of the child—negatively interpreted as irresponsible and sexually permissive, or positively valued as innocent, easily exploited, and grievously mistreated.[64] Their young women betrayed not the least embarrassment when, in the presence of the young cleric translator Hualde, they recounted their offensive exploits:

> Elles ne rougissent du tout poinct, quelque impudente et sordide question ou sale interrogatoire qu'on leur face: de maniere que nostre interprete [Hualde, the future inquisitor]... auoit plus de honte de leur faire nos interrogatoires, qu'elles à y respondre. (216)[65]

The mood conveyed by Lancre's description of the Labourdins and their satanic escapades is one of youth, vigor, freedom, and female independence. Their poverty, the marginality of their lives amidst the rough and violent environment of the Labourt, recede into the background of the magistrate's and the readers' gaze.

While the task of leading the very young children to Satan was a crime committed primarily by the older women, Lancre's witch is, on the whole, young, either still a teenager or in her early twenties; many of them are children. These children play a prominent role in Lancre's observations; bewitchment had become increasingly a family affair; the younger victims seemed to join their elders at the sabbath in greater numbers. Possessed children freely—often without prompting by the magistrates—denounced the participation of their parents and other members of the community in the sabbath. They also denounced the adults who forced them to come along to the sabbath dances. Families developed into veritable witch dynasties, since becoming a witch seemed to have become a familial fate. Of one of the accused priests, Pierre Bocal, it was said that "d'ailleurs les tesmoins deposoient, que la mere, les seurs, et toute la famille de Bocal estoient Sorciers, et diffamez de tout temps de ce crime" [besides the witnesses testified that the mother, the sisters, and the whole Bocal family were witches and were defamed for all time because of this crime] (423). The probability of a familial rather than an individual inclination pertained as well to questions of heresy, prompting the Spanish Inquisition to check carefully into the backgrounds of each of their potential officials. The candidates had to produce documentary proof that their ancestors had remained clear of any taint of heresy.[66] This "certificate of family purity" had to be assembled at no small cost to the candidate. Together with the vow of keeping total secrecy in all inquisitorial matters, it was intended to help the inquisition to avoid satanic contamination.

During Lancre's stay in the Labourt, the number of children who accused their elders of taking them to the sabbath had grown steadily on both sides of the border. Lancre mentioned that as many as five hundred children, once even two thousand, had been part of the proceedings in the later stages of his work. At the height of the craze, there was hardly a village in the region where panic-stricken parents were not moved to demand the execution of suspected witches who had allegedly taken their children to Satan. They tied the children to their beds or endeavored to keep them awake, terrified that once the children closed their eyes, even for an instant, they would be unable to resist satanic abduction. Or parents brought them to church in the vain hope of seeking protection: "Sathan commence à posseder non seulement les Prestres: Mais bien encore certaines Eglises pollues et profanees" [Satan has begun to possess not only the priests but also certain polluted and profaned churches] (39). In this atmosphere of suspicion of even the youngest members of the community, it was not a coincidence that Hualde became one of the most fervent prosecutors of Spanish child-witches after he had assisted in Lancre's inquests (551).

The use of children's testimony posed the same procedural problems for Lancre as that of women had for Kramer and Bodin.[67] How could one evaluate the testimony of persons who did not fit the category of legally recognized adult males? He knew that for any testimony to be valid, two girls "de bon aage" (sexually mature young women) were needed in place of one man. Trying to avoid the difficulty of legitimating child-witnesses, Lancre somehow let the numbers speak where age could not: "sauf des enfans de six ans, sept et huict ans et au dela, la desposition desquels nous receuions en ce seulement que *chacun d'eux maintenoit* virilement et sans iamais varier" [Except for children of six, seven, and eight years of age and older, whose depositions we accepted on the condition that *each of them maintained* his position like a man and without ever changing what was said] (552). It remains unclear if by "enfans" Lancre means only male children. At one point he alludes to this possibility: "nous ayons faict valoir la desposition des filles, si elles n'auoient passe la puberté qui est douze ans, ny des enfans s'ils auoyent passé les quatorze" [we validated the depositions of the girls if they had not yet reached puberty, which is twelve years, or of [male] children if they were older than fourteen] (551).[68] It was judicial practice as well as general custom to accept twelve as the age of maturity for girls and fourteen as that for boys. The children were initially presented to the Devil at age two or three. At nine years of age, sometimes earlier, they acknowledged "de bonne volonté" Satan as their lord and the queen of the sabbath as their "pedagogue" (391). At puberty, the "bon age," they rose to the status of full-fledged members of the sect and became active participants in the sabbath (179). But even at a young age, they followed satanic temptations for pragmatic ends. Like junior Dr. Faustusses, they willingly sold their souls to the Devil "que pour auoir le pris en leurs classes, ils se fussent volontiers donnez à Satan" [and in order to have the prize in their classes, they gave themselves willingly to Satan] (176). For a reward, Satan inspired them to write "des vers si excellents que leur regent les admiroit" [such excellent verses that their teacher admired them] (176). Faust and his pupil, Wagner, had given their souls for rewards no less mundane. While the *Malleus* mentioned child-witches only in passing, Lancre regarded them as active, albeit apprentice, participants in the sabbath. They guard the toads, and they seem to join in the dances.[69] Kramer had mentioned the crimes of *Hexenhebammen*, who either killed the newborn or dedicated the child to Satan at birth. More than a century later, the child-witch had become a dreaded phenomenon. Both Salazar and Lancre tell of children who denounce their elders as witches who had initiated them into the sect. The child-witch craze on both sides of the border brought much suffering to the children: many were severely punished, some even burned at the stake (208–33).[70]

In the end, Lancre's tract returns to the severity of judgment and the pervasiveness of the threat of adult witch activity. Italy, Germany, and Spain needed the inquisition to prosecute their heretics and their witches. In the name of royal majesty, Lancre strove to punish these people with the full weight of the law behind him. He was not entirely successful. "Making justice" meant more to him than prosecuting individuals accused of practicing witchcraft; his work had broader implications. Commenting on the two priests who were burned for their satanic activities, he declared:

> il est fort dangereux de pardonner la sorcelerie, la magie, et crimes semblables, à vn Prestre, mesmement à vn qui a charge d'ames. Car c'est vne clemence mal assise et tres-dangereuse *pour la Republique*, et sur tout en vn pais si infecte que celuy de Labourt. (522)[71]

The results of leniency were *atheisme, heresie, idolatrie*. Satan and his minions wanted more than to destroy souls; they wanted to annihilate the society of Christian men and women (524).

6

Magic and Religious Diversity: The Discourses of Belonging and Exclusion

When Lancre would recall his stay among the Labourdins, one impression persisted in his consciousness. Time and time again he mentioned the "liberté," "diversité," the "inconstance," and the "legereté" that characterized his subjects' lives and personalities. Freedom, diversity, inconstancy, and a certain devilish existential lightness appeared to govern the Labourdins' lives and feelings. Moreover, their priests, whom the women adored as if they were demigods, seemed to share these emotions.[1]

However, the witches' sect, whose existence seemed a virtual certainty to Bodin, Lancre, and many of their colleagues, was not the only transgression disturbing the peace of mind of the orthodox Catholic and Protestant leadership. Since the middle of the century, other sects had made their presence increasingly known. Their number grew in the period of uncertainty toward the end of the century; their names are ubiquitous in all religious and political conflicts of the period. Much can be read about the atheists, Epicureans, libertines, and deists.[2] Bodin, for example, associated the "Epikurer / Atheisten vnd ruchloss leut" (Vom aussgelasnen wütigen Teuffelsheer, 11), the "sceptici" (14), with religious heterodoxy and sexual deviance; and they had been the object of much political and religious attention in Fischart's native Strasbourg as well.[3] Alongside the condemnations leveled against these presumed spiritual derelicts, frequent mention is made of yet another group that appears synonymous with the above, the libertines. Bodin does not name this fourth group in the *Démonomanie*, although invectives against them were popular at the time. They were often cited during the sixteenth and early seventeenth centuries; indeed, they became an indispensable ingredient in the bitter polemics against religious diversity and dissidence. As early as 1535, a synod at Strasbourg legislated against atheism, defining it as a crime.[4] David Wootton rightly points to the "rich vocabulary of disbelief" in Latin as well as in the vernacular leveled by Jean Calvin, Guillaume Farel, and their associates against their opponents.[5] Ten years after the publication of his witch tract, in 1622, Lancre described how he brought many magicians to the stake, among them numerous *alumbrados* and Rosicrucians. No doubt he thought both groups equally dangerous and, worse, in collusion in their battle against the public good.[6]

Despite the frequency with which these epithets were used, a precise definition of such terms is lacking. However, libertinism, atheism, and Epicureanism were generally associated by their critics with debauchery, ignorance, the search for pleasure and prosperity, even effeminacy.[7] Libertines and atheists were said to not fear God and to defend religion only as an ordering principle needed to impose and sustain social discipline. The literal meaning of libertine refers to a sect, a category of (free) thinkers; although they were frequently associated with satanic dalliance, members of this group were equally often accused of denying the existence of demons and the immortality of the soul. Spiritually, they often stood accused of "liberté de l'Esprit," which meant that they considered themselves free of theological and religious dogmatism. This last characteristic appears to be what Lancre had in mind when he harshly condemned the *liberté* of the Labourt women.[8]

According to their numerous critics, libertines and all those associated with them had religious dereliction in common, and, even more dangerously, they were suspected of inciting civil disobedience, mutiny, and in this way endangering the state.[9] Bodin's and Lancre's relentless pronouncements against the public danger of witches and their satanic activities must be seen in the context of these anxieties, whose object was the religiously or socially infirm women or men and their danger to the moral and spiritual fiber of the individual and the community. Neither Bodin nor Lancre would have assented to Cyrano de Bergerac's irreverent remarks: "le Diable seroit-il un ribaud, de chercher avec tant d'ardeur l'accouplement des femmes; non, non mais j'en devine la cause, une femme a l'esprit plus leger qu'un homme, et plus hardy par consequent à resoudre des Comedies de cette nature" [The Devil would be a true rascal to seek with such ardor to have sex with women; no, no, but I know why; a woman is much more easygoing than a man and consequently tougher in coming to terms with such pleasure].[10] The satanic threat was no laughing matter to the men who sought to legislate against witchcraft.

The alleged witch distinguished and condemned by the spirit "plus leger qu'un homme" was equally familiar to Kramer, Bodin, and Lancre; for more than an entire century, they agreed on her deadliness. Even Weyer concurred with the reality, if not the gravity, of the threat implied by a woman's susceptibility to satanic temptation. At the time of their discussions, during the post- and Counter-Reformation years, questions of religious orthodoxy were also argued with increased fervor. In the face of rapidly spreading religious diversity and dissidence, however, the ability to define such orthodoxy became ever more difficult. Women suspected of witchcraft were persecuted with escalating judicial and theological severity; so were men who were believed to have strayed too far from orthodoxy. All the while, belief in magical powers seemed to grow, and with it the anxious accusations of irreligiosity and apostasy among clergy and lay people. This situation did not abate as the century wore on, rather it assumed new dimensions as Europe significantly broadened its geographic, ethnographic, horticultural, and astronomical horizons.[11]

In this discursive Babel, survival meant cultivating the ability to argue one's religious convictions effectively, efficiently, and—when needed— evasively if isolation or even death at the hands of those in charge of the authoritative discourses was to be avoided. Women could remain inside the protective parameters of orthodoxy only when they managed to remain socially, morally, and religiously unmarked. If for any reason they became stigmatized—either by accusations from their neighbors or, as a close reading of Bodin and Lancre documents, by the very fact that they were women and poor or daughters of suspected witches or members of marginalized ethnic groups such as the Labourdins—the protective discourse of the community gave way quickly to an isolating, potentially fatal inquest by the authorities. The witch, whose traits had been authoritatively and systematically enumerated in the *Malleus Maleficarum*, could not, for the most part, participate in the intellectually and theologically challenging climate of discussion that grew out of the fall of Constantinople in 1453, an unforeseen event of unprecedented consequence.[12] Most women, certainly those who were caught in the net of persecution, never did share in the enthusiastic optimism of men like Ficino, the Picos, Ulrich von Hutten, and even Erasmus. The earth and the cosmos expanded, as did knowledge of *scientia magica* and the world of the spirits; ever greater levels of diversity and novelty found their way into printed texts, which people read voraciously.[13] But woman remained outside, rarely an actor, most often acted upon. She became even more vulnerable as she was exposed to the scientific and theological inquiry that pursued her into realms where only she was alleged to have access: the world of the sabbath and familiar, even intimate, dealings with Satan.

At a time when the discourse of religious diversity and learned magic expressed the individual's theological autonomy, assertion, and inquiry, witchcraft became the discourse of fear and—for the learned and lay public—titillation. The sexual explicitness of Lancre's *Tableav* and the immediate and avid response of readers and listeners to the Logroño auto-da-fé, as well as the sheer volume and detail of court records, witch tracts, and sermons, all affirm that witchcraft had become an object of intense judicial and theological scrutiny. Witch tracts and broadsheets had become early modern intellectual and popular best-sellers, widely circulated pornographic texts of sexual deviance and violence against women. Nor was their enduring attraction diminished by the fact that the content had changed little since the publication of the *Malleus* more than a century before. Rather, the witches' story had remained stable and had survived largely unchallenged by clerics and jurists, even among the skeptics, since Kramer had presented it in its canonical form. For centuries the discourse on witchcraft stood as the monument to man's abiding inability to know woman. His attitude toward alleged witches retained the fascination and the aggression of an anger that seemed generated by this inability to comprehend and control her.

The very social nature of her alleged misdeeds (much at the center of Kramer's, Weyer's, Bodin's, and Lancre's writings), such as the abandon with which she gave herself to her night rides and her murderous tendencies, made the witch an uncommon legal, intellectual, and social challenge to early modern men and institutions, all the more so because she was a creation of their own making. In endless variations throughout some two hundred years of history, witchcraft was the epitome of all other crimes of nonconformity. Witches were evil; their persecution and, if needed, extermination were ways of attacking deviance with greater efficiency than was possible among the religious dissidents who appeared everywhere in Europe. The witch's trial—conducted in seclusion, as opposed to her punishment, which was most often part of a public spectacle, used to depict either reconciliation or physical penance—served multiple purposes. It had legal, theological, social, and scientific ramifications: legal, because a crime had to be punished; theological, because the crime had been identified as a sin; social, because more often than not the witch had been accused of antisocial, hostile acts; and finally, each inquest and trial was also a scientific inquiry. Rational, learned men wanted to know exactly what happened in a world from whose experience they were excluded. This *curiositas* provoked jealous reactions; precisely who controlled the space beyond the scope of masculine power and reason was hotly contested.

The demand to conquer the witch and her space grew ever more urgent during the later sixteenth century. If a clear delineation between scientific and demonic magic could not be achieved, the scholar practicing the magical sciences would always remain vulnerable to accusations that he engaged in demonic exercises, activities punishable by death. The murkiness separating the sanctions of science from the illicitness of magic is evident in Remond's Saturday search for Mélusine, Kramer's attempt to locate the devil's mark, and Lancre's travel in the border regions of France, where he was distressed over the strange elusiveness of his charges and frustrated by his inability to speak their language.[14] For all these examples suggest how men's actions were motivated by a desire for knowledge, which inevitably led to their exploration of the mysteries of the forbidden practices.

The space inaccessible to the investigator was geographic (the place of the sabbath), physical (the body of the witch), and, most importantly, intellectual (the woman's knowledge of the satanic ritual). The witch's confession was intended to satisfy both the curiosity of her inquisitors and, at the public reading of her sentence or of her reconciliation with the church and with the community, the commoners' thirst for the comfort of the avenging or forgiving justice of God. Her confession was always framed in the language of the inquisitors. However many witnesses they induced to testify, their curiosity could not, in the last analysis, ever be satisfied. The list of questions that Fischart added to his translation of Bodin's *Démonomanie* for the instruction of the inquisitor is very similar in tone to the *Mainzer Interrogatorien* of 1612.[15] Significantly, the witch was for the most part unable to articulate her own defense effectively. More often than not, she seemed unable to argue the finer doctrinal points; she could not allay the inquisitors' fears concerning sect activity. The interrogators' preconceived idea that the witch was a threat to the community is still detectable in the writings under discussion here. The *Wissensvorsprung,* the projection of the accusers' own biases both inside and outside of the courtroom, constituted a considerable obstacle to the woman's survival. Help could only come from efforts to scrutinize court procedures, from skepticism of the kind that the bishop of Pamplona and the inquisitor Salazar had brought to bear on the trial proceedings in northern Spain. If no one interceded on the alleged witch's behalf, her admission of guilt was issued directly to her in the very language of the inquest. Her guilty testimony was, if not literally, then by direct and inescapable suggestion, put into her mouth.[16] Witch prosecutions had little of the "gute zwanck," the benevolent authority, that, according to the reformers, should be practiced by those in power toward those given into their care.

Responding to the religious, intellectual, and social turmoil that marked the second half of the sixteenth century, doctrinal disputes were articulated in a language molded to express ever finer points of religious difference with ever greater clarity.[17] The failure to avail oneself of authoritative, orthodox discourse meant the failure to participate in the discourse of power. Marginalization and isolation within the community were the inevitable result. The power of language carried with it the ability to protect one's spiritual sovereignty, to control one's social and economic space: within its bounds lay safety and the promise of a future; outside of it stood banishment, homelessness, imprisonment, and even death. During the middle and latter half of the sixteenth century, the intellectual and social environment of early modern Europe erupted with symptoms of religious diversity and dissidence that, together with information about the New World and the renewal of the witch menace, led to a profound crisis in representation that fostered the dogmatization of discourses on all fronts.

When Luther failed to reform the church universal, he was forced to establish his own church as a bastion of the new orthodoxy. He was the victor whose influence on the reforming discourse was formidable and far-reaching. He expected the new, reformed *ecclesia* to stand beside and ultimately replace the old church. But competing religious discourses immediately sprang up.[18] Within twenty short years after Luther's separation from the Roman Church, a multitude of confessions became locked in increasingly heated debates over more and more subtle points of theological orthodoxy. Each group developed its own creed and its own understanding of the major tenets of the Christian faith and community; the role and proper time for baptism; the nature of marriage;

and the duties of men and women to the family, to political and church authorities, and to each other. The need to remain within the bounds of orthodoxy, however narrowly defined, encouraged the proliferation of more narrowly defined theological precepts based on fine distinctions in language and religious dogmas.[19] During the second half of the sixteenth century, theology as the indisputably masculine discourse of intellectual and religious inquiry and study became richly varied and powerfully heterogeneous. In this heterogeneity theology often moved dangerously close to heterodoxy. On occasion it touched magic; we can already hear it in Paracelsus's and Agrippa's repeated and urgent assurances that their thoughts on the nature and the role of magic in God's universe remained within the bounds of the authorized.[20]

Diverse as they were, the religious and theological discourses rose quickly to rhetorical and spiritual maturity in the shadow of the growing threat of heterodoxy. Religious diversity—expressed either as the severely fundamentalist observance of the Spiritualists, Anabaptists, or the *Schwärmer*—and the growing spiritual distance, disenchantment, and separation of those condemned as libertines or of even the atheists emerged as a potential threat to the major orthodoxies, be they Lutheran, Calvinist, Zwinglian, or Catholic.[21] This factionalization within religion in turn led to intense polemics directed by those in power—those in charge of the authoritative discourse—against religious dissidents and their subversive theologies and social utopias. Calvin and Martin Bucer frequently proclaimed the new orthodoxy that Protestant dissidents posed a greater threat to the body politic than the Papists.[22] Bucer's definition indicates the danger that was sensed in the proliferation of dissident—in this case Epicurean—thought: "Der Epicurus meinet den leuten diser furcht ab und inen deshalb etwas zu rugen zu helffen, das er sie understunde zu bereden Gott kümmerte sich nit, was wir uff erden thun und wurde es nit richten" [Epicurus wants to convince people (talk them out of their fear) that they need not fear God, that God does not care what we do on this earth and that he will not judge them].[23] Far from being to the people's advantage, religious diversity can be frightening:

> c'est premierement chose effroyable de la grande diversité des religions, qui a esté et est au monde, et encore plus de l'estrangeté d'aucunes, si fantastique et exhorbitante, que c'est merveille que l'entendement humain aye peu estre fort abesty et enyvré d'imposture car il

> semble qu'il n'y a rien au monde haut et bas, qui n'aye esté deifié en quelque lien, et qui n'aye trouvé place pour y estre adoré.[24]

The accustomed points of orientation for what was right and what was wrong seemed to lose their fixity and predictability. What was praised at one time as God-pleasing righteousness and as a correct understanding of the Bible could at other times be quickly and unequivocally condemned. Struggling to establish order in his city-state(s), Calvin preached and wrote untiringly against the enemies of the faith, against such dangerous religious variants. His zealous invectives against such teachings, which he condemned as hostile to the soul and dangerous to the community, sound a warning of their diabolic traits. The libertine's inclination toward "false liberty" of the flesh robs the "Epicurean swine" of all reason and delivers him into a rage of frantic searching to satisfy all his desires. His language is marked by "un jargon plein de toute confusion,... [ils] ne taschent qu'à confondre et abysmer tout" [a language full of confusion,... they only want to confound and destroy everything].[25]

A few decades later, the situation had changed in such a way that Calvin, in turn, was condemned as an atheist, a veritable religious imposter. In 1572, the year of the St. Bartholomew's Day Massacre and its murderous consequences, Claude de Sainctes published his *Declaration d'aucuns athéismes de la doctrine de Calvin et Bèze contre les premiers fondements de la chrestineté*. The author left no doubt that he considered Calvin and his followers satanic impostors whose doctrine had wrought nothing but violence and destruction: "[Calvin's doctrine] n'est qu'un pur et détestable athéisme, que par subtilité, imposture et violence on avance et pour lequel on faict voye au monde à l'Antichrist contre Jesus Christ" [(Calvin's doctrine) is nothing but pure and despicable atheism, which they advance through subtlety, pretending, and violence and for which they prepare in this world the path for the Antichrist against Christ].[26] The accusations, even though published in a polemical tract and not formally presented in a court of law, sounded remarkably like the witch accusations. Calvin stood accused of "un athéisme, qui abolit la nature de Dieu, la foy chrestienne, la conscience, societé et tranquillité des hommes" [an atheism that destroyed the nature of God, the Christian faith, the conscience, society, and tranquillity of humankind] (106).

As the century progressed, recriminations intensified. In 1584, two years after Bodin first published the *Démonomanie,* the German Wilhelm Lindanus (Guillaume Lindan) produced a strong attack against the

Calvinists, the *Christomachia Calvinistica et sacramentariorum omnium vere Sathanica, qua invidus Diabolus nunc Antichristo suo in dies adventurienti certum praeparat iter.*[27] Calvin here appears as a devil worshipper and practitioner of incest. The discursive closeness to witch accusations is inescapable. Lancre likewise reported on Calvinist and Lutheran heretics who were punished at the auto-da-fé at Logroño, condemned to spend the rest of their lives in prison after abjuring their false beliefs (*Tableav*, 386).

Atheism, libertinism, and sectarianism became inseparable from heresy; their practitioners were men "sans fois, sans loy et sans religion" [men without faith, with neither laws, nor religion].[28] Calvin, Bodin, and Lancre judged their alleged objective to be the retention of all goods in common, the observation of equality among men and women, and the denial that virginity and a pledge of marital fidelity were necessary preconditions to conjugal vows—all even more dangerous than the threat to communal religiosity.[29] The libertines were accused of believing religion to be a mere tool used to pacify the people and to keep them under the control of the religious and lay authorities, who treated adults like children requiring discipline by their elders and employed demons and angels as part of this plot to scare them into obedience. Bodin's and Lancre's passionate indictments against those who denied the reality of demons and the witches' sabbath indicate how seriously deviant beliefs were taken. Hope for recompense and fear of punishment were, to quote the Paduan skeptic Pomponazzi, major impulses to act or to refrain from acting: "this is why it is not far from my thoughts or from the truth to say that Plato taught the existence of angels and demons; not that he believed in them, but because his purpose was to instruct the ignorant."[30] Pomponazzi believed that the world and all creation existed for the sole benefit of humanity. The ignorance and easy fears of the vulgar, simple folk compelled them to blame demons and angels for phenomena beyond their understanding (225).[31] Pomponazzi's *Tractatus de immortalitate animae* (1516/1556), which accumulated arguments tending to deny the immortality of the soul, must be viewed as a major influence on the discussion of religious dissidence.[32] Step by step, Pomponazzi moved to disprove the immortality of the soul, calling the fiction of a future life the bridle that people needed to control their behavior.[33] Half a century later, people stood the risk of being burned alive for such pronouncements. The reduction of, and disregard for, religious ceremony in the wake of the reforming movements—even by those capable of enforcing new orthodoxies—contributed to the growing fear of libertinism and atheism. In an atmosphere where the discourses of religious ceremony seemed to be reduced to mere symbols, to the sparsest expression of communal worship, suspicions arose that Satan and his demons might be part of a plot to rob the people of the reconciling power of religious observance. Hence, owing to their fear of social anarchy, even libertines insisted that religion served many useful functions and was preferable to a people free of religious anxieties.

Looking to define the libertine in a more acceptable and affirmative political and social fashion at a time of rapid change and spiritual uneasiness, Charron (1541-1603) presented a different kind of a man, a sage. Charron's popular *De la sagesse livres trois* (1601) describes this man as "plaine, entière, généreuse et seigneurale" [whole, complete, generous, and noble]. We hear echoes of Giovanni Pico's *Oration on the Dignity of Man* when we read that God is "le dernier effort de notre imagination vers la perfection, chacun amplifiant l'idée suyvant sa capacité" [the final effort of our imagination to reach perfection, each amplifying the idea according to his ability to imagine].[34] The true libertine is free to formulate his own judgment in all things; Charron's concept of *liberté* even seems to include matters of religion, a conviction that did not go unnoticed by some of his sterner contemporaries.

Lancre had completed his mission in the Labourt a year before Charron published his tract. For Lancre, the "estrangé, fantastique et exhorbitante" [strange, fantastic, and exhorbitant qualities] that distinguished the atheists, libertines, and Epicureans had found its most frightening realization among the women of the Labourt. Their seeming deification of Satan was as beastly and as base to him as the religious diversity that shocked Charron and Bodin.

The perilous affinity that Lancre and Bodin observed between satanic magic and dissident religious practices was also the subject of a tract of Pierre Le Loyer (1550-1634), *IIII Livres des spectres* (1589), which was followed in the early seventeenth century by his *Discours, et histoires des spectres, visions et apparitions des esprits*....[35] Le Loyer theorized that Christians first fell into doubting their faith, then became heretics, then libertines, and finally atheists. He delineated intellectual evolution and a mental space similar to that of Dr. Faustus. Unlike many of his contemporaries, Le Loyer separated atheism from libertinism and Epicureanism; whereas the latter two concepts presumed irrational thought, he saw in atheism a discourse of alarming but inescapable logic and of not inconsiderable persuasive power.

Many who found themselves to be the targets of the violent invectives leveled by their opponents argued that they merely sought what they considered to be a responsible, God-pleasing faith; that not they, but rather their accusers, needed to amend their spirituality.[36] When they found themselves charged with irreligion or libertinist leanings, they either attempted to argue their cases publicly, or they chose, in increasing numbers—if one is to believe the invectives against them—to go into spiritual hiding. Many assumed "the attitude of compromise and deceit which came to be known as Nicodemism."[37] To protect life and to preserve a domain where religious preference could be expressed without interference, religious dissimulation became a standard and much criticized practice for many who found themselves cast in the role of a censored and potentially exiled religious minority. Their number grew rapidly in the wake of the religious wars: "ce sont nos guerres pour la religion qui nous ont fait oublie la religion" [It is our wars for religion that made us forget religion], as the Protestant François de La Noue explains the reasons for the rapid increase in atheism and irreligion.[38] People learned to live in a way that hid their true religious alliances; they cultivated the ability to dissimulate—to separate what was said from what was believed.[39] This talent, born out of the spiritual necessities of the sixteenth century, remained, however, closed to the women suspected of witchcraft. Acquiring the art of religious subterfuge was imperative if one was to survive in the community. Soon it became praised as the virtue of the self-proclaimed select, who—though they did not feel bound by religious constraints—believed that without the fear of hell, social order would soon crumble. The intellectual and religious obsession that led to dissimulation or to religious radicalism also enabled many to argue more specific points of doctrine within the bounds of orthodoxy. Some of them, denounced as Epicureans, demanded tolerance and freedom in the church to allow the Holy Spirit to be present in individuals and individual congregations.[40] The personal decision to camouflage one's religious loyalties, to practice Nicodemism, became a political statement about the fundamental question of who controlled thinking and/or behavior, and whether the community could and should intrude into one's personal life.

In Fischart's Strasbourg, just as in Bodin's Laon, in Lancre's Bordeaux, and in many early modern communities, the question was answered with a clear affirmative: by the middle of the century, the well-being of the community superseded any notion of religious tolerance or even individual freedom. Radical religion meant radical politics, and, according to Thomas A. Brady, Jr., "toleration [was] a matter of policy, not of conviction, and the problem of toleration was never faced by those writers, such as Erasmus, who never assumed a public position."[41] Those not active in politics therefore never had to struggle to establish and uphold order in a community churning with religious dissension and contentious opinions and weakened by the activities of what were believed to be heretical sects. Responding to the requirements of public positions and civil authority, the Bodin of the *Heptaplomeres* and the *Démonomanie* and the Lancre of the *Tableau* and the *Livre des princes* inhabit different mental spaces that made differing, even seemingly exclusive discourses available to them.

Nonetheless, the relentless persecution of the witch advocated by men who also spent considerable energies in developing new ideas about the politics of government—as did Lancre and Bodin—indicates that witchcraft was perceived as a significant obstacle to civic calm. Struggling for control in their communities, Protestant magistrates tried and, in the majority of cases, succeeded in establishing their authority over the spiritual, educational, political, cultural, and economic realms. Those suspected of not being aligned with the forces of the confessed orthodoxy were almost always suspected and accused publicly of libertine or atheistic sympathies. More dangerous still, they were believed to be less interested in the law and order of the community than in the pursuit of knowledge, however arcane or unorthodox. These men emphasized the "necessity of dissimulation and reserve for reasons of safety and for keeping dangerous thoughts from the multitude."[42] The elitist notion of Nicodemism made its members—about whom little is known—less than sympathetic to the plight of alleged witches. Theirs was a public fate, more often rural than urban. In their ignorance they hoped for justice, but justice at that time was not the justice of proving their innocence but rather the justice of submitting to an implacable and increasingly efficient judicial process.

Nicodemism provided a substantial discursive challenge to a religious and administrative elite that was struggling against duplicity and deceit, against avoidance and equivocation, and against the whole casuistry of the religious conscience that claimed much attention in the inquisitors' manuals and in the tracts against unbelievers. Not surprisingly, invectives against lying and warnings of equivocating language in witch inquests abound.

In the *Excuse à Messieurs les Nicodémites* (1544), Calvin identified five groups that might be prone to become members of a Nicodemite sect. First, he pointed his accusing pen at the preachers, who, for want of money, were too lenient with their parishioners, and at the clerics, who adhered to religious orthodoxy only when it did not interfere with their pleasures. Another category of concern to him was those intellectuals, judges, lawyers, physicians, teachers, and philosophers for whom religion was but a philosophical proposition, a Platonic idea, as easily argued as discarded. These men proved to be especially vexing antagonists because they were manipulators of language; they were the opinion makers. They were also most afraid of being silenced and/or censored, were they to speak too freely on matters of religious controversy. The third group in need of sharper discipline was the merchants and the common people, who were only interested in their profits and who had little interest in religious practices that would harshly regulate their lives. The last and worst group was the Epicureans, men "more disgusting than the papists," because they feigned adherence to religion while in their hearts they mocked theology. They were suspected of considering faith nothing but a fable invented to make the weak obedient to the powerful.[43]

It is not surprising, given the allegedly widespread practice of religious dissidence and dissimulation, that the struggle against disguise, deceit, and deception found its way into much of the legal, medical, political, and religious writing of the time. In this light Lancre's anxiety over the necessity of translating and, by inference, interpreting the testimony of sabbath participants assumed greater urgency and significance. Paracelsus, who had much to say about magic in his explorations of human physiology and psychology, wrote only a small, equivocating tract on the nature of the witch, which emphasized the public dimension of her marginality. However, he mentioned as a defining trait her refusal to fulfill her social role as woman and wife, her "turning away from men, fleeing men, hiding, wanting to be alone, not attracting men, not looking men in the eye, lying alone, refusing men" (DS, 446–47). In the early modern community, such behavior epitomized not only aberrant sexuality and satanic dependence but also the wish to turn from society into a secretive life of seclusion. At a time when members of the community were often suspected of subterfuge, such behavior could and would not be tolerated. It was judged destructive to the individual as well as to the whole of society.

The third book of the *Malleus* and the last pages of Fischart's translation of the *Démonomanie* are devoted to questions that, used alone or accompanied by the appropriate level of torture, would enable the inquisitors to force a confession. Both guides are divided into carefully and tightly formulated inquiries: Kramer's is of a more general nature; Fischart's deals with an actual trial, the inquest against a certain Elsa, who is accused of having caused a child's death by witchcraft. The *Malleus* deals mostly with the method for asking the right questions, for discerning lying, and for judging how and when to torture. Fischart simply lists a number of pointed questions that could not help but lead to self-incrimination (331–35). Torture, "peinlich Befragung," was only to be used when the statements of the accused did not conform to an established notion of truth. The form and progression of the questions make it clear that the reality of religious dissimulation and the practice of religious subterfuge were well known to urban magistrates and to the inquisitors. Such evasive tactics made them, as recording agents for the early modern judicial and administrative community, extremely suspicious of all witch testimony, especially since they knew that in dealing with the Devil, a reliable concept of truth was not available. For this reason, court records of witch trials, where they do exist, are exceedingly detailed and evidence an almost ritualistic predictability. At each inquest a recording clerk had to be present; it was his task to write down everything that was said in an effort to protect all participants in case of an appeal or in the unlikely event of judicial wrongdoing. These clerks were not to interject themselves into the proceedings: "nos Conseillers Clercs és Cours souueraines, n'assistent iamais aux condannations de mort et n'y peuuent non seulement opiner mais non pas mesme assister, ouir, ny escouter vn attest de mort" [the clerks of the courts never take part in the death sentences and they cannot voice an opinion nor assist, hear or listen to a death sentence] (Lancre, *Tableav*, 402). Any accusations about judicial impropriety aside, magistrates such as Bodin and Lancre took seriously this separation of the recording and the judging of the proceedings. The fear of harboring unbelievers, coupled with the weakening of the religious ties that bound all members of a community together in one and the same public confession of faith, made the Nicodemite and the witch doubly dangerous. Her confession was infinitely more accessible than his beliefs; thus witchcraft inquests became a battleground where belief systems, pastoral concerns, and censure collided. She could be punished and expunged from the community; he could continue to go about his business undetected by the authorities.

As mentioned above, the witch persecutions can be divided into three periods that center around, and are determined by, the publication of the *Malleus Maleficarum*. During the centuries preceding the publication of Kramer's handbook, magic and witchcraft were part of the popular imagination and were of learned, philosophical, and theological interest. While earlier tracts contained the first allusions to a witches' sabbath, to witches, who venerated the Devil presiding over the sabbath in the form of a he-goat, who flew through the night to their secret meeting places and their cannibalistic orgies, Richard Kieckhefer calls Kramer's tract "the famed culmination of the tradition."[44] However, during the years following the publication of the *Malleus,* the discussion assumed a decidedly uglier and more threatening tone. While almost a century passed before the deadly impact of the debate would be felt, the distancing from the dark, satanic side of magic became an obligatory discursive gesture for almost all writers on this or, as Paracelsus's writings evidence, related subjects. From 1486 until the last witch was executed several centuries later, Kramer's manual was the gauge for judging orthodoxy in witch beliefs. Arguing for or against the reality of witches and, later in the century, for their physical presence at the sabbath—which had become a code for the physical mingling with the Devil and for unimaginable but excitingly suggestive debauchery—provided a base for the learned writer's humanist learning on the subject. It mattered little whether the stress was laid more on judicial, medical, or theological aspects of the phenomenon. The tracts—Weyer's, Bodin's, and Lancre's stand for many others of this kind—always represented the witch problematic within the larger context of the author's own intellectual formation and his doctrinal sympathies. Belief in the immortality of the soul, in the Trinity, in demons, and in witches became the mark of orthodoxy, the definition of a social and religious insider.

The fate of a mythical-historical figure like Mélusine makes clear the satanization of the witch discourse brought about by Kramer. Paracelsus's naturalist and scientific definition of her nature as an elemental spirit and/or victim of ascendantal influence notwithstanding, over time Mélusine's name came to be associated with a more negative kind of magic. Luther's, Bodin's, and even Lancre's remarks on this topic confirm her devaluation from founding mother of a noble lineage to a condemned spirit. Kramer brought system and order into the portrait of the woman as witch. While he did not add anything new, he did construct a coherent, judicially and psychologically consistent portrait in the imagination of the time that was to remain officially in force far into the future. All that changed, and then only occasionally, was the age and number of witches and the increasing importance and location of the sabbath. From the original marginalized position prepared for her in religious and philosophical traditions, the woman suspected of witchcraft was moved further and further to the outside. She was thereby excluded from the discourse that concerned her most of all, the discourse that marked her salvation and her social position. Bodin and Lancre could not have been clearer on this subject.

Given the fact that the *Malleus* stood at the beginning of the alleged witch's theological, judicial, and cultural isolation and banishment, it is clear that the persecution of women as witches would and could not be overcome until the principles of the *Malleus* were—for whatever reason—proven to be no longer tenable. The first and, as chapter 4 illustrated, singularly ineffectual effort was Weyer's publication of the *De praestigiis,* which heated up an already simmering debate and contributed to the renewed popularity of the *Malleus*. Bodin's massive attack and Weyer's own admitted belief that Satan could bodily possess women led to the public dispute over these tenets but not to any affirmative rejection of Kramer's theses.

From time to time, however, cautionary remarks indicated the presence of fissures in the belief system. This fracturing was caused less by a sudden disbelief in the power of Satan and his potential ability to delude women into thinking that they had sexual contact with him than by an abiding faith in the righteousness and incorruptibility of the judicial system. Henningsen has shown how this faith affected the inquisitor Salazar. Wishing to calm the witch craze that threatened the judicial supremacy of the inquisition by revising the inquisitorial rules, Salazar quoted an instructional letter from November 27, 1538, that expressed some of the sentiments prompting the inquisitor to moderate his stance on the persecutions. The writer of this letter warned fellow jurists not to believe everything they read in the *Malleus:* "he [the author] writes about it [the sabbath] as something he himself has seen and investigated, for the cases are of such nature that he may have been mistaken, or others may have been."⁴⁵ Salazar continued in what Henningsen calls a "crushing indictment" of inquisitorial procedures:

> we [the inquisitors] failed to write down all important things which related to the defendants both within and outside the Tribunal, for we omitted to record the disputes and rejoinders, writing only the final resolution of each point. We thus suppressed inconsistencies and irrelevancies.... nor was mention made of the continued promises and guarantees with which we assured those who denied everything that if they confessed they would be set at liberty.⁴⁶

There were other cautious and skeptical partisans of women, who chose the weapons of ridicule and sarcasm to chastise the learned doctors' fixation on witches' marks and travel to the sabbath. Like Weyer, Augustin Lercheimer, also known as Herman Witekind, a Protestant clergyman, did not deny the reality of intercourse with the Devil. He believed, however, that if people were sufficiently armed by instruction in faith against devilish temptations, their susceptibility to belief in satanic promises would be lessened. The Oettingen-Wallerstein Collection at the university library at Augsburg contains a tract by Lercheimer bound together with the popular book by the Calvinist Antonius Praetorius (Schultze), pseudonym Johann Scultetus, *Grundlich Bericht von Zauberey und Zauberern /... Allen Staenden der Welt in Gemein vnd sonderlich den hohen vnd nidern Obrigkeiten zu notwendiger nachrichtung und nützlich zu lesen*.⁴⁷ Praetorius proved to be a more temperamental writer than most who had chosen to hold forth on this subject. He literally laughs—"ha, ha, he [sic]"—at the crazy suggestions that women who are so poor as to have to beg for their living might be able to do magic (80). Even more scathingly sarcastic are his comments on the matter of the witch's mark. He alternately mocks and accuses the interrogators who shave off and singe with fire not just the hair on the head and under the arms:

> sondern auch an heimlichen Orten: Welche an fremden Menschen anzugreiffen im Gesetz / bey Hand abhauwen verbotten / vnd gestraft. Sie wenden vor / der Teuffel sitze den Hexen im Haaren vnnd Scham / den woellen sie so vertreiben. O deß armen Teufels / der sich mit so klein Liechtsflam vnd Rauch verjagen laesset. (264)⁴⁸

The allusion to rape here is undeniable, not only in the penetration metaphor but also in the violation done to the victim. Praetorius's treatise must be seen in conjunction with sixteenth-century witch skeptics like Weyer (whom Praetorius never mentioned). This group was not at all small; according to Stuart Clark, "there was clearly an important strand of doubt in-built in Protestant demonology."[49] Judging by the number of publications and reeditions of such works between 1550 and 1630, the discussion was energetic and involved no small group of people. After having played his part in enlivening the debate, Weyer remained an active, if increasingly cautious, participant.

Praetorius entered the debate toward the end of the century, after Weyer and Bodin had both died. He expounded on the judicial, theological, and social aspects of the witch phenomenon with great learning and obvious conviction. He left no doubt that he was preaching a long, passionate, and, in many places, accusatory sermon, which is structured to sound like a dialogue between an authoritative "I" and a selfish, inhumane, clearly less-than-Christian "you." Praetorius's use of the rhetorically effective plural collective is much strengthened by the inverse identification of the enemy. Needed, he says, are: "von allem Aberglauben gantz reine Theologi /... vnd rechtglaeubige Medici, Physici, der Vaeter vnnd Artzney kuendige / vnd gottesfuerchtige Iuristeriti / Rechtsgelehrte" [theologians free of all superstitions /... and orthodox physicians, physicists, who know the books of the Fathers and of the medical arts / and also devout jurists / learned in the law] (227). This enumeration suggests that none of the men whom he knew to be involved in trying witches possessed these qualities. In fact, Praetorius did not want the courts involved at all, believing that matters of faith—judging whether a woman had fallen away from God for whatever reason—were not matters of jurisprudence. If the law had to be invoked, scrupulous attention should be paid to the procedures developed for this purpose.[50]

Providing us with yet another example of the epistemological association of witchcraft and religious dissent, which I have been outlining, Praetorius appeared to be convinced that one explanation for the witch persecutions had to be sought in religious dissension and strife. *Zauberey* (sorcery), he felt, was to be found among the Papists, or else it had to be associated with "Widertaeufferischen und Schwenckfeldischen Traeume und Offenbarunge" [anabaptist and Schwenckfeldian dreams and revelations][51] (64). Blind and bloodthirsty religious and judicial zealots were to blame for the innocent blood of women who at most were feebleminded and old, and certainly not Satan's companions. He, too, believed that sorcery was the result of negligence in education. Paracelsus had voiced comparable caution when he warned that children had to be sent to school to neutralize and remove the threat of the ascendant.[52] Instruction in the faith or in the proper care of the household was, Praetorius believed, a defense against Satan: "aber gemache deß gantzen Hauses jmmer wol butzen und sauber halten / mit gutem Rauchwerck / Dunst vnd Gestanck daempffen. Deß Viehes auch warnemen mit Krippenfegen / vnd was darzu gehoeret" [but one should see to it that the whole house is always clean / with a clean chimney / to reduce smoke and smell. And you should care for your animals by cleaning their troughs / and whatever else is needed] (119). Order within the home and the community was the only reliable ally against witchcraft. Praetorius returned to the political implications of life in a multiconfessional society that demanded clear choices: "abschaffen vnnd vertilgen alle oeffentliche Abgoetterey / falsche Lehr.... Kirchen und Schulen mit richtigen Lehrern bestellen" [do away with and exterminate all public idolatry / and false teachings.... Churches and schools should employ good teachers] (343). Following his Protestant tenets, he demanded that churches submit to the care of the secular rulers, "daher werden die Koenige... Seugammen der Kirchen Gottes genannt / daß sie dieselbigen jhnen lassen befohlen / vnnd angelegen seyn... wie Pfleger vnnd Ammen jhren Pfleg Kindern zuthun schuldig" [therefore, kings are called the nursemaids of the church / so that they may look after her / and care for her... as caretakers and nursemaids do with children entrusted to them] (345). This tract was meant as much as a plea for reason in dealing with alleged witches as it was a call to civil obedience and public order and a warning to be mindful of the long-term consequences wrought by a witchcraft accusation; the onus was on succeeding generations: "ihr habt auch das gantze Geschlecht Buergerlich getoedtet / vnd offt viel Zanck / Hader / Balgen / vnnd Mordt erwecket" [You have killed the reputation of all generations / and often caused much dissension / argument / fighting / and murder] (263).

In one brief sentence, Praetorius articulated the gendered injustice implicit in all witch persecutions. He derided the deadly dichotomy that empowered men to accuse women of riding on broomsticks and of doing all kinds of unprovable harm. Meanwhile, men were allowed to consult horoscopes, engage in interpretations of dreams, sorcery, soothsaying, to read "luegenhaffte / aberglaeubische / zaeuberische vnd verfuehrerische Schriften vnd Buecher" [lying / superstitious / magical and seductive tracts and books] in German and in Latin, and to live lives of debauchery, of "fressen / sauffen / Fechten / Spielen / Tantzen / Gauckeln / und dergleichen Teufflische samen" [gluttony / getting drunk / fencing / gambling / dancing / cheating / and much more of such satanic doings] (358). Staying within the bounds of orthodoxy and, therefore, of community safety was, Praetorius would have agreed, infinitely easier for men than for women.

These bounds had to be enforced and rigorously protected. Fear of the dissidents—the Epicureans, libertines, and atheists—never left sixteenth-century clergy and magistrates entirely. Because they were explicitly or implicitly anti-Christian, these attitudes—indeed they seemed more attitudes than religions—accelerated the circulation and discussion of new ideas. Protestants and Catholics, accusing each other of Nicodemism, libertinism, and atheism, showed clearly that both factions were equally afraid of the implied relativism toward all cherished values. They dreaded the constant shifting of loyalties, and they deplored the hard-to-define limits of acceptable behavior more than they feared true and identifiable heresies.[53] A chapter in Stanislas Hossius's tract *De origine haeresium nostri temporis* (Louvain, 1559) expresses much of the fear and apprehension of what was ahead in post-Reformation Germany. Subtitled *Quibus gradibus sathanismus Germaniam occuparit,* this text describes how in the middle of the century, the first mention of the word "athées" (atheists) and the casual attitude toward religious matters by men who were maligned as Epicureans signaled the presence of a "significant and never entirely vanquished opposition among the intelligentsia."[54] This presence unsettled the authorities in the same time period that we observe a growing hysteria over alleged witch activities in Germany, Switzerland, France, and Austria. The religious wars and doctrinal controversies, along with geographical discoveries, caused the number of the doubters and the irreligious to multiply.

The Calvinist Léry, who traveled to Brazil, described his reaction to the gap that seemed to be widening between God and his creation by comparing cannibalism in America and Europe.[55] Léry had been shocked by the Brazilian Tupinamba's supposed custom of eating the flesh of their male enemies. This ritual was used to ensure that the enemy's qualities were transferred to the Tupinamba's own people. While Léry and the German traveler Hans Staden reported that men and women ate human flesh, neither one ever described a woman prisoner being eaten. Léry explained and excused the Brazilians' behavior by their heathen nature; their cannibalism was prescribed by ritual. Léry had heard of other cannibals who devoured their human prey merely to satisfy their hunger, showing themselves more animal than human. After he returned to his native France, he became embroiled in religious strife that reached its climax in the St. Bartholomew's Day Massacre. He describes his horror at watching a hungry populace taking increasingly desperate measures in the attempt to combat their encroaching starvation. Léry talks of one couple, who—in an instant of complete despair—even resorted to eating the flesh of their infant, who had died of hunger.[56] After a year, the besieged city of Sancerre (1573) had run out of all food.[57] According to Léry, atheism among the Tupinamba of Brazil was a natural, if scandalous, evolution from libertinism to the total collapse of civil and religious order:

> I have wished expressly to recount all of this here, to demonstrate that if those worse-than-devil-ridden atheists, with whom our part of the earth is now covered, share with the Tupinamba the delusion... that there is no God.... Since the atheists are utterly unworthy having cited for them what the Scriptures say [about the immortality of the soul] I will rather offer to them the example of the poor Brazilians... who can teach them that there is in man a spirit.... The Indians [of Peru] will give the lie to the accursed atheists, and rise up in judgment against them. (Whatley, trans., 138-39)

Léry's observations about the natives of the New World were influenced by what he had left behind in Europe. In his eyes the natives exhibited satanic mannerisms: they ate human flesh and went about nude; and their singing and dancing evoked in him memories of the witches' sabbath.[58]

Léry's comments can be considered models for the experiential realism that defined reactions to the New World discoveries, religious diversity and dissidence, and the experience and fear of magic and witchcraft during much of the early modern European community. Toward the end of the sixteenth century, the wide spectrum of compromise positions of the high and late Middle Ages concerning the natural and the occult and the known and the unknown was replaced by a growing conflict between what was perceived in the Old World and what was seen in faraway places. The result of such conflict was a sharpened antagonism between scholar, theologian, and licit magician on the one hand, and on the other, those who were accused of practicing magic or sorcery illicitly and who were—to a large extent—women. The potentially antisocial traits that made the religious dissident so dangerous in the minds of the members of the major confessions prompted them to call for increasingly stringent rules of social discipline. Using Strasbourg as an example, Jean Rott has found that during the sixteenth century, rules had to be imposed "to moderate the fury of the lives of the citizens and villagers and to impose a minimum of civil order and moral standards in the town."[59] Singling out a man as an Epicurean, an atheist, or a Nicodemite not only carried with it the attempt to discipline, banish, or formally punish a member of the community. It also brought about his marginalization, for he was moved out of the circle of influence and power. This result is doubly important, since those accused of membership in the dissident sects, such as Sebastian Franck, Sebastian Castellio, Hans Denck, Anton Engelbrecht, and Otto Brunfels—who, according to Ginzburg, was the "father" of Nicodemism—were clearly exceptional men on account of their intelligence, social prestige, and literary activities. Not unlike the women accused of witchcraft, they seemed, by virtue of their participation in the social ferment, to stand in an inverse relation to their numbers.[60] The force of their numbers, however, did not prevent continued efforts to control, expel, or silence them. In 1598 the Strasbourg Formula of Concord established religious coexistence and orthodoxy, and in so doing condemned all rival church groups, naming the Catholics and the Calvinists right alongside the Epicureans and sectarians.[61] This step was the last one in a long line of such moves. The first had been taken by Bucer and the city government in the thirties, when the lay magistracy had taken control of doctrine, discipline, and church organization. Together with the clergy, they undertook to clarify church doctrine, to oversee the religious and moral renewal of the citizens, especially the young, and to pacify religious and political tensions in their communities. Analogous to the bureaucratization of the witch persecution, sins were prosecuted as crimes, and punishment was dispensed by the courts.[62] The majority of people in France and in Catholic or Protestant reformed cities and provinces found themselves having to adjust to a life of renewed civil and religious discipline, which intensified concerns about the reality of witchcraft. They articulated a growing perception that God had moved away from the needs of the people. Far from despairing about this distant God, the Epicurean felt relief at having relinquished him; and God, in turn, could let go of the worry about humanity.[63] Blumenberg affirms that an epoch's profile is determined by the specific answers given to the immutable questions about the nature of the universe, God, and humanity. Recognizing an epoch means being able to identify its characteristic profile, to separate past from present. This ability remains the privilege of those born after an epoch's passing, those who consider history from the outside, from a perspective that, although able to offer a sense of definition, is nonetheless always distorted because it is set off from the period it names. The experience of those involved in the struggle over religious dissidence and orthodoxy was also that of the people who disputed the nature of the satanic and of the alleged witch. God had distanced himself from his creature, who set about discovering and conquering the world geographically, astronomically, and psychologically.[64] Man, but not yet woman, had to reclaim his place in this cosmos as an individual with the right to exist; the libertines, atheists, and Epicureans certainly acted as if in agreement with this conviction.

Some, however, moved too far away from the orthodoxy that they decried; these men were not simply exiled from their cities or put into prisons or enjoined from publishing or subject to having their writings destroyed. They paid with their lives for having stepped beyond the tightened bounds of prescribed behavior. As irreligion, libertinism, atheism, and Epicureanism became progressively associated with heresy and apostasy, the practitioners, these "masterless men," as Calvin scornfully censored them, had finally to acknowledge a master: civil authority.[65] Jacques Gruet, whom Calvin called a libertine, was beheaded; Calvin was also responsible for the execution in 1553 of Michael Servetus, considered a heretic because of his antitrinitarian stance.[66] Bruno was burned at the stake in 1600 after wandering through Europe as one of the most notorious libertines; the same fate was in store for Giulio Vanini, a reputed libertine and follower of Pomponazzi and Cardano, burned at the stake in 1619.[67]

The deaths of these men and others not mentioned were the direct result of religious dissension and dissidence, for such activity brought them into conflict with the political ambitions of the orthodox churches and of the agencies of social control. But compared with the persecution of women as witches, the victims were few, and the fact remains that women had much less of a chance to escape their fate than even the most notorious male dissident. She could not enter into the cacophony of disputes, the give-and-take of doctrinal arguments, the discursive maneuvers of religious debate. During the second half of the sixteenth century, while the discourses of religious diversity multiplied and vied for supremacy in the cultural marketplace, the witch debate gained momentum in a discursive climate that was marked by doctrinal and theological diversity on the one hand, and a surprising stasis in the witch discourse on the other. As I stated earlier, nothing radically new was said about the witch after Kramer had authoritatively defined her nature. The image was so set, so fixed, so indisputably lodged in the early modern mind that it was transferred, sabbath and all, into the New World, wreaking havoc for decades to come.

To the gendered dichotomy that had made woman inferior in the eyes of the church, the state, and herself must be added her inability to participate in the discourse that was really only concerned with her body and her nature. Ironically, when the old religious and political structures seemed to break open and alternative truths could be heard, she could not participate, in spite of the liberation experienced by many of her male contemporaries and their participation in the various authoritative discourses of the age: legal, medical, even religious.[68] Still, categories of discursive marginalization developed through the decades of the witch persecutions; they furnished the weapons with which to attack religious dissidents.

During the first half of the seventeenth century, when the new orthodoxies had established themselves, and France and Germany had moved beyond the seemingly endless religious strife and toward the establishment of absolutism, the persecution of women as witches continued for a while as part of a political program. My readings of Bodin/Fischart and Lancre suggest that no contradiction existed in the minds of the men who wrote on the state, on religious tolerance, and on the true character of the prince while, at the same time, they defined and persecuted the witch. Toward the end of the century, when the threat to the state perceived in the alleged witch was brought under control, at least discursively, she had no further part to play in the political and social theories of system builders. No matter how the discursive margins had been redrawn, she remained outside of the authoritative discourse until such time as sabbath dancing and the bewitchment of people and things were no longer accepted as part of early modern experiential realism—at a point when cosmological, social, political, and intellectual changes began to construct a different image of the world. And her otherness was no longer necessary to affirm man's power, the self-image, that he and Europe created to assure mastery. The inability of the majority of women to develop a language of religious dissidence and dissimulation at a time when these events dominated the religious discourse and practice of her accusers ultimately deprived her of a major defense against this most devastating assault on her life and faith.[69] Hers was a different language, what Muchembled calls the *interlangage féminin* (a language of woman to woman), a language either stigmatizing or consoling to those in her care. She passed on to other women and to female children—Lancre found this to be most horrifying—the secrets of the spinning room and of the grottos by the sea, secrets that in their entirety were never known to men.[70] Hers also was a discourse marked for the most part by exclusion from ritual and public speech. Her language was "incompatible with the sphere of rhetoric," which is also the sphere of power.[71] This incompatibility was what she had in common with the natives of the New World. Like them, she, too, was excluded from all institutions, from all discourses that legitimated power in the context of European culture and politics: preaching, academic writing, the language of law, and, ironically but significantly, learned, licit magic.[72] In the end, it is clear that the woman suffered profoundly, but she did not do so in isolation; the dissident and the native shared aspects of her plight. For decades, those in power were unable and unwilling to relinquish authority and control over these victims, these marginal figures, for fear that in this gesture they would also relinquish their own position of privilege and power.

Notes

Chapter 1

1. Norman R. C. Cohn, *Europe's Inner Demons: An Enquiry Inspired by the Great Witch-Hunt* (New York: Basic Books, 1975), 223.
2. H. C. Erik Midelfort, *Witch Hunting in Southwestern Germany, 1562–1684: The Social and Intellectual Foundations* (Stanford, CA: Stanford University Press, 1972), 18, 19; Edward Peters, *The Magician, the Witch, and the Law* (Philadelphia: University of Pennsylvania Press, 1978).
3. André Schnyder, "*Der Malleus Maleficarum:* Fragen und Beobachtungen zu seiner Druckgeschichte sowie zur Rezeption bei Bodin, Binsfeld und Delrio," *Archiv für Kulturgeschichte* 74, no. 2 (1992): 323–64.
4. Midelfort, *Witch Hunting in Southwestern Germany*, 194; Stuart Clark, "Glaube und Skepsis in der deutschen Hexenliteratur von Johann Weyer bis Friedrich Spee," *Vom Unfug des Hexen-Processes: Gegner der Hexenverfolgungen von Johann Weyer bis Friedrich Spee*, ed. Hartmut Lehmann and Otto Ulbricht, Wolfenbütteler Forschungen 55 (Wiesbaden: Harrassowitz Verlag, 1992), 15–33; Schnyder, "Fragen und Beobachtungen," 349.
5. Beatriz Pastor Bodmer, *The Armature of Conquest: Spanish Accounts of the Discovery of America, 1492–1589*, trans. Lydia L. Hunt (Stanford, CA: Stanford University Press, 1992), 3. Bodmer identifies what she calls three fundamental narrative modes of discourse: mythification, failure, and rebellion.
6. Stuart Clark, "Inversion, Misrule, and the Meaning of Witchcraft," *Past and Present* 87 (1980): 100.
7. Urs Bitterli, *Cultures in Conflict: Encounters between European and Non-European Cultures, 1492–1800*, trans. Ritchie Robertson (Stanford, CA: Stanford University Press, 1989), 1.
8. Michel de Certeau, *The Writing of History*, trans. Tom Conley (1978; reprinted, New York: Columbia University Press, 1988), 25; Anthony Pagden, *European Encounters with the New World: From Renaissance to Romanticism* (New Haven, CT: Yale University Press, 1993), 11, 30. For a critical review of recent scholarship on the Americas, see the two papers from the 1992 national

conference "New Perspectives on the New World": Helen Nader, "The End of the Old World," and Walter D. Mignolo, "The Darker Side of the Renaissance: Colonization and the Discontinuity of the Classical Tradition," *Renaissance Quarterly* 45, no. 4 (1992): 791–807, 808–29.

9. Michel de Certeau, *The Mystic Fable,* trans. Michael B. Smith (1986; reprinted, Chicago: University of Chicago Press, 1992), 19–20.

10. David Wootton, "Unbelief in Early Modern Europe," *History Workshop: A Journal of Socialist and Feminist Historians* 20 (1985): 86.

11. Henri Busson, "Les noms des incrédules au XVIe siècle," *Bibliothèque d'humanisme et Renaissance* 16 (1954): 273–83.

12. Wolfgang Neuber, *Fremde Welt im europäischen Horizont: Zur Topik der deutschen Amerika-Reiseberichte der Frühen Neuzeit,* Philologische Studien und Quellen 121 (Berlin: Erich Schmidt Verlag, 1991), 245.

13. Kurt Goldammer, *Der göttliche Magier und die Magierin Natur: Religion, Naturmagie und die Anfänge der Naturwissenschaft vom Spätmittelalter bis zur Renaissance, mit Beiträgen zum Magie-Verständnis des Paracelsus,* Kosmographie 5 (Stuttgart: Franz Steiner Verlag, 1991), 8.

14. Lynn Thorndike, *A History of Magic and Experimental Science,* vols. 3–5 (New York: Macmillan, 1923–58).

15. Stuart Clark, "French Historians and Early Modern Popular Culture," *Past and Present* 100 (1983): 86.

16. Keith Thomas, *Religion and the Decline of Magic: Studies in Popular Beliefs in Sixteenth and Seventeenth Century England* (London: Weidenfeld and Nicolson, 1971).

17. Marcel Mauss, *A General Theory of Magic,* trans. Robert Brain (London: Routledge and Kegan Paul, 1972); see also the essays in Leander Petzoldt, ed., *Magie und Religion: Beiträge zu einer Theorie der Magie,* Wege der Forschung 337 (Darmstadt: Wissenschaftliche Buchgesellschaft, 1978); Wootton, "Unbelief," 95–97.

18. Valerie J. I. Flint, *The Rise of Magic in Early Medieval Europe* (Princeton, NJ: Princeton University Press, 1991).

19. Brian P. Copenhaver, "Natural Magic, Hermetism, and Occultism in Early Modern Science," *Reappraisals of the Scientific Revolution,* ed. David C. Lindberg and Robert S. Westman (Cambridge: Cambridge University Press, 1990), 261–303; Amos Funkenstein, *Theology and the Scientific Imagination from the Middle Ages to the Seventeenth Century* (Princeton, NJ: Princeton University Press, 1986); R. J. W. Evans, *Rudolf II and His World: A Study in Intellectual History, 1576–1612* (Oxford: Clarendon Press, 1973); Charles Webster, *From Paracelsus to Newton: Magic and the Making of Modern Science* (Cambridge: Cambridge University Press, 1982); Bert Hansen, "Science and Magic," *Science in the Middle Ages,* ed. David C. Lindberg (Chicago: University of Chicago Press, 1978), 483–506.

20. Richard Kieckhefer, *European Witch Trials: Their Foundations in Popular and Learned Culture, 1300–1500* (Berkeley: University of California Press, 1978); *Magic in the Middle Ages* (Cambridge: Cambridge University Press, 1989).

21. H. C. Erik Midelfort, "Recent Witch Hunting Research, or, Where Do We Go from Here?" *The Papers of the Bibliographical Society of America* 62, no. 3 (1968): 373–420; see also the annotated but sometimes unreliable bibliography in Hans-Jürgen Wolf, *Hexenwahn: Hexen in Geschichte und Gegenwart*, 2d ed. (Dornstadt: Historia Verlag, 1990). Wolf calls his study a "modest contribution to greater tolerance"; it is meant to complement the "old" standard study of the witch craze, Wilhelm G. Soldan, *Geschichte der Hexenprozesse*, ed. Heinrich Heppe and Sabine Ries, 2 vols. (1843; reprinted, Essen: Athenaion, 1990).

22. Goldammer, *Der göttliche Magier*, 21. For more about the mentality and self-confidence of Italian Renaissance magic, see Charles Trinkaus, *In Our Image and Likeness: Humanity and Divinity in Italian Humanist Thought*, 2 vols. (Chicago: University of Chicago Press, 1970).

23. Annemarie Lange-Seidl, ed., *Zeichen und Magie: Akten des Kolloquiums der Bereiche Kultur und Recht der Deutschen Gesellschaft für Semiotik, 5.9.1986, Technische Universität München*, Probleme der Semiotik 8 (Tübingen: Stauffenberg Verlag, 1988); Gerd Schwerhoff, "Rationalität im Wahn: Zum gelehrten Diskurs über die Hexen in der frühen Neuzeit," *Saeculum* 37, no. 1 (1986): 45–82; Stuart Clark, "Inversion," 99–101.

24. Gary Tomlinson, *Music in Renaissance Magic: Toward a Historiography of Others* (Chicago: University of Chicago Press, 1993), 11.

25. Jean Delumeau, *La peur en Occident, XVIe–XVIIIe siècles: une cité assiégée* (Paris: Fayard, 1978).

26. Tomlinson, *Music*, 14; Charles G. Nauert, Jr., *Agrippa and the Crisis of Renaissance Thought*, Illinois Studies in the Social Sciences 55 (Urbana: University of Illinois Press, 1965); Michael H. Keefer, "Agrippa's Dilemma: Hermetic 'Rebirth' and the Ambivalences of *De vanitate* and *De occulta philosophia*," *Renaissance Quarterly* 41, no. 4 (1988): 614–53; Gerhild Scholz Williams and Steven Rowan, "Jacob Spiegel on Gianfrancesco Pico and Reuchlin: Poetry, Scholarship, and Politics in Germany in 1512," *Bibliothèque d'humanisme et de Renaissance* 44, no. 2 (1982): 291–305; Paola Zambelli, ed. *"Astrologi hallucinati": Stars and the End of the World in Luther's Time* (Berlin: Walter de Gruyter, 1986); idem, "Scholastiker und Humanisten: Agrippa und Trithemius zur Hexerei: Die natürliche Magic und die Entstehung Kritischen Denkens," *Archiv für Kirchengeschichte* 67, no. 1 (1985): 41–79. For a concise overview, see Goldammer, *Der göttliche Magier*, 10–12, 37–43; and the appropriate chapters in Thorndike, *A History of Magic*.

27. Miriam Usher Chrisman, *Lay Culture, Learned Culture: Books and Social Change in Strasbourg, 1480–1599* (New Haven, CT: Yale University

Press, 1982); Michael Giesecke, *Der Buchdruck in der frühen Neuzeit: Eine historische Fallstudie über die Durchsetzung neuer Informations- und Kommunikationstechnologien* (Frankfurt am Main: Suhrkamp Verlag, 1991); idem, *Sinnenwandel, Sprachwandel, Kulturwandel: Studien zur Vorgeschichte der Informationsgesellschaft,* Suhrkamp Taschenbuch Wissenschaft 997 (Frankfurt am Main: Suhrkamp Verlag, 1992).

28. Peter Segl, ed., Der Hexenhammer: *Entstehung und Umfeld des* Malleus Maleficarum *von 1487,* Bayreuther historische Kolloquien 2 (Cologne: Böhlau Verlag, 1988); Joseph Klaits, *Servants of Satan: The Age of the Witch Hunts* (Bloomington: Indiana University Press, 1985), indicates that the *Malleus* appeared between 1486 and 1521 in only a few editions, while between 1576 and 1680 sixteen editions appeared. Segl mentioned in conversation that with each subsequent edition, the *Malleus* focused increasingly on the woman as witch; see Schnyder, "Fragen und Beobachtungen," 327–28.

29. Pierre de Lancre, *Tableav de l'inconstance des mavvais anges et demons, ov il est amplement traicté des sorciers et de la sorcelerie* (Paris: J. Berjon, 1612).

30. Rudolf van Nahl, *Zauberglaube und Hexenwahn im Gebiet von Rhein und Maas: Spätmittelalterlicher Volksglaube im Werk Johan Weyers (1515– 1586),* Rheinisches Archiv 116 (Bonn: Ludwig Röhrscheid Verlag, 1983); see van Nahl's bibliography and his work on the publishing history.

31. See chapter 4; Wolfgang Behringer, "Erträge und Perspektiven der Hexenforschung," *Historische Zeitschrift* 249, no. 3 (1989): 628.

32. For a detailed discussion of Fischart's translation of Bodin's *Démonomanie,* see my study "Gemeinsame Sache: Johann Fischarts Übersetzung von Jean Bodins *Démonomanie des sorciers* (1580/81)," forthcoming in *Knowledge and Science in German Early Modern Literature,* ed. Gerhild Scholz Williams and Stephan Schindler.

33. The chronology of Bodin's publications appears in Friedrich von Betzold, "Jean Bodin als Okkultist und seine *Démonomanie," Historische Zeitschrift* 105 (1910): 1–64; "Das *Colloquium Heptaplomeres* und der Atheismus im 16. Jahrhundert," *Historische Zeitschrift* 113 (1914): 216–315; 114 (1915): 237– 301. Even to this day the authorship of this text remains in dispute; see Karl F. Faltenbacher, *Das* Colloquium Heptaplomeres, *ein Religionsgespräch zwischen Scholastik und Aufklärung: Untersuchungen zur Thematik und zur Frage der Autorschaft,* Europäische Hochschulschriften XIII, no. 127 (Frankfurt am Main: Peter Lang, 1988).

34. Wootton, "Unbelief," 97.

35. Michel Foucault, *The Order of Things: An Archeology of the Human Sciences* (1971; reprinted, New York: Vintage Books, 1973).

36. Thomas S. Kuhn, *The Structure of Scientific Revolutions,* 2d ed., (Chicago: University of Chicago Press, 1970).

37. Hans Blumenberg, *Die Genesis der kopernikanischen Welt,* 2d ed., Suhrkamp Taschenbuch Wissenschaft 352 (Frankfurt am Main: Suhrkamp Verlag, 1989), 2:596; *The Genesis of the Copernican World,* trans. Robert M. Wallace (Cambridge, MA: MIT Press, 1987).

38. Funkenstein, *Theology and the Scientific Imagination,* 3.

39. Walter Haug, "Über die Schwierigkeiten des Erzählens in 'nachklassischer' Zeit," *Positionen des Romans im späten Mittelalter,* ed. Walter Haug and Burghart Wachinger (Tübingen: Max Niemeyer Verlag, 1991), 339.

40. Wolfgang Behringer, "Kinderhexenprozesse," *Zeitschrift für historische Forschung* 16, no. 1 (1989): 31–47.

41. Eva Labouvie, "Männer im Hexenprozeß: Zur Sozialanthropologie eines 'männlichen' Verständnisses von Magie und Hexerei," *Geschichte und Gesellschaft: Zeitschrift für historische Sozialwissenschaft* 16, no. 1 (1990): 56–78.

42. Joan W. Scott, "Gender: A Useful Category of Historical Analysis," *American Historical Review* 91, no. 5 (1986): 1056, 1070; see also Gisela Bock, "Geschichte, Frauengeschichte, Geschlechtergeschichte," *Geschichte und Gesellschaft: Zeitschrift für historische Sozialwissenschaft* 14, no. 3 (1988): 364–91; Rita Felski, *Beyond Feminist Aesthetics: Feminist Literature and Social Change* (Cambridge, MA: Harvard University Press, 1989), 48.

43. Clark, "Inversion," 105.

44. For a preliminary investigation of these issues, see Gerhild Scholz Williams, "On Finding Words: Witchcraft and the Discourses of Dissidence and Discovery," *The Graph of Sex and the German Text: Gendered Culture in Early Modern Germany, 1500–1700,* Chloe Beihefte zum Daphnis 19 (Amsterdam: Rodopo, 1994), 45–66. See also Alan Charles Kors, *Atheism in France, 1650–1729* (Princeton, NJ: Princeton University Press, 1990).

45. The presence of many witch tracts in almost all larger library collections, such as the Henry Charles Lea Collection at Cornell University, the Oettingen-Wallerstein Collection at the Universitätsbibliothek Augsburg, the Staats- und Stadtbibliothek Augsburg, the Herzog-August-Bibliothek at Wolfenbüttel, the Universitätsbibliothek Munich, the Universitätsbibliothek Zürich, and many more, signals the importance and popularity of such tracts for the literate public. Many contain not only single volumes but many that are bound together for the purposes of practicality and expedience, such as the one at the Universitätsbibliothek Augsburg, which contains Niels Hemmingsen, *Vermanung von dem Schwartzküstlerischen Aberglauben, das man sich dafür hüten soll* (1586); Augustin Lercheimer, *Ein Christlich Bedenken und Erinnerung von Zauberey zum 3. und letzten Mal gemehrt, auch mit zu Ende anghengter Widerlegung etl. irriger Meinungen und Bräuche* (1598); and Johannes Scultetus, *Grundlich Bericht von Zauberey und Zauberern / . . . Allen Staenden der Welt in Gemein vnd sonderlich den hohen vnd nidern Obrigkeiten zu notwendiger nachrichtung und nützlich zu lesen* (1598). See also Nicoline Hortzitz, ed., *Hexenwahn:*

Quellenschriften des 15. bis 18. Jahrhunderts aus der Augsburger Staats- und Stadtbibliothek (Stuttgart: Silberburg Verlag, 1990). For a comprehensive microfilm collection of almost exclusively American holdings, see Diana M. Del Cervo, ed., *Witchcraft in Europe and America: Guide to the Microfilm Collection* (Woodbridge, CT: Research Publications, 1983). For the Wolfenbüttel collection, see Anneliese Staff, "Von Hexen / Zauberern / Unholden / Schwarzkünstlern / und Teufeln . . . : Bibliographie zu den Beständen der Hexenliteratur der Herzog August Bibliothek Wolfenbüttel," *Vom Unfug des Hexen-Processes: Gegner der Hexenverfolgung von Johann Weyer bis Friedrich Spee,* ed. Hartmut Lehmann and Otto Ulbricht, Wolfenbütteler Forschungen 55 (Wiesbaden: Harrassowitz Verlag, 1992), 341–93.

46. The proliferation of research on magic and witchcraft is impressive. Besides those already cited, see Ulrich von Hehl, "Hexenprozesse und Geschichtswissenschaft," *Historisches Jahrbuch* 107, no. 2 (1987): 349–75; Peter Kriedte, "Die Hexen und ihre Ankläger: Zu den lokalen Voraussetzungen der Hexenverfolgungen in der frühen Neuzeit," *Zeitschrift für historische Forschung* 14, no. 1 (1987): 47–71; Behringer, "Erträge und Perspektiven"; Wolfgang Schieder, "Hexenverfolgungen als Gegenstand der Sozialgeschichte," *Geschichte und Gesellschaft: Zeitschrift für historische Sozialwissenschaft* 16 (1990): 5–7.

47. Mauss, *A General Theory,* 91.

48. Stuart Clark, "The Scientific Status of Demonology," *Occult and Scientific Mentalities in the Renaissance,* ed. Brian Vickers (Cambridge: Cambridge University Press, 1984), 364.

49. Jan-Dirk Müller, "'Curiositas' und 'erfarung' der Welt im frühen deutschen Prosaroman," *Literatur und Laienbildung im Spätmittelalter und in der Reformationszeit: Symposion Wolfenbüttel 1981,* ed. Ludger Grenzmann and Karl Stackmann (Stuttgart: J. B. Metzler, 1984), 252–73; "'Erfarung' zwischen Heilssorge, Selbsterkenntnis und Entdeckung des Kosmos," *Daphnis* 15, nos. 2–3 (1986): 307–42. The model for Müller's studies is Hans Blumenberg, *Der Prozeß der theoretischen Neugierde,* Suhrkamp Taschenbuch Wissenschaft 24 (Frankfurt am Main: Suhrkamp Verlag, 1973).

50. Carlo Ginzburg, *The Night Battles: Witchcraft and Agrarian Cults in the Sixteenth and Seventeenth Centuries,* trans. John and Anne Tedeschi (1966; reprinted, Baltimore: Johns Hopkins University Press, 1983); *Ecstasies: Deciphering the Witches' Sabbath,* trans. Raymond Rosenthal (New York: Pantheon Books, 1991), continues to explore the sabbath as the expression of organized witch activity. See also Gustav Henningsen, "'The Ladies from Outside': An Archaic Pattern of the Witches' Sabbath," *Early Modern European Witchcraft: Centres and Peripheries,* ed. Bengt Ankarloo and Gustav Henningsen (Oxford: Clarendon Press, 1990) 191–219.

51. Stuart Clark, "French Historians," 70.

52. Kilian Blümlein, *Naturerfahrung und Welterkenntnis: Der Beitrag des Paracelsus zur Entwicklung des neuzeitlichen, naturwissenschaftlichen Denkens,* Europäische Hochschulschriften 20, no. 300 (Frankfurt am Main: Peter Lang, 1992), 60–64; Margaret Jones-Davies, ed., *La magie et ses langages* (Lille: Université de Lille III, 1980), 65.

53. Neuber, *Fremde Welt,* 50.

54. Frank Lestringant, *Le huguenot et le sauvage: L'Amérique et la controverse coloniale en France, au temps des Guerres de Religion (1555–1589)* (Paris: Aux Amateurs de Livres, 1990), 33, 37.

55. M. A. K. Halliday, "Language as Code and Language as Behavior: A Systemic-Functional Interpretation of the Nature and Ontogenesis of Dialogue," *The Semiotics of Culture and Language,* ed. Robin P. Fawcett et al. (London: Frances Pinter, 1984), 5. See for example David Carroll and Barry Saxe, *Natural Magic: The Magical State of Being* (New York: Arbor House, 1977); Ioan P. Couliano, *Eros and Magic in the Renaissance,* trans. Margaret Cook (Chicago: University of Chicago Press, 1987); Neville Drury, *The Shaman and Magician: Journeys between the Worlds* (London: Routledge and Kegan Paul, 1982); Brian Easlea, *Witch Hunting, Magic and the New Philosophy: An Introduction to the Debates of the Scientific Revolution, 1450–1750* (Brighton, Eng.: Harvester Press; Atlantic Highlands, NJ: Humanities Press International, 1980); William Eamon, *Science and the Secrets of Nature: Books of Secrets in Medieval and Early Modern Culture* (Princeton, NJ: Princeton University Press, 1994); Petzoldt, *Magie und Religion;* Stephen A. McKnight, *Sacralizing the Secular: The Renaissance Origins of Modernity* (Baton Rouge: Louisiana State University Press, 1989).

56. Lange-Seidl, *Zeichen und Magie,* 64.

57. Kurt Goldammer, "Magie," *Historisches Wörterbuch der Philosophie,* ed. Joachim Ritter (Darmstadt: Wissenschaftliche Buchgesellschaft, 1980), 5:631–36. Norbert Henrichs, "Scientia magica," *Der Wissenschaftsbegriff: Historische und systematische Untersuchungen: Vorträge und Diskussionen im April 1968 in Düsseldorf und im Oktober 1968 in Fulda,* ed. Alwin Diemer, Studien zur Wissenschaftstheorie 4 (Meisenheim: Verlag Anton Hain, 1970), 30–32, lists the following: Indo-European *magh* means power, strength, gift, wealth; Iranian *magu,* Old Persian *magus,* means magician, sorcerer—in Latin *magus;* Gothic, *magan*—Gothic *magan* means to like, desire, and *mahts* equals power, force, strength; and Latin *machina* stands for tools, metaphorically also trick, deception.

58. Paracelsus writes in the "Buch Paragranum": "Und alle Künste auf Erden sind göttlich, sind aus Gott und nichts ist aus anderem Grund. Denn der Hl. Geist ist der Anzünder des Lichts der Natur, darum kann niemand die Astronomie, niemand die Alchemie, niemand die Medizin, niemand die Philosophie, niemand die Theologie, niemand die Artisterei, niemand die Poeterei, niemand

die Musik, niemand die Geomantie, niemand die auguria und das andere alles lästern.... Was aber in uns erfunden wird durch das angezündete Licht der Natur... so uns Gott gibt" [And all arts on earth are of divine origin, they are all from God and nothing is of any other cause. Because the Holy Ghost is the lighter of the light of nature, therefore nobody can malign astronomy, or alchemy, or medicine, or philosophy, or theology, or art, or poetry, or music, or geomancy, or augury and all the other arts.... But whatever is found in us is because of the light of nature... as God gives it to us] (571); "Er [Gott] will nit, daß Solomon allein weise sei, sondern daß er der weise Mann sei und wir alle ebensowohl wie er.... So will er auch in seinen Künsten und Weisheiten, daß wirs alles auch seien" [He (God) does not want Solomon to be the only wise one, rather, that he be wise, and all of us as wise as he.... Thus he also wishes in all his arts and wisdom that we all should be this way] (LF, 18, 19).

59. Nauert, *Agrippa;* Manfred Agethen, "Aufklärungsgesellschaften, Freimaurerei, geheime Gesellschaften: Ein Forschungsbericht (1976–1986)," *Zeitschrift für historische Forschung* 14, no. 1 (1987): 439–63.

60. Gabriele Schwab, "Seduced by Witches: Nathanial Hawthorne's *The Scarlet Letter* in the Context of New England Witchcraft Fictions," *Seduction and Theory: Readings of Gender, Representation, and Rhetoric,* ed. Dianne Hunter (Urbana: University of Illinois Press, 1989), 172.

61. Eugene Vance, *From Topic to Tale: Logic and Narrativity in the Middle Ages,* Theory and History of Literature 47 (Minneapolis: University of Minnesota Press, 1987), 23, 44.

62. Dianne Hunter, "Hysteria, Psychoanalysis, and Feminism: The Case of Anna O.," *The (M)other Tongue: Essays in Feminist Psychoanalytic Interpretation,* ed. Shirley Nelson Garner, Claire Kahane, and Madelon Sprengnether (Ithaca, NY: Cornell University Press, 1985), 113–14.

63. Flint, *The Rise of Magic,* 63; Flint refers here to Mary Douglas, ed., *Witchcraft Confessions and Accusations* (New York: Tavistock Publications, 1970), xvii. Flint's book has aroused considerable discussion. The majority of reviews, thoughtful criticism notwithstanding, remain positive and admiring of the wealth of sources assembled by Flint to support her thesis. For some of the most informative reviews, see Frederick S. Paxton, *American Historical Review* 97, no. 3 (1992): 830–31; Robert A. Markus, *English Historical Review* 107, no. 422 (1992): 378–80; Edward Peters, *Catholic Historical Review* 78, no. 1 (1992): 270–73; Alexander Murray, *Past and Present* 136 (1992): 186–205; E. William Monter, *Journal of Social History* 26, no. 1 (1992): 200–201; Jean A. Truax, *Speculum* 68, no. 3 (1993): 768–70.

64. Flint, *The Rise of Magic,* 63, 82. The following quotation from Flint's book is exemplary for these practices: "Do you believe that you can kill, though without visible arms, people baptized and redeemed by the blood of Christ, and can cook and eat their flesh, after putting some straw or piece of wood or

something in the place of the heart?" (123); for the discussion of witchcraft as *crimen exceptum,* see chapter 4, note 39.

65. Flint, *The Rise of Magic,* 123: "Do you believe this, in common with many women who are followers of Satan? Namely that, in the silence of the night, when you are stretched out upon your bed with your husband's head upon your breast you have the power, flesh as you are, to go out of the closed door and traverse great stretches of space with other women in a similar state of self-deception. And do you believe you can kill, though with no visible arms, people who have been baptized and redeemed by the blood of Christ, and can cook and eat their flesh.... And then that you can resuscitate them after you have eaten them and make them live again? If yes, then you must go forty days of penance, that is, a Lent, on bread and water for seven consecutive days." Flint quotes a number of equally astonishing sources.

66. Flint, *The Rise of Magic,* 292.

67. John F. D'Amico, *Theory and Practice in Renaissance Textual Criticism: Beatus Rhenanus between Conjecture and History* (Berkeley: University of California Press, 1988), 121; Alois M. Haas, "Vorstellungen von der Makrokosmos-Mikrokosmosbeziehung im Denken der Zeit vor Paracelsus," *Nova Acta Paracelsica* 6 (1991/92): 50–77.

68. Ingrid Merkel and Allen G. Debus, eds., *Hermetism and the Renaissance: Intellectual History and the Occult in Early Modern Europe* (Washington, D.C.: Folger Shakespeare Library; London: Associated University Presses, 1988); Daniel P. Walker, *The Ancient Theology: Studies in Christian Platonism from the Fifteenth to the Eighteenth Century* (Ithaca, NY: Cornell University Press, 1972); Wayne Shumaker, *The Occult Sciences in the Renaissance: A Study in Intellectual Patterns* (Berkeley: University of California Press, 1972); Elizabeth Ann Ambrose, The *Hermetica: An Annotated Bibliography,* Sixteenth Century Bibliography 30 (St. Louis: Center for Reformation Research, 1992).

69. R. Howard Bloch, *Etymologies and Genealogies: A Literary Anthropology of the French Middle Ages* (Chicago: University of Chicago Press, 1983), 134.

70. How aggression against a woman could lead to accusations and, in one special case, to a significant regional persecution is described in two sources: Robert Muchembled, *Les derniers bûchers: un village de Flandre et ses sorcières sous Louis XIV* (Paris: Ramsay, 1981); and Robert W. Scribner, "Sorcery, Superstition, and Society: The Witch of Urach, 1529," *Popular Culture and Popular Movements in Reformation Germany* (London: Hambledon Press, 1987), 257–75. Sometimes public anxiety and fury over alleged witch activities reached such a fevered pitch that people took it upon themselves to hunt down and prosecute alleged witches. Such events threatened to infringe upon established juridical and political power and put the authorities into a quandary as to how to deal with zealots who had become more dangerous to the public welfare than the suspected

witch. See Walter Rummel, "Soziale Dynamik und herrschaftliche Problematik der kurtrierischen Hexenverfolgungen: Das Beispiel der Stadt Cochem (1593–1595)," *Geschichte und Gesellschaft: Zeitschrift für historische Sozialwissenschaft* 16, no. 1 (1990): 26–55.

71. Gustav Henningsen, *The Witches' Advocate: Basque Witchcraft and the Spanish Inquisition, 1609–1614* (Reno: University of Nevada Press, 1980); Vance, *From Topic to Tale*, xv; idem, *Merveleous Signals: Poetics and Sign Theory in the Middle Ages* (Lincoln: University of Nebraska Press, 1986), 252; Wolfgang Behringer, "Meinungsbildende Befürworter und Gegner der Hexenverfolgung (15. bis 18. Jahrhundert)," *Hexen und Zauberer: Die große Verfolgung, ein europäisches Phänomen in der Steiermark,* ed. Helfried Valentinitsch (Graz: Leykam Buch Verlag, 1987), 230.

72. Some of the most compelling testimony of the presence of magical thought in early modern society can be deduced from the ubiquitous beliefs in horoscopes and in prognostications, and from the pervasiveness of what we would now call superstitious practices. See Immanuel B. Schairer, *Das religiöse Volksleben am Ausgang des Mittelalters nach Augsburger Quellen* (Leipzig: B. G. Teubner, 1913); Dieter Harmening, *Superstitio: Überlieferungs-und theoriegeschichtliche Untersuchungen zur kirchlich-theologischen Aberglaubensliteratur des Mittelalters* (Berlin: Erich Schmidt Verlag, 1979); Behringer, "Erträge und Perspektiven," 630; Christian Degn, Hartmut Lehmann, and Dagmar Unverhau, eds., *Hexenprozesse: Deutsche und skandinavische Beiträge,* Studien zur Volkskunde und Kulturgeschichte Schleswig-Holsteins (Neumünster: Karl Wachholtz Verlag, 1983). On the presence of the Devil in sixteenth-century beliefs and practices, see Wolfgang Brückner and Rainer Alsheimer, "Das Wirken des Teufels: Theologie und Sage im 16. Jahrhundert," and Rainer Alsheimer, "Katalog protestantischer Teufelserzählungen des 16. Jahrhunderts," both in *Volkserzählung und Reformation: Ein Handbuch zur Tradierung und Funktion von Erzählstoffen und Erzählliteratur im Protestantismus,* ed. Wolfgang Brückner (Berlin: Erich Schmidt Verlag, 1974), 394–416, 417–519. Steven Ozment, ed., *Three Behaim Boys: Growing Up in Early Modern Germany, a Chronicle of Their Lives* (New Haven, CT: Yale University Press, 1990), 179, 183, describes young Stephan Carl's fear of an older woman of his mother's household. He calls her a witch and seems not a little afraid of her. See also Michael V. Behaim's letter telling of terrifying signs on March 16–17, 1529. He does not attempt an interpretation, simply commenting, "what this portends one must leave to God" (52). See also Christoph Daxelmüller, *Zauberpraktiken: Eine Ideengeschichte der Magie* (Zurich: Artemis und Winkler, 1993).

73. George Lakoff, *Women, Fire, and Dangerous Things: What Categories Reveal about the Mind* (Chicago: University of Chicago Press, 1987), xv; Funkenstein, *Theology and the Scientific Imagination,* 3.

74. John W. Cook, "Magic, Witchcraft, and Science," *Philosophical Investigations* 6, no. 1 (1983): 4.

75. Clark, "French Historians," 75, 93.

76. Bloch, *Etymologies,* 17. In a different but comparable context, Steven Ozment, "Mysticism, Nominalism, and Dissent," ed. Charles Trinkaus and Heiko A. Oberman (Leiden: E. J. Brill, 1974), 80, observes: "In the final analysis, words are the connecting link between the mind and reality and between the soul and God. Man must come to grips with the world around him through 'signs voluntarily instituted'; and he must work out his salvation on the basis of 'laws voluntarily and contingently established' by God. In the final analysis, all he has is willed verbal relations."

77. Neuber, *Fremde Welt,* 14; de Certeau, *The Writing of History,* 66.

78. Neuber believes that "an increasingly differentiated theory of invention becomes the basis for a system of humanist science... that includes all areas that are accessible and demonstrable by way of intentional investigation" (*Fremde Welt,* 31). He finds the elaboration of a topos-concept that is seen as a "form of thought" [Denkform], as the "deep structure of social discourse" [Tiefenstruktur des sozialen Diskurses] (32).

79. Vance, *From Topic to Tale,* 43.

80. Frank Lestringant, "Fictions cosmographiques à la Renaissance"; "Le déclin d'un savoir: la crise de la cosmographie à la fin de la Renaissance," *Ecrire le monde à la Renaissance: quinze études sur Rabelais, Postel, Bodin et la littérature géographique,* Collection Varia 6 (Caen: Paradigme, 1993), 294-95, 325.

81. Midelfort, *Witch Hunting in Southwestern Germany;* Peters, *The Magician, the Witch, and the Law;* Kieckhefer, *European Witch Trials,* and *Magic in the Middle Ages.*

82. Neal W. Gilbert, *Renaissance Concepts of Method* (New York: Columbia University Press, 1960); de Certeau, *The Mystic Fable,* 127.

83. De Certeau, *The Mystic Fable,* sees the historian's role in a similar light: "The historian 'calms' the dead and struggles against violence by producing a reason for things that overcome their disorder and assure permanence" (11).

84. De Certeau, *The Mystic Fable,* 18.

85. Mary Beth Rose, *The Expense of Spirit: Love and Sexuality in English Renaissance Drama* (Ithaca, NY: Cornell University Press, 1988), 5; Haug, "Über die Schwierigkeiten des Erzählens," 339.

86. For, writes Montaigne, "if you are going to execute people, you must have luminously clear evidence," cited by Stephen Greenblatt, "Psychoanalysis and Renaissance Culture," *Literary Theory/Renaissance Texts,* ed. P. Parker and D. Quint (Baltimore: Johns Hopkins University Press, 1986), 215.

Chapter 2

1. Leo Hoffrichter, *Die ältesten französischen Bearbeitungen der Melusinensage,* Romanistische Arbeiten 12 (Halle: Max Niemeyer, Verlag, 1928), 65. For bibliography and editorial commentary for the German "Melusine" see Thüring von Ringoltingen, "Melusine," *Romane des 15. und 16. Jahrhunderts: Nach den Erstdrucken mit sämtlichen Holzschnitten,* ed. Jan-Dirk Müller, Bibliothek der frühen Neuzeit 1 (Frankfurt am Main: Deutscher Klassiker Verlag, 1990), 9–176, 1012–87. Jean d'Arras, *Mélusine: roman du XIVe siècle,* ed. Louis Stouff (Dijon: Impr. Bernigaud et Privat, 1932). The French rhymed version is reprinted in Coudrette, *Le roman de Mélusine, ou, Histoire de Lusignan,* ed. Eleanor Roach (Paris: Klincksieck, 1982). Concerning the editorial history of the Arras text, see Laurence Harf-Lancner, "Le Roman de Mélusine et le Roman de Geoffroy a la grande dent: les éditions imprimées de l'œuvre de Jean d'Arras," *Bibliothèque d'humanisme et Renaissance* 50, no. 2 (1988): 349–66.

2. I will cite only a select list in view of the fact that recent book-length studies offer comprehensive bibliographies. For the folkloristic aspects, see the numerous works of the French Germanist Claude Lecouteux: "Das Motiv der gestörten Mahrtenehe als Widerspiegelung der menschlichen Psyche," *Vom Menschenbild im Märchen,* ed. Jürgen Janning, Heino Gehrts, and Herbert Ossowski, Veröffentlichungen der europäischen Märchengesellschaft (Kassel: Erich Röth Verlag, 1980); *Mélusine et le chevalier au cygne* (Paris: Payot, 1982); "Le Merwunder," *Etudes germaniques* 32 (1977): 1–11; 45, no. 1 (1990): 1–9; Laurence Harf-Lancner, *Les fées au Moyen Age; Morgane et Mélusine: la naissance des fées,* Nouvelle bibliothèque du Moyen Age 8 (Geneva: Slatkine, 1984), extends Lecouteux's argument. On the book and manuscript tradition, see Françoise Clier-Colombani, *La fée Mélusine au Moyen Age: images, mythes et symboles* (Paris: Léopard d'or, 1991). For historical studies, see Louis Stouff's comment to his 1932 edition: *Essai sur Mélusine: roman du XIVe siècle par Jean d'Arras* (Dijon: Picard, 1930); see also Eleanor Roach's introduction to the Coudrette edition. Regarding literary history, much attention has been focused, especially by German, English, and American scholars, on the Coudrette and the Ringoltingen texts; see especially the studies by Jan-Dirk Müller; in addition to his editorial comments, see Müller's "Melusine in Bern: Zum Problem der 'Verbürgerlichung' höfischer Epik," *Literatur, Publikum, historischer Kontext,* ed. Gert Kaiser, Beiträge zur älteren deutschen Literaturgeschichte 1 (Bern: Peter Lang, 1977), 29–77. Psychoanalytic approaches appear most recently in Ulrike Junk, "'So müssen Weiber sein': Zur Analyse eines Deutungsmusters von Weiblichkeit am Beispiele der *Melusine* des Thüring von Ringoltingen," *Der frauwen buoch: Versuche zu einer feministischen Mediävistik,* ed. Ingrid Bennewitz, Göppinger Arbeiten zur Germanistik 517 (Göppingen: Kümmerle, 1989) 327–57; Jean Markdale, *Mélusine, ou l'androgyne* (Paris: Editions Retz, 1983); for

feminist/gender approaches, see Ingrid Bennewitz, "Melusines Schwestern: Beobachtungen zu den Frauenfiguren im Prosaroman des 15. und 16. Jahrhunderts," *Germanistik und Deutschunterricht im Zeitalter der Technologie: Selbstbestimmung und Anpassung, Vorträge des Germanistentages Berlin 1987*, ed. Norbert Oellers (Tübingen: Max Niemeyer Verlag, 1988), 1:291–300; Ursula Liebertz-Grün, "Das Spiel der Signifikanten in der *Melusine* des Thüring von Ringoltingen," *Ordnung und Lust: Bilder von Liebe, Ehe und Sexualität im Spätmittelalter und Früher Neuzeit*, ed. Hans Jürgen Bachorski, Literatur, Imagination, Realität 1 (Trier: Wissenschaftlicher Verlag, 1991), 211–29. For historical-cultural studies, see Jacques Le Goff, "Melusine: Mother and Pioneer," *Time, Work, and Culture in the Middle Ages*, trans. Arthur Goldhammer (Chicago: University of Chicago Press, 1980), 205–22; Emmanuel Le Roy Ladurie, "Mélusine maternelle et défricheuse," *Annales: Economies, Sociétés, Civilisations* 26, nos. 3–4 (1971): 587–622; "Mélusine ruralisée," *Le territoire de l'historien*, ed. Emmanuel Le Roy Ladurie (Paris: Gallimard, 1973), 281–98; Gerhild Scholz Williams, "Frühmoderne Transgressionen: Sex und Magie in der *Melusine* und bei Paracelsus," *Daphnis* 20, no. 1 (1991): 81–100; idem, "The Death of Love: *Mélusine* (1392) and *Dr. Faustus* (1587)," *Love and Death in the Renaissance*, ed. Kenneth R. Bartlett, Konrad Eisenbichler, and Janice Liedl (Ottawa, Can.: Dovehouse Editions, 1991), 183–97; "*Mélusine/Melusine*: Erfahrungsdeterminierter Realismus im frühneuzeitlichen Roman," *Lili: Zeitschrift für Literaturwissenschaft und Linguistik* 23, no. 89 (1993): 10–23; Anna Mühlherr, *"Melusine" und "Fortunatus": Verrätselter und verweigerter Sinn*, Fortuna vitrea 10 (Tübingen: Max Niemeyer Verlag, 1993).

3. Jean d'Arras, *Mélusine: roman du XIVe siècle*, 4–5: "Je vous entend a traictier comment la noble et puissant [sic] forteresse de Lisignen en Poictou fu fondee par une faee, et la maniere comment, selon la juste cronique de la vraye histoire, sans y appliquier chose qui ne soit veritable et juste de la propre matiere. Et me orrez declairer la noble lignie qui en est yssue, qui regnera jusques en la fin du monde, selon ce qu'il appert qu'elle a regné jusques a ore" [I am about to tell you how the noble and powerful castle of Lusignan in Poitou was founded by a fairy, and how this is so, according to the correct chronicle of the true history, without adding anything that is not truthful and appropriate to the material. And you will hear me tell of the noble lineage that has sprung from it, which will reign until the end of time, according to what is known that it (the noble line) has reigned up to now"].

4. For more information, see Peter Stallybrass and Allan White, *The Politics and Poetics of Transgression* (Ithaca, NY: Cornell University Press, 1986); Mikhail M. Bahktin, *The Dialogic Imagination: Four Essays*, ed. Michael Holquist, trans. Caryl Emerson and Michael Holquist (Austin: University of Texas Press, 1981); Williams, "Frühmoderne Transgressionen," 82.

5. Michel Foucault, "Préface à la transgression," *Critique* 19, 195–96 (1963): 754.

6. For further analysis of humankind as the "late arrival" in the universe decimated by Lucifer's fall, a universe that had been completed before it and that it was to name and by God's decree to rule, see Blumenberg, *Die Genesis der kopernikanischen Welt,* vol. 1, 35, 231.

7. Elaine H. Pagels, *Adam, Eve, and the Serpent* (New York: Random House, 1988), 3–33.

8. See Markdale, *Mélusine,* 181, for more about sexuality and Lilith, Adam's first wife in the creation myth.

9. The pseudo-Paracelsian "Liber Azoth," a tract about all "hidden things," equates sexual desire with the urge to eat of the Tree of Knowledge (LA, 366). Lucifer appears to Eve in the form of Adam, and only then she desires her companion: "Und obwohl die Geschöpfe Gottes Adam und Eva an sich selbst gut geschaffen waren, so hat doch die schöne Gestalt Adams der Eva so gewaltig gefallen, daß sie sich mit den Augen vergafft hat. Denn der Satan ist ihr in Adams Gestalt erschienen. Merkt, so wie Adam jetzt ist, so ist ihr in dieser Gestalt Lucifer erschienen, so wie Adam nach dem Fall ausgesehen hat. Denn Adam hat vor dem Fall keine virgam naturae gehabt, weshalb sich auch Eva an dem Adam nicht vergafft hatte" [And even though God's creatures Adam and Eve were beautiful in themselves, the beautiful form of Adam pleased Eve such that she devoured Adam with her eyes. Because Satan appeared to her in Adam's guise. Note that as Adam is now, that is how Lucifer appeared to her, as Adam looked after the Fall. Since Adam did not have a penis before the Fall, Eve had not, up to this point, lost her senses in looking at Adam] (LA, 375–76).

10. Clemens Lugowski, *Die Form der Individualität im Roman,* Suhrkamp Taschenbuch Wissenschaft 151 (1932; reprinted, Frankfurt am Main: Suhrkamp Verlag, 1976), 66, calls this "Motivation von hinten," which means that the motivation for the action is determined by later results, in this case by the fact that Jean d'Arras's patron has commissioned a history about a noble house whose members are part of European nobility.

11. See Hans Blumenberg, *Arbeit am Mythos* (Frankfurt am Main: Suhrkamp Verlag, 1979), 18; Liebertz-Grün, "Das Spiel der Signifikanten," 213: "Alltägliches" [Everyday interpretation of speech, action, and other sign systems is not a form of knowledge, but a form of experience]; cf. Jürgen Fohrmann and Harro Müller, eds., *Diskurstheorien und Literaturwissenschaft* (Frankfurt am Main: Suhrkamp Verlag, 1988).

12. The whole story of the changing role of women during the sixteenth century can be interpreted in the context of such experiential change. See Steven Ozment, *When Fathers Ruled: Family Life in Reformation Europe* (Cambridge, MA: Harvard University Press, 1983); Merry E. Wiesner, *Working Women in Renaissance Germany* (New Brunswick, NJ: Rutgers University Press, 1986);

Lyndal Roper, *The Holy Household: Women and Morals in Reformation Augsburg* (Oxford: Clarendon Press; New York: Oxford University Press, 1989).

13. Stephen J. Greenblatt, *Shakespearean Negotiations: The Circulation of Social Energy in Renaissance England,* The New Historicism: Studies in Cultural Poetics 4 (Berkeley: University of California Press, 1988), revises and restates his influential notion of "cultural poetics"; one among a number of critical appraisals of Greenblatt's theses appeared in Brook Thomas, "Stephen Greenblatt and the Limits of Mimesis for Historical Criticism," *The New Historicism: And Other Old-Fashioned Topics* (Princeton, NJ: Princeton University Press, 1991), 179–218.

14. Peter Burke, *The Historical Anthropology of Early Modern Italy: Essays on Perception and Communication* (Cambridge: Cambridge University Press, 1987), 4, 122.

15. In his *Tischreden,* Luther uses Mélusine as an example of a satanic being, a succubus: "wie denn die Melusine zu Lucelburg auch ein solcher succubus oder Teufel gewesen ist" [as Mélusine has likewise been such a succubus or devil], quoted in Nora Parkin, "Melusine," (Ph.D. diss., Washington University, 1993); see also Ambroise Paré, *On Monsters and Marvels,* ed. and trans. Janis L. Pallister (1585; reprinted, Chicago: University of Chicago Press, 1982); Katharine Park and Lorraine J. Daston, "Unnatural Conceptions: The Study of Monsters in Sixteenth and Seventeenth Century France and England," *Past and Present* 92 (1981): 20–54; Gerhild Scholz Williams, "The Woman/The Witch: Variations on a Sixteenth-Century Theme (Paracelsus, Wier, Bodin)," *The Crannied Wall: Women, Religion, and the Arts in Early Modern Europe,* ed. Craig A. Monson (Ann Arbor: University of Michigan Press, 1992), 124–27.

16. Anna Mühlherr, "Geschichte und Liebe im Melusineroman," *Positionen des Romans im späten Mittelalter,* ed. Walter Haug and Burghart Wachinger, Fortuna vitrea 1 (Tübingen: Max Niemeyer Verlag, 1991), 328–37.

17. "Tres faulse serpente, par Dieu, ne toy ne tes fais ne sont que fantosme, ne ja hoir que tu ayes porté ne vendra a bon chief en la fin. . . . Or est destruit par l'art demoniacle" [You treacherous serpent, by God, you and your acts are nothing but phantoms, never have you done anything in good faith. . . . Now [all] is destroyed by the demonic art] (255).

18. The reasonable creature of God must understand, according to Aristotle's theories, that invisible things, according to the way he distinguished between things, and that by the presence of their being and nature, certify, also as St. Paul says in the *Epistle of the Romans,* that the things that God has made will be seen and known by humankind.

19. "Chiere dame, plaise vous assavoir que je scay et congois ce pays tout environ, et sachiez que a quatre ou cinq lieues de cy n'a recest, ne forteresse nulle, excepté celle dont je me suy huy partiz, qui est environ a deux lieues de cy" [Dear lady, may it please you to know that I know and am familiar with the land all

around, and please know that four to five leagues from here there is nothing, no fortress except the one from which I have come, which is about two leagues from here] (7).

20. He approached his father and said to him: "My lady, Queen Persine, your wife, has given you three of the most beautiful daughters that you have ever seen. Sir, come and look at them."

21. Liebertz-Grün points to this possibility, albeit with all due caution ("Das Spiel der Signifikanten," 219).

22. James A. Brundage, *Law, Sex, and Christian Society in Medieval Europe* (Chicago: University of Chicago Press, 1987), 162; see also Joyce E. Salisbury, *Medieval Sexuality: A Research Guide,* Garland Medieval Bibliographies 5 (New York: Garland Publishing, 1990); and *Sex in the Middle Ages: A Book of Essays,* Garland Medieval Casebooks 3 (New York: Garland Publishing, 1991).

23. Girls, see before you the realm where you were born and which you would own had it not been for your father's betrayal, who has put you and me into great and unending misfortune, until the Day of the Highest Judge, who will punish all misdeeds and reward all good deeds.

24. "La vertu du germe de ton pere toy et les autres eust attrait a sa nature humaine, et eussiés esté briefment hors des meurs, nimphes et faees, sans y retourner" [The virtue of your father's seed would have granted his human nature to you and the others; and you would have briefly left the state of nymphs and fairies without returning to it] (12). See also Volker Mertens, "Melusinen, Undinen: Variationen des Mythos vom 12. bis zum 20. Jahrhundert," *Festschrift Walter Haug und Burghart Wachinger,* ed. Johannes Janota et al. (Tübingen: Max Niemeyer Verlag, 1992), 1:209.

25. Palestine, although part of her mother's curse, disappears from Jean d'Arras's story.

26. Müller, "Melusine in Bern," 49, defines as the hero of the German version not a person but the house of Lusignan. The same cannot be said for this text. Even if one concedes a collective leading persona, this persona must be found in the Lusignan women, who together constitute the heroism of this history.

27. Count Aimery was a very valiant man, and one who loved all nobles and was the most learned astronomer of his time and since Aristotle. Because, as history recounts, at this time no one dared not to teach his children the Seven Arts.... And so the sciences were held in higher esteem than they are now.

28. When he will have granted it [the request] to you if you ask for as much space in this area as can be encircled by a deer skin.

29. ... and from this take good [legal] letters and charters, sealed with the grand seal of the aforementioned count and the seals of the peers of this realm.

30. ... they embraced each other, and the lady gave him much comfort. And they built in this desert country many a castle, town, and they made other dwellings; and in a short while the country was filled with people.... And then

it happened that between the lady and the knight arose a quarrel... she left him suddenly.

31. Horrible reminds us of a child born by a woman's union with the Devil, a changeling ("Wechselbalg"). In his translation of Bodin's *Démonomanie des sorciers,* Fischart summarizes the century-old description: "Offtgedachter Inquisitor Sprenger [i.e., the *Malleus Maleficarum*] schreibt / die Teutschen / als die vmb der Zeuberer gelegenheit besseren bescheid wissen / dieweil sie allzeit von Uralten zeiten her viel Zauberer vnd Hexen vnter jhnen gehabt / die halten darfür / daß auß solcher Vermischung zu zeiten Kinder entstehn / welche sie Wechsselkind /oder Wechselbälg heissen / vnd vil schwerer dann andere Kinder seind / wiewol stäts Mager bleiben / vnd wol drey Säugammen zu Todt saugten" [The frequently mentioned inquisitor Sprenger writes / the Germans / the ones who know much about magic / because they have had many sorcerers and witches since time immemorial / they think / that from this kind of relationship children are born / who are called changelings / and who weigh much more than ordinary children / but who remain skinny / even though they have been known to kill three wet nurses by their voracious appetites], Jean Bodin, *Vom aussgelasnen wütigen Teuffelsheer,* ed. Hans Biedermann, trans. Johann Fischart (1591; reprinted, Graz: Akademische Druck- und Verlagsanstalt, 1973), 132.

32. By my soul, Madam, if you think that this is a right and proper thing to do, then go right ahead.

33. My sons, see these two rings that I am giving you, whose stones possess the same power. Know that as long as you are loyal, and without trickery or betrayal, and as long as you carry them with you, you will never be defeated by any weapons... no fate, nor any magical enchantments, nor poisons will be able to harm you.

34. Liebertz-Grün, "Das Spiel der Signifikanten," 217. It is important to note that Liebertz-Grün deals with the German version, which indicates that Raymond uses his lord's spear without explaining why he does so. The French prose narrative offers enough detail to suggest that the count had fallen, as had the boar; at this point Remond reaches for the spear in an attempt to kill the boar; the spear glides off the boar's skin and accidentally pierces the count, killing him instantly.

35. By God, said the count, you will know it. And rest assured that I would wish that neither God nor men ask you about it, and the adventure must come to you from me, for I am now old, and I also have enough heirs for my land, and I love you so much that I wish that great honor would come to you.

36. "Et ceulx se teurent atant, qui ne l'oserent courroucier, car ilz doubtoient trop la grant fierté dont il estoit plain" [And they kept quiet, those who did not dare to anger him, for they feared the great pride that filled him.] (240); "Lors fu Gieffroy si courrouciez et fist si cruel semblant qu'il n'y ot si hardy qui entour

lui osast demourer" [And Gieffroy was so enraged and he looked so frightening that there was hardly anybody who dared stay around] (250).

37. Dear Brother, the gossip of the people everywhere says that your wife is dishonoring you and that each Saturday she fornicates with another.... and others say and insist that she is a fairy who does penance on Saturdays.

38. For a discussion of the theological association of the Fall and Mélusine's sinful nature, see Parkin, "Melusine."

39. When Remond heard her approach, he feigned sleep. And she took off her clothes and lay down beside him, naked... and... he thought that she did not know what he had done. But he thought so in vain, for she knew everything.

40. Poor fool, have you not sprung from the line of King Guion, who was the son of Mélusine, my sister, and I am your aunt, and you are too close a relative to me, even if I consented to be yours, the Church would not permit it.

41. The king enters and looks around the bedroom, and he sees many paintings of knights doing battle armed with their coats of arms, half of which are emblazoned with their weapons. And inscribed below were their names, and which lineage and which region they were from.

42. And I would like you to know who I am and who was my father, so that you do not reproach my children for being sons of a bad mother, or of a serpent, or of a fairy, for I am the daughter of King Elinas d'Albanie and of Queen Presine."

In this respect, the German version differs significantly. Following the French verse adaptation, Thüring von Ringoltingen moves the prehistory of Mélusine's story into the last third of the narrative. This means that the reader remains in the dark until Gieffroy stands at the tomb of his father and finds out the truth from the stone tablet that is held by the marble statue, the effigy of his mother.

43. In M. Charles Brunet's edition, the word is "recomptée."

Chapter 3

1. Bea Lundt, *Melusine und Merlin im Mittelalter: Entwürfe und Modelle weiblicher Existenz im Beziehungs-Diskurs der Geschlechter: Ein Beitrag zur historischen Erzählforschung* (Munich: Wilhelm Fink Verlag, 1991); Theresia Klugsberger, *Verfahren im Text: Meerjungfrauen in literarischen Versionen und mythischen Konstruktionen von H. C. Andersen, H. C. Artmann, K. Bayer, C. M. Wieland, O. Wilde,* Stuttgarter Arbeiten zur Germanistik 222 (Stuttgart: Heinz Verlag, 1989); Hanna Moog, ed., *Die Wasserfrau: Von geheimen Kräften, Sehnsüchten und Ungeheuern mit Namen Hans* (Cologne: Eugen Diederichs Verlag, 1987); Anna M. Stuby, *Liebe, Tod und Wasserfrau: Mythen des Weiblichen in der Literatur* (Opladen: Westdeutscher Verlag, 1992). See also Mertens' work

on Mélusine's persisting presence in narrative texts and the reasons for such literary popularity, "Melusinen, Undinen."

2. Theophrastus Paracelsus, "Liber de nymphis," *Theophrastus Paracelsus,* ed. Will-Erich Peuckert (1944; reprinted, Darmstadt: Wissenschaftliche Buchgesellschaft, 1990), 3:462–98. Unless otherwise indicated, all translations are my own. I chose the Peuckert edition because I found it reliable and readily available and accessible to the American scholar and student of early modern German texts. It should be noted, however, that Washington University's Medical School Library holds one of the most extensive collections of primary and secondary materials on Paracelsus, including a complete set of Johann Huser's first edition of the collected works of Paracelsus. See also Gunhild Pörksen, "Die Bewohner der Elemente nach Paracelsus' 'Liber de nymphis,'" *Nova Acta Paracelsica* 6 (1991/92): 29–51.

3. It is more blessed to describe the nature of nymphs than [military or monastic] orders; it is more blessed to describe the nature of giants than courtly manners; it is more blessed to speak about Mélusine than about artillery and canons; more blessed to describe the little people living underground than to fight with swords or to serve the ladies (LN, 464).

4. Kurt Goldammer, "Paracelsus und die Magie," *Paracelsus (1493–1541): "Keines andern Knecht,"* ed. Heinz Dopsch, Kurt Goldammer, and Peter F. Kramml (Salzburg: Verlag Anton Pustet, 1993), 225.

5. Whatever nature does by her power, that is natural magic, whatsoever the divine powers accomplish within us and through [God's actions], that is the heavenly magic [from the light of the Holy Spirit]. Blümlein, *Naturerfahrung und Welterkenntnis,* 45, quoting from the Sudhoff edition, vol. 12, 334.

6. Besides more recent works by Blümlein, Goldammer, and Joachim Telle, one must mention Allen G. Debus, ed., *Science, Medicine, and Society in the Renaissance: Essays to Honor Walter Pagel,* 2 vols. (New York: Science History Publications, 1972); idem, *The Chemical Philosophy: Paracelsian Science and Medicine in the Sixteenth and Seventeenth Centuries* (New York: Science History Publications, 1977); Walter Pagel, Paracelsus: An Introduction to Philosophical Medicine in the Era of the Renaissance (Basel: S. Karger, 1958); idem, *Das medizinische Weltbild des Paracelsus: Seine Zusammenhänge mit Neoplatonismus und Gnosis,* Kosmographie: Forschungen und Texte zur Geschichte des Weltbildes, der Naturphilosophie, der Mystik und des Spiritualismus vom Spätmittelalter bis zur Romantik 1 (Wiesbaden: Franz Steiner Verlag, 1962); Gundolf Keil and Peter Assion, eds., *Fachprosaforschung: Acht Vorträge zur mittelalterlichen Artesliteratur* (Berlin: Erich Schmidt Verlag, 1974); Erwin Metzke, *Coincidentia Oppositorum: Gesammelte Studien zur Philosophiegeschichte,* ed. Karlfred Gründer, Forschungen und Berichte der evangelischen Studiengemeinschaft 19 (Witten: Luther Verlag, 1961); Will-Erich Peuckert, *Gabalia: Ein Versuch zur Geschichte der Magia naturalis im 16. bis 18. Jahrhun-*

dert (Berlin: Erich Schmidt Verlag, 1967); idem, *Theophrastus Paracelsus;* Andrew Wear, R. K. French, and I. M. Lonie, eds., *The Medical Renaissance of the Sixteenth Century* (Cambridge: Cambridge University Press, 1985); Heinrich Schipperges, *Paracelsus: Der Mensch im Licht der Natur* (Stuttgart: Ernst Klett, 1974); Webster, *From Paracelsus to Newton.*

7. Rudolf Allers, "Microcosmus: From Anaximander to Paracelsus," *Traditio* 2 (1944), 319–407; Francis Oakley, *Omnipotence, Covenant and Order: An Excursion in the History of Ideas from Abelard to Leibniz* (Ithaca, NY: Cornell University Press, 1984).

8. He lets us ... search, wander the world over and experience many things. And when we have experienced everything, we should remember whatever we think worthwhile. ... All arts are perfect in the spirits, no matter if they are good or bad; from them they must come down to us.

9. Alois M. Haas, "Sterben und Todesverständnis bei Paracelsus," unpublished paper, 1993; I am grateful to Professor Haas (University of Zürich) for letting me read his manuscript; Kurt Goldammer, "Das religiöse Denken des Paracelsus," *Paracelsus (1493–1541): "Keines andern Knecht,"* ed. Heinz Dopsch, Kurt Goldammer, and Peter F. Kramml (Salzburg: Verlag Anton Pustet, 1993), 195.

10. Blumenberg, *Arbeit am Mythos,* 18.

11. [Magic] is such that it brings divine powers into the medium. ... The medium is the center; the center is humankind. In this way divine power can be placed into humankind by human beings.

12. Ernst Cassirer, "Giovanni Pico della Mirandola: A Study in the History of Renaissance Ideas," *Journal of the History of Ideas* 3, no. 2 (1942): 123–44, 319–46; Ernst Cassirer, Paul Oskar Kristeller, and John Herman Randall, Jr., eds., *The Renaissance Philosophy of Man* (Chicago: University of Chicago Press, 1948); Henri de Lubac, *Pic de la Mirandole: études et discussions* (Paris: Aubier Montaigne, 1974); William G. Craven, *Giovanni Pico della Mirandola, Symbol of His Age: Modern Interpretations of a Renaissance Philosopher,* Travaux d'humanisme et Renaissance 185 (Geneva: Librairie Droz, 1981); Jean Delumeau, *La civilisation de la Renaissance* (1967; reprinted, Paris: Arthaud, 1973); Paul O. Kristeller, *Eight Philosophers of the Italian Renaissance* (1964; reprinted, Stanford, CA: Stanford University Press, 1966); Peter Burke, *The Renaissance* (Atlantic Highlands, NJ: Humanities Press International, 1987); Goldammer, *Der göttliche Magier,* 37–43.

13. Pierre Charron, *De la sagesse livres trois* (Bordeaux: Simon Millanges, 1611), 1: lv, 281.

14. "[Der Arzt muß] nach der gesetzten Ordnung der Natur und nit der Menschen handeln. Denn der Arzt ist nit dem Menschen unterworfen, sondern durch die Natur allein Gott" [(The physician must) act according to the deter-

mined order of nature and not that of humankind. For the physician is not subservient to people but rather through nature alone to God] (PA, 574).

15. Kurt Goldammer, "Die Stellung des Paracelsus in den Wissenschaften," *Paracelsus (1493–1541): "Keines andern Knecht,"* ed. Heinz Dopsch, Kurt Goldammer, and Peter F. Kramml (Salzburg: Verlag Anton Pustet, 1993), 63–65.

16. Goldammer, "Die Stellung des Paracelsus," 3–65.

17. For more on this topic, see Carroll and Saxe, *Natural Magic;* Easlea, *Witch Hunting;* William Eamon, "Arcana Disclosed: The Advent of Printing, the Books of Secret Traditions and the Development of Experimental Science in the Sixteenth Century," *History of Science* 22, no. 2 (1984): 111–50; Daniel P. Walker, *Spiritual and Demonic Magic from Ficino to Campanella* (London: Warburg Institute, University of London, 1958); idem, *The Ancient Theology;* Brian Vickers, "Analogy Versus Identity: The Rejection of Occult Symbolism, 1580–1680," *Occult and Scientific Mentalities in the Renaissance,* ed. Brian Vickers (Cambridge: Cambridge University Press, 1984), 95.

18. Cardinal Nicholas of Cusa, *Die Kunst der Vermutung: Auswahl aus den Schriften von Nikolaus von Cues,* ed. Hans Blumenberg, Sammlung Dieterich 128 (Bremen: Carl Schünemann, 1957), 246.

19. In the tract "Bertheonea," Paracelsus ridicules the false physicians as much as their ignorant patients: "Bei den Bauern sind sie lateinisch, bei den Deutschen welsch... bei den Hebräischen sind sie griechisch, bei den Griechischen hebräisch, bei den Dorfpfaffen theologi, bei den Badern doctores der Arznei.... Etliche sind, die von sich selbst nicht lügen können, die ziehen gen Montpellier, lernens aus dem Avicenna, etliche von Paris aus dem Galen" [(The false physicians) pretend to be Latinist with the peasants, Italian with the Germans... with the Jews they are Greek, with the Greeks, Jews; in front of the village priests they pretend to be theologians, doctors of medicine with the barbers.... There are some who are unable to lie of their own accord, those go to Montpellier, and they learn it (lying) from Avicenna, some go to Paris and learn it from Galen] (BA, 7–10).

20. But as long as your medicine is Jewish, you can speak with the Jews and say that I am a seducer of the people, that I am of the Devil, that I am possessed, that I am learned in the art of nigromancy, that I am a magus; all these things the Jews said of Christ. My nature is such that you would not be able to loosen the laces of my shoe [i.e., you are lower than the lowest creature].

21. Jakob Sprenger and Heinrich Institoris, *Der Hexenhammer (Malleus Maleficarum),* ed. and trans. J. W. R. Schmidt, 9th ed. (Munich: Deutscher Taschenbuch Verlag, 1982); for the English translation, see *The Malleus Maleficarum of Heinrich Kramer and James Sprenger,* ed. and trans. Montague Summers (1928; reprinted, New York: Dover Publications, 1971); Segl, Der Hexenhammer.

22. "... daß niemand frei ist, allein der, der keinen Herrn hat.... Wo der Hl. Geist nicht ist, da ist der freie Wille, denn wo der Hl. Geist ist, da müssen alle Dinge nach dem Hl. Geist gehen, und ist auch in dem ein freier Wille; die den Hl. Geist haben, haben die göttliche Weisheit" [... that nobody is free but the one who has no master.... Where the Holy Spirit does not dwell is free will, because wherever the Holy Spirit does dwell, all things have to go according to his will; those of the Holy Spirit possess divine wisdom] (PS, 381, 383). Paracelsus seems to allude here to an idea that Nicholas of Cusa had expressed decades earlier and that Paracelsus may have taken from Agrippa: "Gott will, so der Kusaner, daß der Mensch das ursprüngliche Eigentumsrecht des Schöpfers an seinem Geschöpf selbst übernimmt und an sich ausübt. Der theologische Begriff der Freisprechung des Menschen entbindet von der Schuld, der philosophische von der Abhängigkeit des Eigentums, das Gott am Menschen als Urheber seines Daseins besitzt" [God desires, says the man from Cusa, that humankind take over from the Creator and exercise the original right of possession and self-determination. The theological concept of human liberation releases humankind from guilt, the philosophical from the right of possession, which God as the Creator claims to have on humankind.) Hans Blumenberg, *Aspekte der Epochenschwelle: Cusaner und Nolaner,* 2d ed., Suhrkamp Taschenbuch Wissenschaft 174 (Frankfurt am Main: Suhrkamp Verlag, 1982), 516; Nicholas of Cusa, *Die Kunst der Vermutung,* 45: "The concept of human freedom thus serves to release God from the responsibility for evil in the world."

23. Georg Luck, trans. and ed., *Arcana mundi: Magic and the Occult in the Greek and Roman Worlds: A Collection of Ancient Texts* (Baltimore: Johns Hopkins University Press, 1985); Harmening, *Superstitio.*

24. Theophrastus Paracelsus, "Philosophia sagax," *Theophrastus Paracelsus,* ed. Will-Erich Peuckert (1944; reprinted, Darmstadt: Wissenschaftliche Buchgesellschaft, 1990), 3:37–406.

25. I am writing as a Christian and not as a heathen, a German, and not an Italian, and interpreter, and not as a sophist.... [I am] not a magician, nor a heathen, nor a Gypsy ... because I have the gift and mercy of the same spirit, which emanates from the Father.

26. Peuckert uses "limus" throughout; it also appears as "limbus": "kommt vom lateinischen 'limus' oder 'lutum' = Schlamm." Everything generates from this "limus," beginning with the four elements: fire, earth, water, air; Blümlein, *Naturerfahrung,* 87, 88.

27. Mankind is the small world, that is, man has all the characteristics of the world in him, therefore he is the microcosmos. He is the fifth being of the elements and of the stars or firmament in the upper sphere and in the lower globe. Thus the large world is the father of the small one.

28. "Wer kann einer Frauen, sie sei gleich, wie sie wolle, feind sein? Denn mit ihren Früchten wird die Welt besetzt, darum läßt sie Gott, ob sie gleich gar

eine Galle wäre, lang leben" [Who can be hostile to a woman, no matter who she might be? With the fruits of her body the world is populated, therefore God grants her long life, no matter if she is nothing but bile] (MI, 262).

29. There is much to note about Melusina, because she is not of the kind, as the theologians have seen her, rather she was a nymph; but this is true: possessed by the Devil, from whom she would have been released, had she stayed to the end with her lord.

30. Girolamo Cardano and Giordano Bruno were also convinced that the native Americans were the result of an alternate creation; see Pagden, *European Encounters*, 11.

31. "Und so kann ich das nit unterlassen, von denen eine kleine Meldung zu tun, die in verborgenen Inseln gefunden worden sind und noch verborgen sind; daß man glauben möge, daß sie von Adam seien, wird nicht festzustellen sein, und daß Adams Kinder in die verborgenen Inseln gekommen seien, sondern es ist wohl zu denken, daß die selbigen Leute von einem anderen Adam seien, denn zu dem Schlusse wird es schwerlich kommen, daß sie Fleisches und Bluts halben mit uns verwandt seien... es sind vielerlei Tiere auf Erden hin und her, vielleicht auch vielerlei Menschen" [And thus I have to report a small piece of news about those who have been found on the hidden islands; it is difficult to determine if they are of Adam, even if we would like to believe this. Rather, it is probably the case that these selfsame people are of a different Adam, because it is difficult to accept that they are related to us through the same flesh and blood... there are many animals throughout this earth, maybe also many different people] (PS, 68).

32. Sergio Landucci, *I filosofi e i selvaggi, 1580–1780,* Biblioteca di cultura moderna 721 (Bari: Editori Laterza, 1972), 23, 78.

33. On the "truth" about the alleged cannibalism of the New World natives, see Philip P. Boucher, *Cannibal Encounters: Europeans and Island Caribs, 1492–1763* (Baltimore: Johns Hopkins University Press, 1992).

34. "Ihr sollt euch... nit verwundern, denn Verwundern kommt aus einem Unwissen und Unverstand" [you must not wonder because wonder comes from ignorance] (VP, 180). For a comparison with the idea of wonder as the dominant reaction to the "new" people in the Americas, see Stephen J. Greenblatt, *Marvelous Possessions: The Wonder of the New World* (Chicago: University of Chicago Press, 1991); and Tzvetan Todorov, *The Conquest of America: The Question of the Other,* trans. Richard Howard (New York: Harper and Row, 1984).

35. It is a topos of early modern reports from the New World that the natives not only live longer but also keep their youthful appearance through old age.

36. Manuel Simon, *Heilige, Hexe, Mutter: Der Wandel des Frauenbildes durch die Medizin im 16. Jahrhundert,* Historische Anthropologie 20 (Berlin: Dietrich Reimer Verlag, 1993), 15–66. Simon's study does not take into account the recent work on gender and medicine.

37. "Nicht alle sind praedestiniert zu der Ehe, zur Erziehung der Kinder, sondern etliche zum Reich Gottes, die können den Frauen nicht nutz sein; etliche, damit die Menschenzahl nit zu groß werde, bleiben von Natur unfruchtbar" [Not all are predestined for marriage, for the raising of children, rather, some are (predestined) for God's realm; they are infertile, so that the population not become too numerous] (PS, 259).

38. Cf. Roper, *The Holy Household.*

39. "So ist der Frau ebenso die gute Art zu behalten, mit einem Manne, der guter Art ist. Wenn so gut und gut zusammenkommt, wird nichts Böses draus.... Die Ehe aber, die Gott zusammenfüget, das ist die Ehe, aus der die Kinder, die Erwählten Gottes geboren werden." [In this way, a woman will remain a good woman if she is married to a good man. When good and good thus come together, nothing evil can result from it. Marriage, arranged by God, is the kind of marriage from which children are born, who will be God's chosen] (OP, 178, 179).

40. Cf. Simon, *Heilige,* 66–74.

41. "Der Mann ist der Same ... die Frau der Acker ist. ... Der Acker ist die Erde, in die gesät wird, so ist die matrix die Erde und ist des Samens besonderes Gefäß.... Der Frauen Blühen, ist wenn sie empfängt; ... und darnach wie nach allem Blühen folgt Frucht, das ist das Kind" [Man is the seed, woman the field.... The field is the earth, into which the seed is sown, the matrix is the earth and is the seed's special vessel.... The woman's time to bloom is the time when she conceives; after the bloom follows the fruit, which is the child] (OP, 140, 154).

42. Cf. Simon, *Heilige,* 107.

43. On the "Weiblichkeit Gottes," see Ute Gause, "Zum Frauenbild im Frühwerk des Paracelsus," *Parerga Paracelsica: Paracelsus in Vergangenheit und Gegenwart,* ed. Joachim Telle, Heidelberger Studien zur Naturkunde der frühen Neuzeit 3 (Stuttgart: Franz Steiner Verlag, 1992), 45–56. In the discussions about the "celestial flesh" of Christ, Paracelsus seems to side here with the thinking of many radical reformers.

44. Paracelsus has nothing to say directly on the issue of a woman's sexual organs being the inverse of a male's (the "one-sex model"); rather, he viewed male-female similarity as a spiritual closeness. On the "one-sex model," see Thomas W. Laqueur, *Making Sex: Body and Gender from the Greeks to Freud* (Cambridge, MA: Harvard University Press, 1990); Jonathan P. Clark, "Inside/out: Body Politics against Large Bodies," *Daphnis* 20, no. 1 (1991): 101–30.

45. Gerhard Harrer, "Paracelsus und die psychischen Erkrankungen," *Paracelsus (1493–1541): "Keines andern Knecht,"* ed. Heinz Dopsch, Kurt Goldammer, and Peter F. Kramml (Salzburg: Verlag Anton Pustet, 1993), 101–109.

46. Bodin, *Vom aussgelasnen wütigen Teuffelsheer*, 266, 267: "So doch die Alten dises für ein Wunder wargenommen vnnd inn Verzeichnussen hinderlassen / daß nie kein Weib von Melancholey oder vnmuth / vnnd nie kein Mann / Freuden gestorben sey... daß die Feuchtigkeiten vnd HUMORES der Weiber / gar der verbranten Melancholey widerstreben... nun seind aber... die Weiber kalter vnnd trockner Natur" [Our forefathers considered it a miracle and left witness to this effect / that no woman ever died of melancholy or sadness / and no man of joy... that the humidity and the humors of women / oppose the burned melancholy... now we know... that females are of a cold and dry nature].

47. Cf. Simon, *Heilige*, 110.

48. *Imaginatio* means "an activity of reason under the influence of objects that affect our senses; imagination is capable of setting one's fantasies outward, and reaching much further than the activity of our senses"; Gregory Zilboorg, *The Medical Man and the Witch during the Renaissance* (Baltimore: Johns Hopkins University Press, 1935); see also Walter Pagel, "Paracelsus als 'Naturmystiker,'" *Epochen der Naturmystik: Hermetische Tradition im wissenschaftlichen Fortschritt*, ed. Antoine Faivre, et al. (Berlin: Erich Schmidt Verlag, 1979), 60–62.

49. Such freak births were signs of great notoriety and wonder, and they were considered powerful portents and presages. Much pamphlet literature explaining these births circulated during the late fifteenth and early sixteenth centuries. One such account, describing the birth and death of twins born in Worms, prompted Sebastian Brant to write a Latin and a German commentary. See Dieter Wuttke, "Sebastian Brants Verhältnis zu Wunderdeutungen und Astrologie," *Studien zur deutschen Literatur und Sprache des Mittelalters: Festschrift für Hugo Moser zum 65. Geburtstag*, ed. Werner Besch et al. (Berlin: Erich Schmidt Verlag, 1974), 272–86; Hans-Joachim Köhler, ed., *Flugschriften als Massenmedien der Reformationszeit: Beiträge zum Tübinger Symposion 1980*, Spätmittelalter und frühe Neuzeit 13 (Stuttgart: Klett-Cotta, 1981).

50. Now note that each young girl is "owned" and given away already in her mother's womb, just as each boy is "owned" already and married to his wife in the womb; that is divine predestination.

51. For more about these concepts of *illiaster*, "the first cause, *chaos* itself, within which all is contained in potentia" and *archeus*, "the force active in all nature," see Blümlein, *Naturerfahrung*, 86, 134, and the literature he cites.

52. Cf. Simon, *Heilige*, 81.

53. Paré, *On Monsters and Marvels*, 1585, ed. and trans. Janis L. Pallister (Chicago: University of Chicago Press, 1982), 5. Ottavia Niccoli, "'Menstruum quasi Monstruum': Monstrous Births and Menstrual Taboo in the Sixteenth Century," *Sex and Gender in Historical Perspective*, ed. Edward Muir and Guido Ruggiero, trans. Mary M. Gallucci (Baltimore: Johns Hopkins University

Press, 1990), 1–25, argues that Paré reintroduced the idea of the monstrous birth resulting from menstrual conception. Paracelsus treated this topic with considerably greater sophistication several decades earlier.

54. In this text, as in the "Philosophia sagax," he calls them *Ascendenten;* they inhabit the planetary sphere and form the connection between the planet and humankind. They constitute part of the *praesagia,* which predict the future: "Und dess' soll sich niemand verwundern oder in einen Spott werfen, denn das Gestirn wirkts und tuts, kein Teufel, kein Gespenst, kein infernalischer Geist, sondern die Natur zeigt's an und eröffnets" [And nobody should be amazed at this or make fun of it, because the stars are responsible for it, not a devil, nor a spirit, nor an infernal being, but rather nature makes it visible and opens it (to the mind)] (PS, 241). While Paracelsus wrote this tract in the early thirties, it was not printed until 1567. It thus appeared at a time when the witchcraft disputes began to heat up (Goldammer, *Der göttliche Magier,* 102; Simon, *Heilige,* 23–27).

55. Now note that all things needed in our old age must be taught to us from our youth, and that education makes a rock for us. For what is taught to us in our youth is the rock, upon which nature builds.

56. Therefore it is useless to present things forever in the same way, for what can a person achieve on earth that is of eternal value? . . . Things disappear with time, and nobody is above time, rather below it.

Chapter 4

1. The same sources are cited repeatedly in the texts under discussion and in the many others that precede or follow: Aristotle, Plato, the Old and the New Testaments, Augustine, Thomas Aquinas, the Canon Episcopi, the neo-Platonists, and Hermes Trismegistus. By the time Kramer penned his tract, he based his arguments on a stable and widely shared body of information about Christian and non-Christian cosmology and demonology. The detailed and often-repeated reproduction of this information in treatises on magic and witchcraft assigned to such representation all the characteristics of a topos; the theological premise had become a rhetorical prescription. Besides the books on magic already mentioned, see Iona A. Opie and Moire Tatem, eds., *A Dictionary of Superstitions* (Oxford: Oxford University Press, 1989).

2. See Henry Charles Lea, *Materials toward a History of Witchcraft,* ed. Arthur C. Howland, 3 vols. (Philadelphia: University of Pennsylvania Press, 1939); idem, *Geschichte der Inquisition im Mittelalter,* ed. and trans. Heinz Wieck, Max Rachel, and Joseph Hansen, 3 vols. (Nördlingen: Greno, 1987); Cohn, *Europe's Inner Demons;* Joseph Hansen, *Zauberwahn, Inquisition und Hexenprozeß im Mittelalter und die Entstehung der großen Hexenverfolgung,*

Historische Bibliothek 12 (Munich: R. Oldenbourg, 1900); idem, *Quellen und Untersuchungen zur Geschichte des Hexenwahns und der Hexenverfolgungen im Mittelalter* (1901; reprinted, Hildesheim: Georg Olms Verlag, 1963); Soldan, *Geschichte der Hexenprozesse;* Gustav Henningsen and John Tedeschi, eds., *The Inquisition in Early Modern Europe: Studies on Sources and Methods* (De Kalb: Northern Illinois University Press, 1986); Stephen Haliczer, *Inquisition and Society in the Kingdom of Valencia, 1478-1834* (Berkeley: University of California Press, 1990); E. William Monter, *Frontiers of Heresy: The Spanish Inquisition from the Basque Lands to Sicily* (Cambridge: Cambridge University Press, 1990); Gerhard Schormann, *Hexenprozesse in Deutschland,* 2d ed. (Göttingen: Vandenhoeck und Ruprecht, 1986); Peters, *The Magician, the Witch, and the Law.*

3. See Wolfgang Behringer, *Mit dem Feuer vom Leben zum Tod: Hexengesetzgebung in Bayern* (Munich: Heinrich Hugendubel Verlag, 1988); Klaits, *Servants of Satan;* Midelfort, *Witch Hunting in Southwestern Germany;* Bengt Ankarloo and Gustav Henningsen, eds., *Early Modern European Witchcraft: Centres and Peripheries* (Oxford: Clarendon Press, 1990).

4. Cf. Pagden, *European Encounters,* 21.

5. Landucci, *I filosofi,* 39, 217, 218; see also Frank Lestringant, "Rage, fureur, folie, cannibales: le Scythe et le Brésilien," *La folie et le corps: études,* ed. Jean Céard (Paris: Presses de l'Ecole normale supérieure, 1985), 56-57.

6. Iohannes Wierus, "Liber apologeticus et Pseudomachia daemonum," *Opera omnia: Edito nova et hactenus desiderata* (Amsterdam: Apud Petrum vanden Berge, 1660), 627: "Ad haec quartum illum de occulta philosophia librum Cornelii Agrippae, furtim arreptum esse ex novissimo Razielis afferis in scholiis Libr. IV de vita longa Theophrasti Paracelsi...suppresso tamen Agrippa nomine" [From the fourth book of Cornelius Agrippa's *De occulta philosophia,* it was taken secretly to appear in the *de vita longa* by Theophrastus Paracelsus without giving Agrippa's name].

7. Johann Weyer, *De praestigiis daemonum,* trans. John Shea, *Witches, Devils, and Doctors in the Renaissance,* ed. George Mora et al., Medieval and Renaissance Texts and Studies 73 (Binghamton, NY: Medieval and Renaissance Texts and Studies, 1991), 257: "People use this example [the Lohengrin legend] to support the claim that sexual relations take place between spirits and women.... Flatterers are wont to embellish the beginnings of powerful kingdoms and distinguished families in this way to convince us more easily that there is something divine about them." I have chosen this edition because it is the translation of Weyer's last personally supervised edition of 1583. The advantage of using this text is not simply its accessibility but also the fact that here Weyer responds to criticism of his work and incorporates new materials that had become available since the first publication in 1563.

8. Fischart's interest in the demonic aspects of the Mélusine myth is further highlighted by his work on the tale of Peter of Stauffenberg; see André Schnyder,

"Johann Fischart als Bearbeiter eines mittelalterlichen Märes: Veränderungen ästhetischer Darstellungsverfahren und kultureller Deutungsmuster im 'Peter von Stauffenberg,'" *Wirkendes Wort* 39, no. 1 (1989): 15–43.

9. Bodin, *Vom aussgelasnen wütigen Teuffelsheer,* 40: "Inn beyder Medicin / das ist / inn Alter vnd Newer / inn Galenischer vnd Paracelsischer ... in Medicamentischer vnd Chyrurgischer Artzenei Doctores promouiret" [In both disciplines of medicine / that is, in the old and the new / in Galenic and Paracelsian ... in medicinal and surgical medicine as doctors graduated]. See also van Nahl, *Zauberglaube und Hexenwahn,* 72–75; Allen G. Debus, *The French Paracelsians: The Chemical Challenge to Medical and Scientific Tradition in Early Modern France* (Cambridge: Cambridge University Press, 1991); idem, *The English Paracelsians* (1965; reprinted, New York: Franklin Watts, 1966).

10. These works were the most influential in the debate, which was to last several centuries. The great number of imitators and commentators only underscores the impact and the currency of their treatises. The translator of Bodin's *Démonomanie des sorciers [Vom aussgelasnen wütigen Teuffelsheer],* Johann Fischart (ca. 1546–90), is known in German literature mainly for his translations of Rabelais's *Gargantua and Pantagruel (Geschichtsklitterung,* 1575), the *Flöhhaz* (1573), and for the collection of funny tales *Glückhafft Schiff von Zürich* (1578). He translated Bodin's tract into German in 1581 and supervised a second edition in 1586 ("wie bei gewissen Völckern man je von fünf zu fünff Jaren pflegt die Tempel auff ein newes zu reinigen ... nicht zwar das ich den Tempel wolt Mutiern vnd endern / das ist / jemans anders / dann demjenigen /so es ein mahl dediciert zubeeigenen / Sondern inn ebenmäßigem erfrischen vnd restauriern" [iii–iv]), which he dedicates to "Herrn Eberhart / Herren zu Rapoltstein Hohenack vnd Geroltzeck am Wasichin" [As is the custom with certain peoples to clean the temple every five years ... not that I wanted to change the temple / that is /dedicate it to anybody else but to the one to whom it was dedicated in the beginning, but rather that I wanted to freshen and restore it]. This translation/edition recommends itself for several reasons. It is accessible in a reprint edition. Furthermore, Fischart did not view his work as a mere translation, rather he offered it as a commentary on a work that he admired and whose message he believed to be timely and needed: "als die gemeynem Nutzen vnnd Vatterland zu vorstand fürgenommen / damit ... Vngewißheit / Zweiffel vnd Zwispalt von straffung der Zauberer vnnd Vnholden dermahln eins eine gründtliche Nachrichtigung / Gewißheit / vnd klare helle Vorleuchtung hiemit hette" [to the general good and to the fatherland's benefit intended / so that ... all uncertainty / doubt and conflict about the punishment of magicians and witches be clarified by detailed reports /certainty / and clear, distinct explanations] (iii). Finally, his editorial work includes marginalia to aid his reader's orientation and to facilitate reference searches, as well as comments that he enclosed in brackets for easy identification ("zusatz, erzehlung anderer Meynung").

11. In his dispute with Weyer, Fischart also mentions Weyer's *De lamiis liber* (1577; reprinted, Basil: Ex Officina Oporiniana, 1582). In this work, Weyer does not go much beyond the *De praestigiis*. I will, therefore, also limit my attention to this work.

12. Behringer, "Erträge und Perspektiven," 628.

13. Cf. Schnyder, "Fragen und Beobachtungen," 328–30; this article on the *Malleus Maleficarum* discusses aspects of the tract's printing history and its reception, concentrating on Bodin, Peter Binsfeld, and Martin Delrio. After the often cited latent period, in the witch persecutions, the time between 1486 and 1560, the *Malleus*, besides being the object of Weyer's scholarly attention, also appeared in 1580 in what Schnyder justly calls a "Neuerung" in the printing history of witch tracts—as part of a collection of demonological tracts never again to be published as a single volume.

14. Wolfgang Behringer, *Hexenverfolgung in Bayern: Volksmagie, Glaubenseifer und Staatsräson in der Frühen Neuzeit* (Munich: R. Oldenbourg Verlag, 1987), 132; Adolf Hauffen, "Fischart-Studien III: Der *Malleus Maleficarum* und Bodins *Démonomanie*," *Euphorion* 4 (1897), 6, many years ago emphasized the legal power unofficially accorded this tract.

15. Bodin, *Vom aussgelasnen wütigen Teuffelsheer*, 21, 26: "Ioannes Goropius Becanus, Historicus der Statt Antorff / in seinem Buch von der älte vnd herrlichkeit der Teutschen Sprach / welches er *Hermathena* nennet / daß er einen alten geschribenen Psalter inn Italien gesehen / darinnen bißweilen ein gantzer Psalm / bißweilen etliche Gesetz mit Roter Dinten vnterstrichen / vnd darbei geschriben geweßt / zu welchem prästen / glück oder vnglück eine jedes so Rubro signirt / dienen vnnd helffen könne.... Die Teutschen nennens Weissagen vnd Warsagen / dieweil man sagen soll was War ist / vnnd was man eigentlich vor für gewiß weiß: Darumb hieß es bei den alten / Gewißsagen / oder Sächßisch / Witsagen" [Ioannes Goropius Becanus, historian of the town of Antdorff / (writes) in his book about the age and beauty of the German language / which he calls *Hermathena* / that he once saw a book of psalms written in Italian / wherein at times a whole psalm / at times a number of paragraphs / were underlined with red ink / and there was written / for which kind of prediction / fortune or misfortune each rubric was designated / the Germans call it predicting or prophecying, since one says what is true and to come / and what one could know for certain: therefore our ancestors called it / soothsaying / or in the Saxon language / *Witsagen*]. Similar examples can be found throughout the text.

16. Hauffen calls Bodin's book crazy, senseless, of great "long-windedness and showing off with empty, tasteless learning," 5. Recent research is not as critical but is equally perplexed by the incongruity between Bodin's other work and this essay. Fischart's translation has, for the same reason, I feel, received little to no attention. Hauffen calls it "eine unerquickliche Sache" [a distasteful matter]; Stefan Janson, *Jean Bodin-Johann Fischart: De la démonomanie des sorciers*

(1580), Vom aussgelassnen wütigen Teuffelsheer (1581) *und ihre Fallberichte,* Europäische Hochschulschriften 1, no. 352 (Frankfurt am Main: Peter Lang, 1980), ii–iii, remains completely baffled by this cooperative venture. But his study is filled with many errors and adds little to our understanding of either text.

17. For more on this topic, see Roland Crahay and Marie Isaac, "La 'bibliothèque' de Bodin démonologue: les bases théoriques," *Bulletin de la classe des lettres et des sciences morales et politiques* 73 (1987): 129–71; Paul Lawrence Rose, *Bodin and the Great God of Nature: The Moral and Religious Universe of a Judaiser,* Travaux d'humanisme et Renaissance 179 (Geneva: Droz, 1980).

18. "Not knowing of Plutarch and never having had any conversations with witches from France, old women are in complete agreement with each other; they speak Greek and Latin without having studied languages and know how to kill a person with the help of an image made of wax with no knowledge of Plato" (noted in Bodin/Fischart, 10, 12, 97, 189).

19. Weyer, *De praestigiis daemonum,* 479: "I should not be faulted because of my medical profession, I should not be accused of going beyond the limits of my calling, when here I add my own opinion as an appendix... quite different from long-standing popular opinion.... If someone wishes to elicit the truth from this labyrinth... he should not be prevented by criticism." Bodin, *Vom aussgelasnen wütigen Teuffelsheer,* 15: "Vnd ist hierinnen der Juristen Weisen Rhat zufolgen / welche sich nit schewen / inn sachen so die Medicisch [sic] Facultet vnnd Kunst betreffen / sich auff die Medicos zuziehen.... Ja wann die gemein Einhelligkeit der Weisen vnnd Gelehrten nicht genugsam ist / vorgedachts zubeweren / was will man dann für kräfftigere beweisung fortan weiter suchen vnnd finden?" [And in all this we should follow the wise council of the jurists / who are not afraid / in things that concern the medical faculty and art / to quote the physicians.... If the community of the wise and learned is not enough / to judge the aforementioned / what better proof can one attempt to seek and find?].

20. Clark, "The Scientific Status of Demonology," 357, 359, points to the great variety of "real-life" reports that characterize these tracts. He suggests that this might be part of the wish to illustrate the wide spectrum of magical phenomena and to avoid the obscure and the spurious. Janson, *Jean Bodin-Johann Fischart,* 124, lists some of the sources and briefly discusses their narrative function.

21. Repeated references to the town and country around Ravensburg and to Innsbruck identify the radius of the inquisitors' action. They also give the area of southwest Germany a notoriety still current when Bodin quotes his predecessor Jakob Sprenger. On the use of sources in the *Malleus,* see Peter Segl, "Henricus Institorius: Persönlichkeit und literarisches Werk," and André Schnyder, "Der *Malleus Maleficarum:* Unvorgreifliche Überlegungen und Beobachtungen zum Problem der Textform," both in *Der* Hexenhammer: *Entstehung und Umfeld des* Malleus Maleficarum *von 1487,* ed. Peter Segl, Bayreuther historische Kolloquien 2 (Cologne: Böhlau Verlag, 1988), 103–26, 127–49. For more about

the witchcraft trials in Innsbruck, see Heide Dienst, "Lebensbewältigung durch Magie: Alltägliche Zauberei in Innsbruck gegen Ende des 15. Jahrhunderts," *Alltag im 16. Jahrhundert: Studien zu Lebensformen in mitteleuropäischen Städten,* ed. Alfred Kohler and Heinrich Lutz, Wiener Beiträge zur Geschichte der Neuzeit 14 (Vienna: Verlag für Geschichte und Politik; Munich: R. Oldenbourg Verlag, 1987), 80–116; "Die Verarbeitung von Materialien des Innsbrucker Hexenprozesses von 1485 durch Institoris im *Hexenhammer,*" unpublished manuscript.

22. Ernst Pitz, "Diplomatische Studien zu den päpstlichen Erlassen über das Zauber- und Hexenwesen," *Der* Hexenhammer*: Entstehung und Umfeld des Malleus Maleficarum von 1487,* ed. Peter Segl, Bayreuther historische Kolloquien 2 (Cologne: Böhlau Verlag, 1988), 23–70. On the basis of his document search, Pitz concludes that the pope could not appoint anyone to the office of inquisitor who did not seek or welcome such an office. Pitz asserts that "the Roman Curia was, as a rule, not the source of evil, rather it tolerated it," (68), which would make him what is known in German as a "Schreibtischtäter" [perpetrator bureaucrat]. The papal bull does not presuppose any great papal interest but rather great energy on the part of Kramer and Sprenger in securing for themselves the permission to be active as inquisitors, specifically in southern Germany (54). Early editions list Sprenger as the second author of the *Malleus,* but Peter Segl has identified Kramer (Henricus Institores) as the sole author; see Segl, "Henricus Institorius," 103–26.

The untimely death of Professor Sigrid Brauner in December 1992 cut short the career of a promising scholar of early modern German culture. Her 1989 dissertation, *Fearless Wives and Frightened Shrews: The Concept of the Witch in Early Modern Germany,* ed. Robert H. Brown (Amherst: University of Massachusetts Press, 1995) and several articles on the *Malleus Maleficarum* have returned this work to the center of discussion, from which it had been missing for far too long—much cited, but seldom read.

23. [It is] short because of the paraphrasing of many authors.... Therefore, you should not consider this our labor, but rather the labor of the many from whose works this has been gleaned.... Thus we leave it to our colleagues to look through this work; the completion we leave to those who exercise the strictest justice, because they are installed by God to exercise revenge against the evil ones."

For more on this procedure, see Christel Beyer, *Hexen-Leut, so zu Würzburg gerichtet: Der Umgang mit Sprache und Wirklichkeit in Inquisitionsprozessen wegen Hexerei,* Europäische Hochschulschriften 1, no. 948 (Frankfurt am Main: Peter Lang, 1986), 16.

24. See pt. 3, 140, 141, 149, for gender changes within a sentence.

25. The main task of this work is to help us inquisitors to rid the lands of upper Germany of witches, as far as it can happen by the grace of God, in that we deliver them to their judges for punishment.

178   *Notes to Pages 72-74*

26. "Um dies zu verstehen, und damit die Prediger wenigstens einen Kern für ihre Predigt haben, ist zuerst von den Engeln zu reden.... Der Prediger sei endlich vorsichtig bei gewissen Argumenten der Laien oder auch einiger Gelehrten, die insoweit die Existenz der Hexen leugnen" [In order to understand this, and to give the preachers a basic concept for their sermons, they should start by talking about angels.... The preacher must be careful with certain arguments articulated by lay people and certain scholars, insofar as they deny the existence of witches] (pt. 1, 198, 206; see also pt. 2., 148; pt. 3, 142.) Cf. Beyer, *Hexen-Leut*, 39.

27. Everything happens from lust, which in women is insatiable.... Three things are insatiable and the fourth, which never speaks: that is the womb. Therefore they have dalliance with the demons, so that they might still their lust.

28. Sigrid Brauner makes this point in "Cannibals, Witches, and Evil Wives in the 'Civilizing Process,'" *"Neue Welt"/"Dritte Welt": Interkulturelle Beziehungen Deutschlands zu Lateinamerika und der Karibik,* ed. S. Bauschlinger and S. L. Cocalis (Tübingen: Francke Verlag, 1994), 1–28.

29. For more on the topic of early physiology, see Clark, "Inside/out," 101–30; Thomas W. Laqueur, *Making Sex: Body and Gender from the Greeks to Freud* (Cambridge, MA: Harvard University Press, 1990).

30. ... that is certain according to what very many people have seen and heard; also because of the public discussion that brought to light the truth after the seeing and touching of such member.

31. For more on the relation of witchcraft to marriage, see Heide Wunder, "Hexenprozesse im Herzogtum Preussen während des 16. Jahrhunderts," *Hexenprozesse: Deutsche und skandinavische Beiträge,* ed. Christian Degn, Hartmut Lehmann, and Dagmar Unverhau, Studien zur Volkskunde und Kulturgeschichte Schleswig-Holsteins 12 (Neumünster: Karl Wachholtz Verlag, 1983), 193; Ozment, *When Fathers Ruled;* Roper, *The Holy Household;* and Maria Mies, "Colonization and Housewifeization," *Patriarchy and Accumulation on a World Scale: Women in the International Division of Labour,* ed. Maria Mies (London: Zed Books, 1986), 74–111.

32. In the juridical prescriptions of part 3, Kramer explained that informing on the activities of a heretic or a "witch" is to be encouraged because of the danger she represents to the state: "was zur Schädigung der Menschen, der Haustiere oder der Feldfrüchte und zum Schaden des Staatswesens auszuschlagen vermag... [der Denunziant] denunziere mit Rücksicht auf das verhängte Urteil der Exkommunikation oder aus Glaubenseifer und zum Besten des Staatswesens" [whatsoever causes damage to people, to animals, to the fruits of the fields, or to the state... people denounce because of the threatened excommunication or because of their zealous faith or for the best interest of the state] (pt. 3, 34).

33. Because the Devil knows that [children who have been killed before baptism do not enter into Heaven]. Therefore, the more time it takes to assemble the number of the just, the longer it will be until Judgment Day: once the number is completed, the world will be at an end.

34. "The woman remains forever a minor," claims Robert Muchembled, *Sorcières: justice et société aux 16e et 17e siècles* (Paris: Editions Imago, 1987), 61. See also Ian Maclean, *The Renaissance Notion of Woman: A Study in the Fortunes of Scholasticism and Medical Science in European Intellectual Life* (Cambridge: Cambridge University Press, 1980).

35. Bodin, *Vom aussgelasnen wütigen Teuffelsheer*, Vorwarnung: "Jetzund legt er einen ort vnd Spruch der H. Schrifft seinem gutduncken nach auß / hernach auff gut Jüdisch Rabinisch / folgends Allegorisch... sehr viel Gelehrten dieses an jhm als sträfflich taxieren vnnd halten / das er viel zu viel auff der Rabiner Schrifften / Außlegungen vnd Glossen angebracht [sic] vnd verpicht ist" [At first he interprets Holy Scriptures as he pleases / then according to Jewish rabbinical custom / then allegorically... many scholars find this objectionable / and consider that he values the rabbis' writings / interpretations and glosses much too much]. For more on Bodin's alleged preference for Jewish sources, see Rose, *Bodin and the Great God*. For a discussion of Bodin's possibly Jewish ancestors, see Jacques Saillot, "Jean Bodin, sa famille, ses origines," *Jean Bodin: actes du colloque interdisciplinaire d'Angers, 24 au 27 mai 1985* (Angers: Presses de l'Université d'Angers, 1985), 1:111-19.

36. "Daher scheint der böse Wille des Teufels die Ursache [that is, the inclination] des bösen Willens zu sein, besonders bei den Hexen" [Therefore it seems that the evil intentions of the Devil are the cause of evil, especially in witches] (pt. 1, 65).

37. See Dagmar Unverhau, "Akkusationsprozeß-Inquisitionsprozeß: Indikatoren für die Intensität der Hexenverfolgung in Schleswig-Holstein? Überlegungen und Untersuchungen zu einer Typologie der Hexenprozesse," *Hexenprozesse: Deutsche und skandinavische Beiträge,* ed. Christian Degn, Hartmut Lehmann, and Dagmar Unverhau, Studien zur Volkskunde und Kulturgeschichte Schleswig-Holsteins 12 (Neumünster: Karl Wachholtz Verlag, 1983), 93, 98; Wolfgang Behringer, "Kinderhexenprozesse: Zur Rolle von Kindern in der Geschichte der Hexenverfolgung," *Zeitschrift für historische Forschung*, 19, no. 1 (1989): 31-47.

38. Note that the excommunicated, as well as accomplices of the crime, as well as infamous persons and criminals and slaves against their masters, can be admitted to the proceedings to give testimony in all matters of faith; likewise heretics can be admitted for testimony against heretics, likewise sorcerers against sorcerers, however only if there is not other testimony, and only against and not for [the accused].

39. Around the thirteenth century, this category of crime began to appear in legal tracts. *Crimen exceptum* refers to a crime so dangerous to society and of such grave insult to God that its proceedings were characterized by more exceptions than usual. In the case of witchcraft, it meant the participation of ecclesiastical as well as secular authorities. In the sixteenth century, the court had taken over the function of the accuser; the crime was defined as secular (*maleficium*) and religious (*apostasy*). In the formulation of the laws that governed such procedures, social privilege excepting some people from torture was removed. Although they were clerics, inquisitors were henceforth allowed to torture the victim—albeit by carefully circumscribed methods—after giving each other absolution. See Edward Peters, *Torture* (New York: Basil Blackwell, 1985), 6, 61; John Tedeschi, "Inquisitorial Law and the Witch," *Early Modern European Witchcraft: Centres and Peripheries,* ed. Bengt Ankarloo and Gustav Henningsen (Oxford: Clarendon Press, 1990), 83–118; Midelfort, *Witch Hunting in Southwestern Germany,* 17, 68; Christina Larner, "Crimen Exceptum? The Crime of Witchcraft in Europe," *Crime and the Law: The Social History of Crime in Western Europe since 1500,* ed. V. A. C. Gatrell, Bruce Lenman, and Geoffrey Parker (London: Europa Publications, 1980), 49–75. For more information about the resources available on inquisitorial methods and differences, see Henningsen and Tedeschi, eds., *The Inquisition in Early Modern Europe.*

40. But the Roman emperors and jurists / when they realized / that / in the case where these convictions could not find expression / the larger part of the misdeeds and crimes would go unpunished.... So it is that we are convinced / that one should in such a case give credence to the women / regardless of / whether they already have been slandered and considered without honor / as our learned doctors say / truly because of a [bad] deed / or ... cursed or if they were ignominous / no matter how dishonorable or obscene the woman might be.

41. Peters, *Torture,* 70–73; Henningsen, *The Witches' Advocate,* 357–87, describes Salazar's efforts to curb excessive violence and to pacify the people with the help of more humane and reasonable inquisitorial laws. We find that even some of the most dedicated witch hunters, preceding his work, such as Delrio and Binsfeld, voice their doubts about the efficacy of torture in witch investigations and discuss alternative ways of questioning and punishing suspected witches. Cf. Schnyder, "Fragen und Beobachtungen," 345, 349, 356.

42. Burke, *The Historical Anthropology of Early Modern Italy,* 80.

43. Behringer, *Hexenverfolgung in Bayern,* 89.

44. At least thirty-four editions of the *Malleus Maleficarum* appeared between 1486 and 1669, mainly during the periods 1486–1520 and 1574–1621. Between 30,000 and 50,000 copies were put on the market by publishers in Frankfurt, the Rhenish cities (fourteen editions), Lyon (eleven editions), Nuremberg (four editions), Venice (three editions), and Paris (two editions). See introduction to *Witches, Devils, and Doctors in the Renaissance,* ed. George Mora et al., trans.

John Shea, collaborators Erik Midelfort and Helen Bacon, Medieval and Renaissance Texts and Studies 73 (Binghamton, NY: Medieval and Renaissance Texts and Studies, 1991), lxxxiv.

45. Introduction to *Witches, Devils, and Doctors,* lvi.

46. Benjamin Keen, "The Vision of America in the Writings of Urbain Chauveton," *First Images of America: The Impact of the New World on the Old,* ed. Fredi Chiappelli, Michael J. B. Allen, and Robert L. Benson (Berkeley: University of California Press, 1976), 1:107, 117.

47. André Thevet, *Les singvlaritez de la France Antarctique, avtrement nommée Amerique* (Anvers: De l'imprimerie de Christophle Plantin a la licorne d'or, 1558). For the difference between "good" cannibals, whose anthropophagism restricted itself to the ritual killing and eating of human flesh, and "bad" cannibals, who ate human flesh mainly for nourishment, see Lestringant, "Rage, fureur, folie, cannibales."

48. Only he who had cleansed his body and soul, who had abstained from the "work of Venus," would expect divine illumination.

For more on the topic, see Heinrich Cornelius Agrippa von Nettesheim, *De occulta philosophia,* ed. Karl Anton Nowotny (1533; reprinted, Graz: Akademische Druck- und Verlagsanstalt, 1967), pt. 3, 64.

49. Pagden, *European Encounters,* 17, 21; Richard Godbeer reports on comparable suspicions among the Puritans in New England toward their indigenous neighbors. He tells of the accusers at the Salem witch trials who had convinced themselves that the Devil looked like a native American. Cotton Mather described them as Satan's "most devoted and resembling children." See Richard Godbeer, *The Devil's Dominion: Magic and Religion in Early Modern New England* (Cambridge: Cambridge University Press, 1992), 192. See also Sophie Houdard, *Les sciences du diable: quatre discours sur la sorcellerie (XVe–XVIIe siècle)* (Paris: Cerf, 1992), 97.

50. For this reason Weyer's writings have been of great interest to medical historians and to psychologists. Most of the secondary literature is cited in the notes of the new edition and translation and in Rudolf van Nahl, *Zauberglaube und Hexenwahn* as well as in H. C. Erik Midelfort, "Johann Weyer in medizinischer, theologischer und rechtsgeschichtlicher Hinsicht," *Vom Unfug des Hexen-Prozesses: Gegner der Hexenverfolgungen von Johann Weyer bis Friedrich Spee,* ed. Hartmut Lehmann and Otto Ulbricht, Wolfenbütteler Forschungen 55 (Wiesbaden: Harrassowitz Verlag, 1992), 63. See also Sidney Anglo, "Melancholia and Witchcraft: The Debate between Wier, Bodin, and Scot," *Folie et déraison à la Renaissance,* ed., A. Gerlo (Brussels: Editions de l'Université de Bruxelles, 1976), 209–28.

51. See Gustav Henningsen and Bengt Ankarloo, introduction to *Early Modern European Witchcraft: Centres and Peripheries,* ed. Bengt Ankarloo and Gustav Henningsen (Oxford: Clarendon Press, 1990), 8; Andreas Blauert, "Hexen-

verfolgung in einer spätmittelalterlichen Gemeinde," *Geschichte und Gesellschaft: Zeitschrift für historische Sozialwissenschaft* 16, no. 1 (1990): 8–25; Labouvie, "Männer im Hexenprozeß," 76–78; Muchembled, *Les derniers bûchers*. Thomas W. Robisheaux, *Rural Society and the Search for Order in Early Modern Germany* (Cambridge: Cambridge University Press, 1989), 99, describes the village as "A small number of the privileged and of well-to-do peasants, a number of laborers of small and medium incomes, a great number of the poor and miserable: . . . [a] world without movement and seething at the same time." Similarly, Robisheaux speaks of the "pauperization of the countryside" in sixteenth-century Germany, which led to a loss of order and to decay. The gap between the village poor and the village rich became unbridgeable, and the poorer among the population began to show a high degree of mobility (71, 86).

52. Jonathan Dollimore, *Sexual Dissidence: Augustine to Wilde, Freud to Foucault* (Oxford: Clarendon Press; New York: Oxford University Press, 1991), 284n. 1.

53. Stuart Clark, "Protestant Demonology: Sin, Superstition, and Society (c.1520–c.1630)," *Early Modern European Witchcraft: Centres and Peripheries*, ed. Bengt Ankarloo and Gustav Henningsen (Oxford: Clarendon Press, 1990), 56, concurs that the Lutheran demonologists are less inclined to attribute excessive power to Satan. He claims that Protestant witch tracts, most of them written by pastors, are typically more interested in educating their parishioners in being good citizens: "their tone is not so much intellectual as evangelical and homiletic."

54. Although I could demonstrate the point by examples from our own time and our own country, even in the case of maidens whom we believe to be most religiously chaste, nevertheless, since the examples would be odious, let us omit them and choose an example from a distant country (248).

55. Joy D. Wiltenburg, *Disorderly Women and Female Power in the Street Literature of Early Modern England and Germany* (Charlottesville: University Press of Virginia, 1992), lists many such tales as the subjects of popular, widely circulated texts.

56. I will return to the history of Bodin's reception below. On Weyer's role, see van Nahl, *Zauberglaube und Hexenwahn*, 50–79. The 1583 edition, on which the text I am using is based, shows a clearer chapter structure, including main and subheadings, making orientation much easier. Van Nahl points out that the sixth chapter distinguishes between the notorious magicians and the poisoner, whom Weyer wanted punished, and the *lamiae*, whose punishment, if any had to be levied, was to be lighter than that for men; cf. Weyer, 439; van Nahl, *Zauberglaube und Hexenwahn*, 64). Van Nahl's research on the reception of Weyer's works has shown that first reactions (1563) were positive. Approbation, however, was followed quickly by negative voices, which, in the end, proved to be the most influential during subsequent decades. The first general

reaction seems to have been one of relief and hope that the burning of women might have become a thing of the past (69). Opposition, however, came promptly from jurists and theologians, who found Weyer irritating for his "meddling" in their areas of expertise and for his new kind of biblical interpretation (72). In 1596 the work landed on the "Index librorum prohibitorum," from which it had disappeared by 1627. For more on the history of Weyer's reception, see also Wolfgang Ziegeler, *Möglichkeiten der Kritik am Hexen- und Zauberwesen im ausgehenden Mittelalter: Zeitgenössische Stimmen und ihre soziale Zugehörigkeit,* Kollektive Einstellungen und sozialer Wandel im Mittelalter 2 (Cologne: Böhlau Verlag, 1973).

57. Clark, "Glaube und Skepsis," 15–33.

58. Perez Zagorin, *Ways of Lying: Dissimulation, Persecution, and Conformity in Early Modern Europe* (Cambridge, MA: Harvard University Press, 1990).

59. Van Nahl observes: "In the end, Weyer failed with his new and promising ideas because he had dared to enter into areas of theology and law without having the appropriate training and authority to do so" (*Zauberglaube und Hexenwahn,* 72).

60. Bodin, *Vom aussgelasnen wütigen Teuffelsheer,* 112: "Doctor Weir, Schirmer vnnd Beschützer der Zauberer" [Doctor Weir, protector of sorcerers].

61. Bodin dedicated the *Démonomanie* to Christophe de Thou, first president of the Parliament of Paris, where Bodin sat in judgment over Johanna. She was condemned on April 30, 1578, after confessing "sans question ny torture" [without either questioning or torture] her relationship with the Devil. See Gilles Roussineau, "Peur et répression du mal dans la *Démonomanie des sorciers* de Jean Bodin," *Jean Bodin: actes du colloque interdisciplinaire d'Angers, 24 au 27 mai 1985* (Angers: Presses de l'Université d'Angers, 1985), 2:416. See also Houdard, *Les sciences du diable,* 57.

62. Her horrible depravity and murderous actions / the divine and human laws provided punishment for this kind of evil actions / as did generally the common customs among Christians / which have been practiced in this kingdom since the times of old.

63. Peter Blumenthal, "Zu Bodin's *Démonomanie des sorciers*," *Ketzerei und Ketzerbekämpfung in Wort und Text: Studien zur sprachlichen Verarbeitung religiöser Konflikte in der westlichen Romania,* ed. Peter Blumenthal, Zeitschrift für französische Sprache und Literatur 14 (Wiesbaden: Franz Steiner Verlag, 1989), 90.

64. From this we will know / how it is possible / although taking place among different peoples / at different times / that these stories fit together / just as they do when it comes to magicians and the deeds of witches and their confessions. Similar references can be found in Bodin, *Vom aussgelasnen wütigen Teuffelsheer,* 122, 128, 135, 157; Bodin's often repeated argument that demons

and witches were active in all parts of the world since time immemorial made Weyer appear ignorant—he did not know history—or arrogant—he did not care about its heuristic value. Bodin had been a keen observer of supernatural phenomena since 1550 in Toulouse. He himself was suspected of witchcraft in 1587 but not tried; after the Catholic League took Laon, his case was reopened. He saved himself from more serious proceedings by declaring his allegiance to the League; cf. Maxime Préaud, "La *Démonomanie,* fille de la *République,*" *Jean Bodin: actes du colloque interdisciplinaire d'Angers, 24 au 27 mai 1985* (Angers: Presses de l'Université d'Angers, 1985), 2:419. In 1596, the year of his death, Pope Clement VIII placed the *Démonomanie* on the "Index." Bodin was accused of having used too many rabbinical sources and of having neglected the New Testament (cf. Betzold, "Jean Bodin als Okkultist und seine *Démonomanie,*" 54). Delrio also lists the *Démonomanie* among the books "that smack of heresy and demonic influences" that should be placed on the "Index"; quoted in Houdard, *Les sciences du diable,* 96.

65. Bodin believes that there are "100 000 Hexen vnd Hexenmeister inn Franckreich" [100,000 witches and sorcerers in France] and that they will poison the country if they are not destroyed (Vorred, 5).

66. Jean de Léry, *Au lendemain de la Saint-Barthélemy: Guerre civile et famine: Histoire mémorable du siège de Sancerre,* ed. Gérald Nakam (1573; reprinted, Paris: Editions Anthropos, 1975). For a more detailed comparison of Léry's writings on Sancerre and Brazil to the religious controversies of the time, see Frank Lestringant, *Le huguenot et le sauvage,* chaps. 2, 3.

67. . . . they murdered their hapless fellow Christians and compatriots at Lyon / and threw them into the river Saone / only to pull them out again / cut them open / take out the fat. . . . Also / they ate their livers and hearts / and other pieces of human flesh. . . . If then according to the law / those / who eat human flesh should be put to death / why does one not start proceedings against such dogs just as one does against the death-devouring witches / since they introduced without shame a level of inhumanity unheard of among Christians.

68. Jean Bodin, *La méthode de l'histoire,* ed. and trans. Pierre Mesnard (1566; reprinted, Paris: Société d'édition "Les Belles Lettres," 1941), 114; cf. Ann M. Blair, "Le nature théâtre de Dieu, selon Jean Bodin," *Revue du seizième siècle* 7 (1989): 73–93.

69. Olaus Magnus (Archbishop of Uppsala [1490–1558]), *Historia de gentibvs septentrionalibvs* (Roma: apvd Ioannem Mariam de Viottis, 1555). Writers on witchcraft cited Olaus Magnus most frequently as a witness for the fact that the northernmost parts of Europe were infested with demons and witches.

70. Fischart wrote: "Newe Insuln voll Sodomy"; for fear of insulting the innocent ears of his German audience, he will not translate these words: "vnnd bei den Teutschen jhrer dieses lasters vnschuld halben nit vnvertolmetschen steht" [(and he would not) translate for the Germans because they were innocent

of such depravity] (178). About the conquerers' attempts at eradicating sodomy among the natives, see Jonathan Goldberg, *Sodometries: Renaissance Texts, Modern Sexualities* (Stanford: Stanford University Press, 1992).

71. It is not surprising that Léry adds to the 1585 edition of his travelogue about the Tupinamba of Brazil a description of the witches' sabbath, which he had taken out of Bodin's text. In the same instance, Léry also comments on the witchcraft controversy between Weyer and Bodin. Cf. Lestringant, *Le huguenot et le sauvage*, 50.

72. The new is only acceptable in the context of the old. Bodin was familiar with the works of Peter Martyr and Benzoni, whose *Novae novi orbis historiae* had been a much translated, adapted, and excerpted best-seller of the second half of the sixteenth century. Bodin and Fischart must have also known about the controversy over the treatment of the indigenous people, which by then had reached Europe in the form of the "Black Legend," a dispute that Bartholomé de Las Casas's passionate engagement with the natives helped to create. While in agreement with the negative assessment of the natives, Bodin's comments on the behavior of the Spanish appear at least ambivalent if not downright critical: "Wiewol andere / so jnen [den Spaniern] nicht gönsig / als die Ständ im Niderland / solchs jhrer angebornen Blut vnd Goltgirigkeit zumessen / vnnd vermeynen / sie solten mit gedachten Lasteren / die sie an andern straffen wöllen / nit weniger / dann dieselbigen behenckt vnd beschlept sein" [As others / who did not like the Spanish / as did the Dutch Estates / blamed this on their greed for money and gold / and they proclaim / that they are said to have those vices / that they like to punish in others in great quantity]. Fischart notes in the margin his source, "a book was published in the eighties with the title *Of the Cruelty of the Spanish in the New Islands.*" (178).

73. Hauffen, "Fischart-Studien III," 254.

Chapter 5

1. For more about learned writers in Italy, Spain, and France and their similar or dissimilar views, see Julio Caro Baroja, "Witchcraft and Catholic Theology," *Early Modern European Witchcraft: Centres and Peripheries*, ed. Bengt Ankarloo and Gustav Henningsen (Oxford: Clarendon Press, 1990), 31–40.

2. Beroja, "Witchcraft and Catholic Theology," 40.

3. Houdard, *Les sciences du diable*, 183.

4. Robert Muchembled, "Satanic Myths and Cultural Reality," *Early Modern European Witchcraft: Centres and Peripheries*, ed. Bengt Ankarloo and Gustav Henningsen (Oxford: Clarendon Press, 1990), 153.

5. Henningsen, *The Witches' Advocate*, 24–25.

6. Lancre, *Tableav de l'inconstance des mavvais anges et demons*, title page.

7. Lancre was in fact a distant relative of Montaigne's, having married his grandniece in 1588. For more on this topic, see Alan M. Boase, "Montaigne et la sorcellerie," *Humanisme et Renaissance* 2 (1935): 401–21; Henri Busson, "Montaigne et son cousin," *Revue d'histoire littéraire de la France* 4 (1960): 481–99.

8. Isa Dardano Basso, *L'ancora e gli specchi: lettura del* Tableau de l'inconstance et instabilité de toutes choses *di Pierre de Lancre*, Biblioteca di cultura 162 (Rome: Bulzoni Editore, 1979), 42. Lancre produced this tract in 1607 and issued a new edition in 1610. Twelve years later a third and final study on the subject of the magical arts appeared: *L'incredvlité et mescreance dv sortilege plainment convaincue* (Paris: Chez Nicolas Bvon, 1622). By then he had become advisor to the king in the government. He died in 1630.

9. Baroja, "Witchcraft and Catholic Theology," 40.

10. Pastor Bodmer, *The Armature of Conquest*, 142.

11. Travelers coming in search of wine in this city of Bordeaux assured us that on their way they saw great numbers of demons appearing as horrific human beings passing through France. This is the reason why the number of sorcerers is so great in the Labourt.

12. See Gerhild Scholz Williams, "Der Zauber der neuen Welt: Reise und Magie im sechzehnten Jahrhundert," *German Quarterly* 65, no. 3–4 (1992): 294–305, for more information on the visual and literary presentations of supposedly magical and satanic ritual and behavior among the natives of the New World.

13. In his book *The Incorruptible Flesh: Bodily Mutation and Mortification in Religion and Folklore* (Cambridge: Cambridge University Press, 1988), 17–19, Piero Camporesi speaks of bread enriched with substances such as hemp seeds. Ingesting it caused strange behavior, almost like drunkenness, and led to manifestations of collective delirium, which sometimes expressed itself in wild dancing. Camporesi speaks about such phenomena as indicators of a "culture of hunger" in early modern Europe.

14. These comments occur, respectively, in Jacques Ferrand, *A Treatise on Lovesickness*, ed. and trans. Donald A. Beecher and Massimo Ciavolella (Syracuse, NY: Syracuse University Press, 1990), 519; Cohn, *Europe's Inner Demons*, 137; Robert Mandrou, *Magistrats et sorciers en France au XVIIe siècle: une analyse de psychologie historique* (Paris: Plon, 1968), 138. Note that Lancre's *Tableav* is available in an abridged edition: *Tableau de l'inconstance des mauvais anges et démons: où il est amplement traité des sorciers et de la sorcellerie*, ed. Nicole Jacques-Chaquin (Paris: Editions Aubier, 1982).

15. Jean Céard, "The Inside Other: Witchcraft in Pierre de Lancre's *Tableau de l'inconstance des mauvais anges et démons*" (paper presented at the American

1930), 215 (trans. of *Petri Pomponatii... opera. De naturalium effectuum admirandorum causis, sen de incantationibus liber. Item de fato: libero arbitrio: praedestinatione: prouidentia Dei* [Basel: Henriepetrina, 1567]).

31. Pintard, *Le libertinage érudit*, 43.

32. Martin L. Pine, "Pomponazzi and the Problem of 'Double Truth,'" *Journal of the History of Ideas* 29 (1968): 163–76; *Pietro Pomponazzi: Radical Philosopher of the Renaissance*, Saggi e testi 21 (Padua: Editrice Antenore, 1986).

33. Henri Busson, *Le rationalisme dans la littérature française de la Renaissance (1533–1601)* (Paris: J. Vrin, 1957), 46, 50, makes this point. Many of the writers on magic and witchcraft return to the concept of sectarian beliefs and their association with demonic activity. For example, René Dupont, *La philosophie des esprits* (Paris, 1602), defines libertines as those who "n'ont horreur de prononcer que tout ce qui se dict des Demons ou Diables, sont invention et artifices pour faire peur aux hommes" [are not afraid of saying that all that is said about demons or devils is invention and artifice intended to frighten people] (223).

34. Charron, *De la sagesse*, 2:5, 358; Alberto Tenenti, "Milieu XVIe siècle: libertinisme et hérésie," *Annales: Economies, Sociétés, Civilisations* 18, no. 1 (1963): 15.

35. The tract appeared in 1605 with Nicolas Buvon, the same printer who did Lancre's work. Buvon seemed to have specialized in publishing on demonology and witchcraft.

36. Kors, *Atheism in France*, 27.

37. Carlos M. N. Eire, "Prelude to Sedition? Calvin's Attack on Nicodemism and Religious Compromise," *Archiv für Reformationsgeschichte* 76 (1985): 122.

38. Quoted in Zagorin, *Ways of Lying*, 11; see also Pintard, *Le libertinage érudit*, 5.

39. Wootton, "Lucien Febvre," 712.

40. Werner Bellardi, "Anton Engelbrecht (1485–1558): Helfer, Mitarbeiter und Gegner Bucers," *Archiv für Reformationsgeschichte* 64 (1973): 191.

41. Brady, "Architect of Persecution," 263.

42. Zagorin, *Ways of Lying*, 11.

43. Zagorin, *Ways of Lying*, 77. For more on the topic, see Carlos M. N. Eire, "Calvinism and Nicodemism: A Reappraisal," *Sixteenth Century Journal* 10, no. 1 (1979): 45–69.

44. Kieckhefer, *Magic in the Middle Ages*, 196.

45. Henningsen, *The Witches' Advocate*, 347.

46. Henningsen, *The Witches' Advocate*, 347–48.

47. Lercheimer, *Ein Christliche Bedenken*. For more on Scultetus, see Soldan, *Geschichte der Hexenprozesse*, 2:22; Clark, "Protestant Demonology," 58.

48. . . . but rather also in private places: which normally strangers are forbidden by law to touch / lest they have their hands cut off as punishment. They pretend / that the Devil might hide in the witch's hair or in her vagina / this is the way they want to drive him out. Oh what a small devil / that can be driven out with such a small flame.

49. Clark, "Protestant Demonology," 76.

50. Praetorius repeatedly refers to the *Carolina,* the *Peinliche Halsgerichtsordnung Kaiser Karls V* (1538), which provides that "in allen peinlichen sachen [involving torture], den Rechten schleunig [that is, without undue delay] nachgegangen [sei]" [in all matters of torture, all rights must be observed] (205).

51. Caspar Schwenckfeld (1489–1561), religious radical, sympathized with Anabaptists. See R. Emmet McLaughlin, *Caspar Schwenckfeld: Reluctant Radical: His Life to 1540* (New Haven: Yale University Press, 1986).

52. "Wenn nun das Kind aus der schulmeisterlichen Erziehung kommt, so stiften und reizen sie das Kind. . . . So werden Diebe. . . . Auf dieses merkt, daß alle Dinge, die wir im Alter gebrauchen sollen, von Jugend auf in uns erzogen werden müssen, und das Erziehen bringt und macht in uns einen Felsen" [When the child has finished school, then they start inciting and tempting the child. . . . Thus they become thieves. . . . Note that all things that we need in old age we must learn when we are young, and that education creates a foundation for us] (DS, 442, 444).

53. Lienhard, "Les épicuriens à Strasbourg," 25; Tenenti, "Milieu XVIe siècle," 6.

54. Quoted in Brady, *Ruling Class, Regime, and Reformation,* 247. See also Marcel Bataillon, ed., *Aspects du libertinisme au XVIe siècle: actes du colloque international de Sommières, exposés,* De Pétrarque à Descartes 30 (Paris: J. Vrin, 1974), 18.

55. Frank Lestringant, "Rage, fureur, folie, cannibales"; "Catholiques et cannibales: le thème du cannibalisme dans le discours protestant au temps des guerres de religion," *Pratiques et discours alimentaires à la Renaissance: actes du colloque de Tours de mars 1979, Centre d'études supérieures de la Renaissance,* ed. Jean-Claude Margolin and Robert Sauzet (Paris: G. P. Maisonneuve et Larose, 1982), 233–45.

56. Lestringant, *Le huguenot et le sauvage,* 51–60.

57. Léry, *Au lendemain de la Saint-Barthélemy;* Janet Whatley comments on the same event in the foreword to Lery, *History of a Voyage to the Land of Brazil, Otherwise Called America,* Latin American Literature and Culture 6 (Berkeley: University of California Press, 1990), xvii (trans. of Jean de Léry, *Histoire d'un voyage fait en la terre de Brézil: autrement dite Amérique . . . ,* ed. Jean-Claude Morisot and Louis Necker, Les classiques de la pensée politique 9 [Geneva: Librairie Droz, 1975]). This is a reprint, with commentary and introduction, of the second edition of 1580; the first edition had appeared two years

earlier, in 1578, twenty years after Léry's return from Brazil. In one of his longer asides in the Bodin text, Fischart also expounds on the cannibalism of native Americans and Spaniards; he indicates that he, Fischart, like Léry, did not see much difference between the two: "[the Spanish acted as if] they only punished those who ate human flesh, but everyone knows / . . . that they had only killed a few of them . . . and that they, too, had eaten the flesh of their enemies." Fischart continues by quoting Léry as further proof of the inhumanity of his contemporaries: "that the French, on St. Bartholomy's Night 1572, had cut open and eaten the livers and hearts of their countrymen" (239).

58. The third edition (Geneva: A. Chuppin, 1585) contains a description of the sabbath from Bodin's *Démonomanie* and a comment on the Weyer/Bodin dispute (1580); Lestringant, *Le huguenot et le sauvage,* 50. Léry's text affirms the association that witches of the Old World had found their counterparts in the New World, and that the religious dissidents (atheists, libertines, Epicureans) were of the same irreligious sort: "I have concluded that they have the same master: that is, the Brazilian women and the witches over here were guided by the same spirit of Satan; neither the distance between the places nor the long passage over the sea keeps the father of lies from working both here and there on those who are handed over to him by the just judgment of God" (Léry, *History of a Voyage to the Land of Brazil,* 248n. 14).

59. Quoted in Lienhard, *Croyants et sceptiques,* 13.

60. John Yoder, "Comments on Lienhard," 52; Cornelis H. W. van den Berg, "Anton Engelbrecht: un 'épicurien' strasbourgeois," 111–21, both in *Croyants et sceptiques au XVIe siècle: le dossier des "Epicuriens": actes du colloque organisé par le GRENEP, Strasbourg, 9–10 juin 1978,* ed. Marc Lienhard (Strasbourg: Librairie ISTRA, 1981); Ozment, *Mysticism and Dissent,* 116–89; Carlo Ginzburg, *Il Nicodemismo: simulazione e dissimulazione religiosa nell'Europa del '500, Biblioteca di cultura storica,* 107 (Turin: Einaudi, 1970). As Tenenti, "Milieu XVIe siècle," 4, states, "they were certainly very numerous"; Zagorin also posits a large unknown when he accounts for the number of actual Nicodemites.

61. Abray, *The People's Reformation,* 156–59.

62. Abray, *The People's Reformation,* 45.

63. Lienhard, "Les épicuriens à Strasbourg," 32.

64. Blumenberg, *Die Genesis der kopernikanischen Welt;* on Blumenberg's concept of the early modern epoch, see Gerhild Scholz Williams, "Provokation und Antwort: Hans Blumenbergs Frühe Neuzeit," *"Der Buchstab tödt, der Geist macht lebendig": Festschrift zum 60. Geburtstag von Hans-Gert Roloff von Freunden, Schülern und Kollegen,* ed. James Hardin and Jörg Jungmayr (Bern: Peter Lang, 1992), 1:109–26.

65. Ozment, *The Age of Reform,* 356, argues that civil codes assumed the role of final authority.

66. Ozment, *The Age of Reform*, 386–96.

67. Ferrand, *A Treatise on Lovesickness*, 28, 89, details the history; see also Pintard, *Le libertinage érudit*, 62.

68. Although not quite on the same topic, Marion Kobelt-Groch confirms my thesis nonetheless in "Von 'armen frouwen' und 'bösen wibern': Frauen im Bauernkrieg zwischen Anpassung und Auflehnung," *Archiv für Reformationsgeschichte* 79 (1988): 103–37. Roper, in *The Holy Household*, also claims that the Reformation was not a liberating experience for womankind.

69. Ferrand, *A Treatise on Lovesickness*, 156.

70. Muchembled, *Sorcières*, 61.

71. Deborah Cameron, *Feminism and Linguistic Theory* (New York: St. Martin's Press, 1985), 146.

72. Felski, *Beyond Feminist Aesthetics*, 62.

Works Cited

Primary Literature

Agrippa von Nettesheim, Heinrich Cornelius. *De occulta philosophia*. 1533. Ed. Karl Anton Nowotny. Graz: Akademische Druck- und Verlagsanstalt, 1967.

Arras, Jean d'. *Mélusine: roman du XIVe siècle*. Ed. Louis Stouff. Dijon: Impr. Bernigaud et Privat, 1932.

———. *Mélusine*. 1478. Ed. M. Charles Brunet. Paris: P. Jannet, 1854.

Binsfeld, Peter. *Traktat von Bekanntnuß der Zauberer und Hexen*. 1589. Munich: Adamberg, 1591.

Bodin, Jean. *La méthode de l'histoire*. 1566. Ed. and trans. Pierre Mesnard. Paris: Société d'édition "Les Belles Lettres," 1941.

———. *De la démonomanie des sorciers*. Paris, 1580. Reprinted, Hiedesheim-Zürich-New York: Olms, 1988.

———. *Vom aussgelasnen wütigen Teuffelsheer*. 1591. Trans. Johann Fischart. Ed. Hans Biedermann. Graz: Akademische Druck- und Verlagsanstalt, 1973.

Calvin, Jean. *Commentaires sur le Nouveau Testament*. Ed. Pierre Marcel. 4 vols. Paris: Ch. Meyrueis, 1854–55.

———. *Excuse à Messieurs les Nicodémites*. Geneva, 1544.

———. *Des scandales*. Ed. Olivier Fatio and C. Rapin. Textes littéraires français 323. Geneva: Librairie Droz, 1984.

———. *Three French Treatises*. Ed. Francis M. Higman. London: Athlone Press, 1970.

Charron, Pierre. *De la Sagesse livres trois*. 1601. Bordeaux: Simon Millanges, 1611.

Couldrette. *Le roman de Mélusine, ou, Histoire de Lusignan*. Ed. Eleanor Roach. Paris: Klincksieck, 1982.

Douglas, Mary Tew, ed. *Witchcraft Confessions and Accusations*. London: Travistock Publications, 1970.

Dupont, Réne. *La philosophie des esprits*. Paris, 1602.

Farel, Guillaume. *Le glaive de la parolle veritable, tiré contre le Bouclier de *defense: duquel un Cordilier Libertin s'est voulu servir, pour approuver ses fausses et damnables opinions.* Geneva, 1550.

Ferrand, Jacques. *A Treatise on Lovesickness*. Ed. and trans. Donald A. Beecher and Massimo Ciavolella. Syracuse, NY: Syracuse University Press, 1990.

Garasse, François. *La doctrine cvrievse des beavx esprits de ce temps, ov, Pretendvs tels*. Paris: Sebastien Chappelet, 1623.

Grillando, Paulo. *Tractatus de hereticis: sortilegijs omnifariam coitu*. Lyon: Apud Jacobu Glúcti, 1536.

Hemmingsen, Niels. *Vermanung von den Schwartzkünstlerischen Aberglauben, das man sich dafür hüten soll*. Wittenberg: Hans Kraffts Erben, 1586.

Hildebrand, Wolffgang. *Goetia, vel Theurgia, sive praestigiarum magicarum descriptio revelatio, resolutio, inquisitio, et executio. Das ist, WAHRE und eigentliche entdeckunge declaration oder erklärunge fürnehmer articulder zauberey....* Leipzig: Johann Francken, 1631.

Hortzitz, Nicoline, ed. *Hexenwahn: Quellenschriften des 15. bis 18. Jahrhunderts aus der Augsburger Staats- und Stadtbibliothek*. Stuttgart: Silberburg Verlag, 1990.

Lancre, Pierre de. *L'incredvlité et mescreance dv sortilege plainment convaincue*. Paris: Chez Nicolas Bvon, 1622.

———. *Le livre des princes, contenant plusieurs notables discours pour l'instruction des Roys, Empereurs et Monarques*. Paris: Buon, 1617.

———. *Tableau de l'inconstance des mauvais anges et démons: où il est amplement traité des sorciers et de la sorcellerie*. Ed. Nicole Jacques-Chaquin. Paris: Editions Aubier, 1982.

———. *Tableav de l'inconstance des mavvais anges et demons, ov il est amplement traicté des sorciers et de la sorcelerie*. Paris: J. Berjon, 1612.

———. *Tableau de l'inconstance et instabilité de toutes choses, où il es montré qu'en Dieu seul gît la vraie constance, à laquelle l'homme sage doit viser*. Paris, 1607/1610.

Las Casas, Bartolomé de. *The Devastation of the Indies: A Brief Account*. Trans. Herma Briffault. Baltimore: Johns Hopkins University Press, 1992.

Lercheimer, Augustin [Hermann Witekind]. *Ein Christlich Bedenken und Erinnerung von Zauberey zum 3. und letzten Mal gemehrt, auch mit zu Ende angehengter Widerlegung etl. irriger Meinungen und Bräuche*. Cologne: Nicolai Erben, 1598.

Léry, Jean de. *Histoire d'vn voyage faict en la terre dv Bresil, avtrement dite Amerique*. 1578. 3d ed. Geneve: A. Chuppin, 1585.

———. *Histoire d'un voyage fait en la terre de Brézil*. 1580. Ed. Frank Lestringant. Montpellier: M. Chaleil, 1975.

———. *Histoire d'un voyage fait en la terre de Brézil: autrement dite Amérique....* 1580. Ed. Jean-Claude Morisot and Louis Necker. Les classiques de la pensée politique 9. Geneva: Librairie Droz, 1975.

———. *History of a Voyage to the Land of Brazil, Otherwise Called America.* Ed. and trans. Janet Whatley. Latin American Literature and Culture 6. Berkeley: University of California Press, 1990.

———. *Au lendemain de la Saint-Barthélemy: Guerre civile et famine: Histoire mémorable du siège de Sancerre. 1573.* Ed. Gérald Nakam. Paris: Editions Anthropos, 1975.

Luck, Georg, ed. and trans. *Arcana Mundi: Magic and the Occult in the Greek and Roman Worlds: A Collection of Ancient Texts.* Baltimore: Johns Hopkins University Press, 1985.

Magnus, Olaus. *Historia de gentibvs septentrionalibvs.* Roma: Apud Ioannem Mariam de Viottis, 1555.

Naudé, Gabriel. *Considerazione politiche sui colpi di stato.* Trans. Piero Bertolucci. Turin: P. Boringhieri, 1958.

Nicholas, of Cusa, Cardinal. *Die Kunst der Vermutung: Auswahl aus den Schriften von Nikolaus von Cues.* Ed. Hans Blumenberg. Sammlung Dieterich 128. Bremen: Carl Schünemann, 1957.

Paré, Ambroise. *On Monsters and Marvels. 1585.* Ed. and trans. Janis L. Pallister. Chicago: University of Chicago Press, 1982.

Pomponazzi, Pietro. *Petri Pomponatii... opera. De naturalium effectuum admirandorum causis, sen de incantationibus liber. Item de fato: libero arbitrio: praedestinatione: prouidentia Dei.* Basel: Henriepetrina, 1567.

———. *Les causes des merveilles de la nature, ou, Les enchantements.* Ed. and trans. Henri Busson. Textes du christianisme 8. Paris: Rieder, 1930.

Ringoltingen, Thüring von. *Melusine. Romane des 15. und 16. Jahrhunderts: Nach den Erstdrucken mit sämtlichen Holzschnitten,* ed. Jan-Dirk Müller, 9–176, 1012–87. Bibliothek der frühen Neuzeit 1. Frankfurt am Main: Deutscher Klassiker Verlag, 1990.

Rudinger, Johann. *De magia illicita. decas concionum; zehen müthliche Predigten von der Zauber- vnd Hexenwerck....* Jena: Johan Reissernberger, 1630.

Samson, Hermann. *Neun Auszerlesen vnd Wolgegründete Hexen Predigt / Darinnen der Terminus Magiae oder Zäuberey nach den logicalischen terminis richtig vnd kürzlich ausz Gottes Wort....* Riga in Liefflandt: Gerhard Schröders, 1626.

Sanctes, Claude de. *Declaration d'aucuns athéimes de la doctrine de Calvin et Bèze contre les premiers fondements de la chrestineté.* Paris, 1572.

[Schilling, Wolfgang.] *Newer Tractat von der verführten Kinder Zauberey.* Cologne: Peter von Brachel, 1629.

Scultetus, Johannes [Antonius Praetorius/Schultze]. *Grundlich Bericht von Zauberey und Zauberern /... Allen Staenden der Welt in Gemein vnd sonderlich den hohen vnd nidern Obrigkeiten zu notwendiger nachrichtung und nützlich zu lesen.* Cologne: Nicolai Erben, 1598.

204 Works Cited

Sprenger, Jakob, and Heinrich Institoris. *Der Hexenhammer (Malleus Maleficarum)*. Ed. and trans. J. W. R. Schmidt. 1905. Reprint, 9th ed. Munich: Deutscher Taschenbuch Verlag, 1982, 1990.

———. *The* Malleus Maleficarum *of Heinrich Kramer and James Sprenger*. Ed. and trans. Montague Summers. 1928. Reprint, New York: Dover Publications, 1971.

Theophrastus Paracelsus. *Theophrastus Paracelsus*. Ed. Will-Erich Peuckert. 5 vols. 1944. Reprint, Darmstadt: Wissenschaftliche Buchgesellschaft, 1990.

Thevet, André. *Les singularités de la France antarctique: le Brésil des cannibales au XVIe siècle*. 1558. Ed. Frank Lestringant. Paris: La Découverte/Maspero, 1983.

———. *Les singvlaritez de la France Antarctique, avtrement nommée Amerique*. Anvers: De l'imprimerie de Christophle Plantin a la licorne d'or, 1558.

Wierus, Iohannes [Johann Weyer, Johann Wier]. *De lamiis liber*. 1577. Basil: Ex Officina Oporiniana, 1582.

———. "Liber apologeticus et Pseudomachia daemonum." In *Opera omnia: Edito nova et hactenus desiderata*, 623–34. Amsterdam: Apud Petrum vanden Berge, 1660.

———. *De praestigiis daemonum*. 1583. Trans. John Shea. *Witches, Devils, and Doctors in the Renaissance*. Ed. George Mora et al. Medieval and Renaissance Texts and Studies 73. Binghamton, NY: Medieval and Renaissance Texts and Studies, 1991.

Secondary Literature

Abray, Lorna Jane. *The People's Reformation: Magistrates, Clergy, and Commons in Strasbourg, 1500–1598*. Ithaca, NY: Cornell University Press, 1985.

Agethen, Manfred. "Aufklärungsgesellschaften, Freimauerei, geheime Gesellschaften: Ein Forschungsbericht (1976–86)." *Zeitschrift für historische Forschung* 14, no. 1 (1987): 439–63.

Allers, Rudolf. "Microcosmus: From Anaximander to Paracelsus." *Traditio* 2 (1944): 319–407.

Alsheimer, Rainer. "Katalog protestantischer Teufelserzählungen des 16. Jahrhunderts." In *Volkserzählung und Reformation: Ein Handbuch zur Tradierung und Funktion von Erzählstoffen und Erzählliteratur im Protestantismus*, ed. Wolfgang Brückner, 417–519. Berlin: Erich Schmidt Verlag, 1974.

Ambrose, Elizabeth Ann. *The* Hermetica: *An Annotated Bibliography*. Sixteenth Century Bibliography 30. St. Louis, MO: Center for Reformation Research, 1992.

Anglo, Sidney. "Melancholia and Witchcraft: The Debate between Wier, Bodin, and Scot." In *Folie et déraison à la Renaissance*, 209–28. Ed. A. Gerlo.

Travaux de l'Institut pour l'étude de la Renaissance et de l'humanisme 5. Brussels: Editions de l'Université de Bruxelles, 1976.

Ankarloo, Bengt, and Gustav Henningsen, eds. *Early Modern European Witchcraft: Centres and Peripheries.* Oxford: Clarendon Press, 1990.

Bahktin, Mikhail M. *The Dialogic Imagination: Four Essays.* Ed. Michael Holquist. Trans. Caryl Emerson and Michael Holquist. Austin: University of Texas Press, 1981.

Baroja, Julio Caro. "Witchcraft and Catholic Theology." In *Early Modern European Witchcraft: Centres and Peripheries,* ed. Bengt Ankarloo and Gustav Henningsen, 19–43. Oxford: Clarendon Press, 1990.

Bataillon, Marcel, ed. *Aspects du libertinisme au XVIe siècle: actes du colloque international de Sommières, exposés.* De Pétrarque à Descartes 30. Paris: J. Vrin, 1974.

Behringer, Wolfgang. "Erträge und Perspektiven der Hexenforschung." *Historische Zeitschrift* 249, no. 3 (1989): 619–40.

———. *Hexenverfolgung in Bayern: Volksmagie, Glaubenseifer und Staatsräson in der Frühen Neuzeit.* Munich: R. Oldenbourg Verlag, 1987.

———. "Kinderhexenprozesse: Zur Rolle von Kindern in der Geschichte der Hexenverfolgung." *Zeitschrift für historische Forschung* 16, no. 1 (1989): 31–47.

———. "Meinungsbildende Befürworter und Gegner der Hexenverfolgung (15. bis 18. Jahrhundert)." In *Hexen und Zauberer: Die große Verfolgung, ein europäisches Phänomen in der Steiermark,* ed. Helfried Valentinitsch, 219–237. Graz: Leykam Buch Verlag, 1987.

———. *Mit dem Feuer vom Leben zum Tod: Hexengesetzgebung in Bayern.* Munich: Heinrich Hugendubel Verlag, 1988.

Bellardi, Werner. "Anton Engelbrecht (1485–1558): Helfer, Mitarbeiter und Gegner Bucers." *Archiv für Reformationsgeschichte* 64 (1973): 183–206.

Bennewitz-Behr, Ingrid. "Melusines Schwestern: Beobachtungen zu den Frauenfiguren im Prosaroman des 15. und 16. Jahrhunderts." *Germanistik und Deutschunterricht im Zeitalter der Technologie: Selbstbestimmung und Anpassung, Vorträge des Germanistentages Berlin 1987.* Ed. Norbert Oellers. Tübingen: Max Niemeyer Verlag, 1988. 1:291–300.

Berg, Cornelis H. W. van den. "Anton Engelbrecht: un 'épicurien' strasbourgeois." In *Croyants et sceptiques au XVIe siècle: le dossier des "Epicuriens": actes du Colloque organisé par le GRENEP, Strasbourg, 9–10 juin 1978,* ed. Marc Lienhard, 111–21. Strasbourg: Librairie ISTRA, 1981.

Berriot, François. *Athéisme et athéistes au XVIe siècle en France.* Lille: Atelier national de reproductions des theses, Université de Lille III, 1984.

Bertaud, Madeleine. "Pierre de Lancre et la femme." *Travaux de linguistique et de littérature* 14, no. 2 (1976): 51–70.

Betzold, Friedrich von. "Das *Colloquium Heptaplomeres* und der Atheismus im 16. Jahrhundert." *Historische Zeitschrift* 113 (1914): 216–315; 114 (1915): 237–301.

———. "Jean Bodin als Okkultist und seine *Démonomanie*." *Historische Zeitschrift* 105 (1910): 1–64.

Beyer, Christel. *Hexen-Leut, so zu Würzburg gerichtet: Der Umgang mit Sprache und Wirklichkeit in Inquisitionsprozessen wegen Hexerei*. Europäische Hochschulschriften 1, no. 948. Frankfurt am Main: Peter Lang, 1986.

Bitterli, Urs. *Cultures in Conflict: Encounters between European and Non-European Cultures, 1492–1800*. Trans. Ritchie Robertson. Stanford, CA: Stanford University Press, 1989.

Blair, Ann M. "Le nature théâtre de Dieu, selon Jean Bodin." *Revue du seizième siècle* 7 (1989): 73–93.

Blauert, Andreas. "Hexenverfolgung in einer spätmittelalterlichen Gemeinde." *Geschichte und Gesellschaft: Zeitschrift für historische Sozialwissenschaft* 16, no. 1 (1990): 8–25.

Bloch, Marc L. B. *The Royal Touch: Sacred Monarchy and Scrofula in England and France*. Trans. J. E. Anderson. London: Routledge and Kegan Paul, 1973.

Bloch, R. Howard. *Etymologies and Genealogies: A Literary Anthropology of the French Middle Ages*. Chicago: University of Chicago Press, 1983.

Blümlein, Kilian. *Naturerfahrung und Welterkenntnis: Der Beitrag des Paracelsus zur Entwicklung des neuzeitlichen, naturwissenschaftlichen Denkens*. Europäische Hochschulschriften 20, no. 300. Frankfurt am Main: Peter Lang, 1992.

Blumenberg, Hans. *Arbeit am Mythos*. Frankfurt am Main: Suhrkamp Verlag, 1979.

———. *Aspekte der Epochenschwelle: Cusaner und Nolaner*. 2d ed. Suhrkamp Taschenbuch Wissenschaft 174. Frankfurt am Main: Suhrkamp Verlag, 1982.

———. *Die Genesis der kopernikanischen Welt*. 2d ed. 3 vols. Suhrkamp Taschenbuch Wissenschaft 352. Frankfurt am Main: Suhrkamp Verlag, 1989.

———. *The Genesis of the Copernican World*. Trans. Robert M. Wallace. Cambridge, MA: MIT Press, 1987.

———. *The Legitimacy of the Modern Age*. Trans. Robert M. Wallace. Cambridge, MA: MIT Press, 1983.

———. *Der Prozeß der theoretischen Neugierde*. Suhrkamp Taschenbuch Wissenschaft 24. Frankfurt am Main: Suhrkamp Verlag, 1973.

———. "Das Universum eines Ketzers." *Das Aschermittwochsmahl*, by Giordano Bruno. Trans. Ferdinand Fellmann. Frankfurt am Main: Insel Verlag, 1969.

Blumenthal, Peter. "Zu Bodin's *Démonomanie des sorciers*." In *Ketzerei und Ketzerbekämpfung in Wort und Text: Studien zur sprachlichen Verarbeitung religiöser Konflikte in der westlichen Romania*, ed. Peter Blumenthal, 89–97.

Zeitschrift für französische Sprache und Literatur 14. Wiesbaden: Franz Steiner Verlag, 1989.
Boase, Alan M. "Montaigne et la sorcellerie." *Humanisme et Renaissance* 2 (1935): 401–21.
Bock, Gisela. "Geschichte, Frauengeschichte, Geschlechtergeschichte." *Geschichte und Gesellschaft: Zeitschrift für historische Sozialwissenschaft* 14, no. 3 (1988): 364–91.
Boucher, Philip P. *Cannibal Encounters: Europeans and Island Caribs, 1492–1763*. Baltimore: Johns Hopkins University Press, 1992.
Boureau, Alain. *Le simple corps du roi: l'impossible sacralité des souverains français XVe–XVIIIe siècle*. Paris: Les Editions de Paris, 1988.
Bouwsma, William J. *John Calvin: A Sixteenth-Century Portrait*. New York: Oxford University Press, 1988.
———. "The Two Faces of Humanism: Stoicism and Augustinianism in Renaissance Thought." In *Itinerarium Italicum: The Profile of the Italian Renaissance in the Mirror of Its European Transformations, Dedicated to Paul Oskar Kristeller on the Occasion of his Seventieth Birthday*, ed. Heiko A. Oberman and Thomas A. Brady, 3–60. Studies in Medieval and Renaissance Thought 14. Leiden: E. J. Brill, 1975.
Brady, Thomas A., Jr. "Architect of Persecution: Jacob Sturm and the Fall of the Sects at Strasbourg." *Archiv für Reformationsgeschichte* 79 (1988): 262–81.
———. *Protestant Politics: Jacob Sturm (1489–1553) and the German Reformation*. Atlantic Highlands, NJ: Humanities Press International, 1993.
———. *Ruling Class, Regime, and Reformation at Strasbourg, 1520–1555*. Studies in Medieval and Reformation Thought 22. Leiden: E. J. Brill, 1978.
Brauner, Sigrid. "Cannibals, Witches, and Evil Wives in the 'Civilizing Process.' " In *"Neue Welt"/"Dritte Welt": Interkulturelle Beziehungen Deutschlands zu Lateinamerika und der Karibik*, ed. S. Bauschinger and S. L. Cocalis, 1–28. Tübingen: Francke Verlag, 1994.
———. *Fearless Wives and Frightened Shrews: The Concept of the Witch in Early Modern Germany*. Ed. Robert H. Brown. Amherst: University of Massachusetts Press, 1995.
Brückner, Wolfgang, and Rainer Alsheimer. "Das Wirken des Teufels: Theologie und Sage im 16. Jahrhundert." In *Volkserzählung und Reformation: Ein Handbuch zur Tradierung und Funktion von Erzählstoffen und Erzählliteratur im Protestantismus*, ed. Wolfgang Brückner, 394–416. Berlin: Erich Schmidt Verlag, 1974.
Brundage, James A. *Law, Sex, and Christian Society in Medieval Europe*. Chicago: University of Chicago Press, 1987.
Burke, Peter. *The Historical Anthropology of Early Modern Italy: Essays on Perception and Communication*. Cambridge: Cambridge University Press, 1987.

———. *The Renaissance*. Atlantic Highlands, NJ: Humanities Press International, 1987.
Busson, Henri. "Montaigne et son cousin." *Revue d'histoire littéraire de la France* 4 (1960): 481–99.
———. "Les noms des incrédules au XVIe siécle." *Bibliothèque d'humanisme et Renaissance* 16 (1954): 273–83.
———. *Le rationalisme dans la littérature française de la Renaissance (1533–1601)*. Paris: J. Vrin, 1957.
Cameron, Deborah. *Feminism and Linguistic Theory*. New York: St. Martin's Press, 1985.
Camporesi, Piero. *The Incorruptible Flesh: Bodily Mutation and Mortification in Religion and Folklore*. Cambridge: Cambridge University Press, 1988.
Carroll, David, and Barry Saxe. *Natural Magic: The Magical State of Being*. New York: Arbor House, 1977.
Cassirer, Ernst. "Giovanni Pico della Mirandola: A Study in the History of Renaissance Ideas." *Journal of the History of Ideas* 3, no. 3 (1942): 123–44, no. 4 (1942): 319–46.
Cassirer, Ernst, Paul Oskar Kristeller, and John Herman Randall, Jr., eds. *The Renaissance Philosophy of Man*. Chicago: University of Chicago Press, 1948.
Céard, Jean. "The Inside Other: Witchcraft in Pierre de Lancre's *Tableau de l'inconstance des mauvais anges et démons*." American Historical Association Convention, Chicago, 1992.
Chrismann, Miriam Usher. *Lay Culture, Learned Culture: Books and Social Change in Strasbourg, 1480–1599*. New Haven, CT: Yale University Press, 1982.
Clark, Jonathan P. "Inside/out: Body Politics against Large Bodies." *Daphnis* 20, no. 1 (1991): 101–30.
Clark, Stuart. "French Historians and Early Modern Popular Culture." *Past and Present* 100 (1983): 62–99.
———. "Glaube und Skepsis in der deutschen Hexenliteratur von Johann Weyer bis Friedrich Spee." In *Vom Unfug des Hexen-Processes: Gegner der Hexenverfolgungen von Johann Weyer bis Friedrich Spee*, ed. Hartmut Lehmann and Otto Ulbricht, 15–33. Wolfenbütteler Forschungen 55. Wiesbaden: Harrassowitz Verlag, 1992.
———. "Inversion, Misrule and the Meaning of Witchcraft." *Past and Present* 87 (1980): 98–127.
———. "Protestant Demonology: Sin, Superstition, and Society (c.1520–c.1630)." In *Early Modern European Witchcraft: Centres and Peripheries*, ed. Bengt Ankarloo and Gustav Henningsen, 45–81. Oxford: Clarendon Press, 1990.
———. "The Scientific Status of Demonology." In *Occult and Scientific Mentali-*

ties in the Renaissance, ed. Brian Vickers, 351–74. Cambridge: Cambridge University Press, 1984.

Clier-Colombani, Françoise. *La fée Mélusine au Moyen Age: images, mythes et symboles.* Paris: Léopard d'or, 1991.

Cohn, Norman R. C. *Europe's Inner Demons: An Enquiry Inspired by the Great Witch-Hunt.* New York: Basic Books, 1975.

Cook, John W. "Magic, Witchcraft, and Science." *Philosophical Investigations* 6, no. 1 (1983): 2–36.

Copenhaver, Brian P. "Natural Magic, Hermetism, and Occultism in Early Modern Science." In *Reappraisals of the Scientific Revolution,* ed. David C. Lindberg and Robert S. Westman, 261–303. Cambridge: Cambridge University Press, 1990.

Couliano, Ioan P. *Eros and Magic in the Renaissance.* Trans. Margaret Cook. Chicago: University of Chicago Press, 1987.

Crahay, Roland, and Marie Isaac: "La 'bibliothèque' de Bodin démonologue: les bases théoriques." *Bulletin de la classe des lettres et des sciences morales et politiques* 73 (1987): 129–71.

Craven, William G. *Giovanni Pico della Mirandola, Symbol of His Age: Modern Interpretations of a Renaissance Philosopher.* Travaux d'humanisme et Renaissance 185. Geneva: Librairie Droz, 1981.

D'Amico, John F. *Theory and Practice in Renaissance Textual Criticism: Beatus Rhenanus between Conjecture and History.* Berkeley: University of California Press, 1988.

Dardano Basso, Isa. *L'ancora e gli specchi: lettura del Tableau de l'inconstance et instabilité de toutes choses di Pierre de Lancre.* Biblioteca di cultura 162. Rome: Bulzoni Editore, 1979.

Davidson, Nicholas. "Unbelief and Atheism in Italy, 1500–1700." In *Atheism from the Reformation to the Enlightenment,* ed. Michael Hunter and David Wootton, 55–85. Oxford: Clarendon Press; New York: Oxford University Press, 1992.

Daxelmüller, Christoph. *Zauberpraktiken: Eine Ideengeschichte der Magie.* Zurich: Artemis und Winkler, 1993.

Debus, Allen G. *The Chemical Philosophy: Paracelsian Science and Medicine in the Sixteenth and Seventeenth Centuries.* New York: Science History Publications, 1977.

———. *The English Paracelsians.* 1965. Reprint, New York: Franklin Watts, 1966.

———. *The French Paracelsians: The Chemical Challenge to Medical and Scientific Tradition in Early Modern France.* Cambridge: Cambridge University Press, 1991.

Debus, Allen G., ed. *Science, Medicine, and Society in the Renaissance: Essays* to Honor Walter Pagel. 2 vols. New York: Science History Publications, 1972.

De Certeau, Michel. *The Mystic Fable*. Trans. Michael B. Smith. Chicago: University of Chicago Press, 1992.

———. *La possession de Loudun*. 1970. Reprint, Paris: Gallimard, 1980.

———. *The Writing of History*. Trans. Tom Conley. New York: Columbia University Press, 1988.

Degn, Christian, Hartmut Lehmann, and Dagmar Unverhau, eds. *Hexenprozesse: Deutsche und skandinavische Beiträge*. Studien zur Volkskunde und Kulturgeschichte Schleswig-Holsteins 12. Neumünster: Karl Wachholtz Verlag, 1983.

De Kroon, Marijn. *Martin Bucer und Johannes Calvin: Reformatorische Perspektiven: Einleitung und Texte*. Trans. Hartmut Rudolph. Göttingen: Vandenhoeck und Ruprecht, 1991.

———. *Studien zu Martin Bucers Obrigkeitsverständnis: Evangelisches Ethos und politisches Engagement*. Gütersloh: Reinhard Mohn, 1984.

Del Cervo, Diana M., ed. *Witchcraft in Europe and America: Guide to the Microfilm Collection*. Woodbridge, CT: Research Publications, 1983.

Delumeau, Jean. *La civilisation de la Renaissance*. 1967. Reprint, Les grandes civilisations 7. Paris: Arthaud. 1973.

———. *La peur en Occident, XIVe–XVIIIe siècles: une cité assiégée*. Paris: Fayard, 1978.

Dienst, Heide. "Lebensbewältigung durch Magie: in Alltägliche Zauberei in Innsbruck gegen Ende des 15. Jahrhunderts." In *Alltag im 16. Jahrhundert: Studien zu Lebensformen in mitteleuropäischen Städten*, ed. Alfred Kohler and Heinrich Lutz, 80–116. Wiener Beiträge zur Geschichte der Neuzeit 14. Vienna: Verlag für Geschichte und Politik; Munich: R. Oldenbourg Verlag, 1987.

———. "Die Verarbeitung von Materialien des Innsbrucker Hexenprozesses von 1485 durch Institoris im *Hexenhammer*." Unpublished manuscript.

Dollimore, Jonathan. *Sexual Dissidence: Augustine to Wilde, Freud to Foucault*. Oxford: Clarendon Press; New York: Oxford University Press, 1991.

Douglas, Mary, ed. *Witchcraft Confessions and Accusations*. New York: Tavistock Publications, 1970.

Drury, Neville. *The Shaman and Magician: Journeys between the Worlds*. London: Routledge and Kegan Paul, 1982.

Eamon, William. "Arcana Disclosed: The Advent of Printing, the Books of Secrets Tradition and the Development of Experimental Science in the Sixteenth Century." *History of Science* 22, no. 2 (1984): 111–50.

———. *Science and the Secrets of Nature: Books of Secrets in Medieval and Early Modern Culture*. Princeton, NJ: Princeton University Press, 1994.

Easlea, Brian. *Witch Hunting, Magic, and the New Philosophy: An Introduction to the Debates of the Scientific Revolution, 1450–1750*. Brighton, Eng.: Harvester Press; Atlantic Highlands, NJ: Humanities Press International, 1980.

Eire, Carlos M. N. "Calvinism and Nicodemism: A Reappraisal." *The Sixteenth Century Journal* 10, no. 1 (1979): 45–69.

———. "Prelude to Sedition? Calvin's Attack on Nicodemism and Religious Compromise." *Archiv für Reformationsgeschichte* 76 (1985): 120–45.

Evans, R. J. W. *Rudolf II and His World: A Study in Intellectual History, 1576–1612*. Oxford: Clarendon Press, 1973.

Faltenbacher, Karl F. *Das* Colloquium Heptaplomeres, *ein Religionsgespräch zwischen Scholastik und Aufklärung: Untersuchungen zur Thematik und zur Frage der Autorschaft*. Europäische Hochschulschriften 13.127. Frankfurt am Main: Peter Lang, 1988.

Faracovi, Ornella Pompeo. "L'antropologia della religione nel libertinismo francese de Seicento." In *Ricerche su letteratura libertina e letteratura clandestina nel seicento: atti del convegno di studio di Genova (30 ottobre–1 novembre 1980)*, ed. Tullio Gregory et al., 119–42. Florence: La nuova Italia Editrice, 1981.

Fawcett, Robin P. et al., eds. *The Semiotics of Culture and Language*. London: Frances Pinter, 1984.

Febvre, Lucien P. V. "Aux origines de l'esprit moderne: libertinisme, naturalisme, mécanisme." *Au cœur religieux du XVIe siècle*. 2d ed. Paris: SEVPEN, 1957. 337–58.

———. *The Problem of Unbelief in the Sixteenth Century: The Religion of Rabelais*. Trans. Beatrice Gottlieb. Cambridge, MA: Harvard University Press, 1982.

Felski, Rita. *Beyond Feminist Aesthetics: Feminist Literature and Social Change*. Cambridge, MA: Harvard University Press, 1989.

Flint, Valerie I. J. *The Rise of Magic in Early Medieval Europe*. Princeton, NJ: Princeton University Press, 1991.

Fohrmann, Jürgen, and Harro Müller, eds. *Diskurstheorien und Literaturwissenschaft*. Frankfurt am Main: Suhrkamp Verlag, 1988.

Foucault, Michel. *The Order of Things: An Archeology of the Human Sciences*. 1971. Reprint, New York: Vintage Books, 1973.

———. "Préface à la transgression." *Critique* 19, nos. 195–96 (1963): 751–69.

Funkenstein, Amos. *Theology and the Scientific Imagination from the Middle Ages to the Seventeenth Century*. Princeton, NJ: Princeton University Press, 1986.

Gauna, Max. *Upwellings: First Expressions of Unbelief in the Printed Literature of the French Renaissance*. London and Toronto: Associated University Presses, 1992.

Gause, Ute. "Zum Frauenbild im Frühwerk des Paracelsus." In *Parerga Paracelsica: Paracelsus in Vergangenheit und Gegenwart*, ed. Joachim Telle, 45–56. Heidelberger Studien zur Naturkunde der frühen Neuzeit 3. Stuttgart: Franz Steiner Verlag, 1992.

Giesecke, Michael. *Der Buchdruck in der frühen Neuzeit: Eine historische Fallstudie über die Durchsetzung neuer Informations- und Kommunikationstechnologien*. Frankfurt am Main: Suhrkamp Verlag, 1991.

———. *Sinnenwandel, Sprachwandel, Kulturwandel: Studien zur Vorgeschichte der Informationsgesellschaft*. Suhrkamp Taschenbuch Wissenschaft 997. Frankfurt am Main: Suhrkamp Verlag, 1992.

Gilbert, Neal W. *Renaissance Concepts of Method*. New York: Columbia University Press, 1960.

Ginzburg, Carlo. *Ecstasies: Deciphering the Witches' Sabbath*. Trans. Raymond Rosenthal. New York: Pantheon Books, 1991.

———. *Il Nicodemismo: simulazione e dissimulazione religiosa nell'Europa del '500*. Biblioteca di cultura storica 107. Turin: Einaudi, 1970.

———. *The Night Battles: Witchcraft and Agrarian Cults in the Sixteenth and Seventeenth Centuries*. Trans. John and Anne Tedeschi. Baltimore: Johns Hopkins University Press, 1983.

Godard de Donville, Louise. *Le libertin des origines à 1665: un produit des apologètes*. Paris: Papers on French Seventeenth-Century Literature, 1989.

Godbeer, Richard. *The Devil's Dominion: Magic and Religion in Early New England*. Cambridge: Cambridge University Press, 1992.

Goldammer, Kurt. *Der göttliche Magier und die Magierin Natur: Religion, Naturmagie und die Anfänge der Naturwissenschaft vom Spätmittelalter bis zur Renaissance, mit Beiträgen zum Magie-Verständnis des Paracelsus*. Kosmographie 5. Stuttgart: Franz Steiner Verlag, 1991.

———. "Magie." *Historisches Wörterbuch der Philosophie*. Ed. Joachim Ritter. Darmstadt: Wissenschaftliche Buchgesellschaft, 1980. 5:631–36.

———. "Paracelsus und die Magie." In *Paracelsus (1493–1541): "Keines andern Knecht,"* ed. Heinz Dopsch, Kurt Goldammer, and Peter F. Kramml, 219–27. Salzburg: Verlag Anton Pustet, 1993.

———. "Das religiöse Denken des Paracelsus." In *Paracelsus (1493–1541): "Keines andern Knecht,"* ed. Heinz Dopsch, Kurt Goldammer, and Peter F. Kramml, 195–201. Salzburg: Verlag Anton Pustet, 1993.

———. "Die Stellung des Paracelsus in den Wissenschaften." In *Paracelsus (1493–1541): "Keines andern Knecht,"* ed. Heinz Dopsch, Kurt Goldammer, and Peter F. Kramml, 3–65. Salzburg: Verlag Anton Pustet, 1993.

Goldberg, Jonathan. *Sodometries: Renaissance Texts, Modern Sexualities*. Stanford: Stanford University Press, 1992.

Greenblatt, Stephen J. *Marvelous Possessions: The Wonder of the New World*. Chicago: University of Chicago Press, 1991.

———. "Psychoanalysis and Renaissance Culture." In *Literary Theory/Renaissance Texts,* ed. P. Parker and D. Quint, 215. Baltimore: Johns Hopkins University Press, 1986.

———. *Shakespearean Negotiations: The Circulation of Social Energy in Renaissance England.* The New Historicism: Studies in Cultural Poetics 4. Berkeley: University of California Press, 1988.

Gulielmetti, Angela. "The 'Exploitation' of Colonial Discourse in Bartholomé de Las Casas' *Brevisima Relación de la Destrucción de las Indias.*" Unpublished paper, Department of Germanic Languages and Literatures, Washington University, 1993.

Haas, Alois M. "Sterben und Todesverständnis bei Paracelsus." Unpublished paper, 1993.

———. "Vorstellungen von der Makrokosmos-Mikrokosmosbeziehung im Denken der Zeit vor Paracelsus." *Nova Acta Paracelsica* 6 (1991/92): 50–77.

Haliczer, Stephen. *Inquisition and Society in the Kingdom of Valencia, 1478–1834.* Berkeley: University of California Press, 1990.

Halliday, M. A. K. "Language as Code and Language as Behavior: A Systemic-Functional Interpretation of the Nature and Ontogenesis of Dialogue." In *The Semiotics of Culture and Language,* ed. Robin P. Fawcett et al., 3–35. London: Frances Pinter, 1984.

Hansen, Bert. "Science and Magic." In *Science in the Middle Ages,* ed. David C. Lindberg, 483–506. Chicago: University of Chicago Press, 1978.

Hansen, Joseph. *Quellen und Untersuchungen zur Geschichte des Hexenwahns und der Hexenverfolgungen im Mittelalter.* 1901. Reprint, Hildesheim: Georg Olms Verlag, 1963.

———. *Zauberwahn, Inquisition und Hexenprozeß im Mittelalter und die Entstehung der großen Hexenverfolgung.* Historische Bibliothek 12. Munich: R. Oldenbourg, 1900.

Harf-Lancner, Laurence. *Les fées au Moyen Age: Morgane et Mélusine: la naissance des fées.* Nouvelle bibliothèque du Moyen Age 8. Geneva: Slatkine, 1984.

———. "Le Roman de Mélusine et le Roman de Geoffroy à la grande dent: les éditions imprimées de l'œuvre de Jean d'Arras." *Bibliothèque d'Humanisme et de Renaissance* 50, no. 2 (1988): 349–66.

Harmening, Dieter. *Superstitio: Überlieferungs- und theoriegeschichtliche Untersuchungen zur kirchlich-theologischen Aberglaubensliteratur des Mittelalters.* Berlin: Erich Schmidt Verlag, 1979.

Harrer, Gerhard. "Paracelsus und die psychischen Erkrankungen." In *Paracelsus (1493–1541): "Keines andern Knecht,"* ed. Heinz Dopsch, Kurt Goldammer, and Peter F. Kramml, 101–9. Salzburg: Verlag Anton Pustet, 1993.

Hauffen, Adolf: "Fischart-Studien III: Der *Malleus Maleficarum* und Bodins *Démonomanie.*" *Euphorion* 4 (1897): 1–17, 251–61.

Haug, Walter. "Über die Schwierigkeiten des Erzählens in 'nachklassischer' Zeit." In *Positionen des Romans im späten Mittelalter,* ed. Walter Haug and Burghart Wachinger, 338-65. Fortuna vitrea 1. Tübingen: Max Niemeyer Verlag, 1991.

Hehl, Ulrich von. "Hexenprozesse und Geschichtswissenschaft." *Historisches Jahrbuch* 107, no. 2 (1987): 349-75.

Henningsen, Gustav. "'The Ladies from Outside': An Archaic Pattern of the Witches' Sabbath." In *Early Modern European Witchcraft: Centres and Peripheries,* ed. Bengt Ankarloo and Gustav Henningsen, 191-219. Oxford: Clarendon Press, 1990.

———. *The Witches' Advocate: Basque Witchcraft and the Spanish Inquisition, 1609-1614.* Reno: University of Nevada Press, 1980.

Henningsen, Gustav, and Bengt Ankarloo. Introduction to *Early Modern European Witchcraft: Centres and Peripheries,* ed. Bengt Ankarloo and Gustav Henningsen, 1-15. Oxford: Clarendon Press, 1990.

Henningsen, Gustav, and John Tedeschi, eds. *The Inquisition in Early Modern Europe: Studies on Sources and Methods.* De Kalb: Northern Illinois University Press, 1986.

Henrichs, Norbert. "Scientia magica." In *Der Wissenschaftsbegriff: Historische und systematische Untersuchungen: Vorträge und Diskussionen im April 1968 in Düsseldorf und im Oktober 1968 in Fulda,* ed. Alwin Diemer, 30-46. Studien zur Wissenschaftstheorie 4. Meisenheim: Verlag Anton Hain, 1970.

Hillerbrand, Hans Joachim, ed. *Radical Tendencies in the Reformation: Divergent Perspectives.* Sixteenth Century Essays and Studies 9. Kirksville, MO: Sixteenth Century Journal Publishers, 1988.

Hoffrichter, Leo. *Die ältesten französischen Bearbeitungen der Melusinensage.* Romanistische Arbeiten 12. Halle: Max Niemeyer Verlag, 1928.

Houdard, Sophie. *Les sciences du diable: quatre discours sur la sorcellerie (XVe-XVIIIe siècle).* Paris: Cerf, 1992.

Hunter, Dianne. "Hysteria, Psychoanalysis, and Feminism: The Case of Anna O." In *The (M)other Tongue: Essays in Feminist Psychoanalytic Interpretation,* ed. Shirley Nelson Garner, Claire Kahane, and Madelon Sprengnether, 89-115. Ithaca, NY: Cornell University Press, 1985.

Hunter, Michael, and David Wootton, eds. *Atheism from the Reformation to the Enlightenment.* Oxford: Clarendon Press; New York: Oxford University Press, 1992.

Janson, Stefan. *Jean Bodin-Johann Fischart: De la démonomanie des sorciers* (1580), *Vom aussgelasnen wütigen Teufelsheer* (1581) *und ihre Fallberichte.* Europäische Hochschulschriften 1.352. Frankfurt am Main: Peter Lang, 1980.

Joisten, Hartmut. *Der Grenzgänger Martin Bucer: Ein europäischer Reformator.* Stuttgart: Quell und Meyer Verlag, 1991.
Jones, Howard. *The Epicurean Tradition.* London: Routledge, 1989.
Jones-Davies, Margaret, ed. *La magie et ses langages.* Lille: Université de Lille III, 1980.
Junk, Ulrike. "'So müssen Weiber sein'": Zur Analyse eines Deutungsmusters von Weiblichkeit am Beispiele der *Melusine* des Thüring von Ringoltingen." In *Der frauwen buoch: Versuche zu einer feministischen Mediävistik,* ed. Ingrid Bennewitz, 327–57. Göppinger Arbeiten zur Germanistik 517. Göppingen: Kümmerle, 1989.
Kantorowicz, Ernst H. *The King's Two Bodies: A Study in Mediaeval Political Theology.* 1957. Reprint, Princeton, NJ: Princeton University Press, 1970.
Keefer, Michael H. "Agrippa's Dilemma: Hermetic 'Rebirth' and the Ambivalences of *De vanitate* and *De occulta philosophia.*" *Renaissance Quarterly* 41, no. 4 (1988): 614–53.
Keen, Benjamin. "The Vision of America in the Writings of Urbain Chauveton." In *First Images of America: The Impact of the New World on the Old,* ed. Fredi Chiappelli, Michael J. B. Allen, and Robert L. Benson, 1:107–20. Berkeley: University of California Press, 1976.
Keil, Gundolf, and Peter Assion, eds. *Fachprosaforschung: Acht Vorträge zur mittelalterlichen Artesliteratur.* Berlin: Erich Schmidt Verlag, 1974.
Kieckhefer, Richard. *European Witch Trials: Their Foundations in Popular and Learned Culture, 1300–1500.* Berkeley: University of California Press, 1976.
———. *Magic in the Middle Ages.* Cambridge: Cambridge University Press, 1990.
Klaits, Joseph. *Servants of Satan: The Age of the Witch Hunts.* Bloomington: Indiana University Press, 1985.
Klugsberger, Theresia. *Verfahren im Text: Meerjungfrauen in literarischen Versionen und mythischen Konstruktionen von H. C. Andersen, H. C. Artmann, K. Bayer, C. M. Wieland, O. Wilde.* Stuttgarter Arbeiten zur Germanistik 222. Stuttgart: Heinz Verlag, 1989.
Kobelt-Groch, Marion. "Von 'armen frouwen' und 'bösen wibern': Frauen im Bauernkrieg zwischen Anpassung und Auflehnung." *Archiv für Reformationsgeschichte* 79 (1988): 103–37.
Köhler, Hans-Joachim, ed. *Flugschriften als Massenmedien der Reformationszeit: Beiträge zum Tübinger Symposion 1980.* Spätmittelalter und frühe Neuzeit 13. Stuttgart: Klett-Cotta, 1981.
Kors, Alan Charles. *Atheism in France, 1650–1729.* Princeton, NJ: Princeton University Press, 1990.
Kriedte, Peter. "Die Hexen und ihre Ankläger: Zu den lokalen Voraussetzungen der Hexenverfolgungen in der frühen Neuzeit." *Zeitschrift für historische Forschung* 14, no. 1 (1987): 47–71.

Kristeller, Paul O. *Eight Philosophers of the Italian Renaissance*. 1964. Reprint, Stanford, CA: Stanford University Press, 1966.

Kuhn, Thomas S. *The Structure of Scientific Revolutions*. 2d ed. Chicago: University of Chicago Press, 1970.

Labouvie, Eva. "Männer im Hexenprozeß: Zur Sozialanthropologie eines 'männlichen' Verständnisses von Magie und Hexerei." *Geschichte und Gesellschaft: Zeitschrift für historische Sozialwissenschaft* 16, no. 1 (1990): 56–78.

Lakoff, George. *Women, Fire, and Dangerous Things: What Categories Reveal about the Mind*. Chicago: University of Chicago Press, 1987.

Landucci, Sergio. *I filosofi e i selvaggi, 1580–1780*. Biblioteca di cultura moderna 721. Bari: Editori Laterza, 1972.

Lange-Seidl, Annemarie, ed. *Zeichen und Magie: Akten des Kolloquiums der Bereiche Kultur und Recht der Deutschen Gesellschaft für Semiotik, 5.9.1986, Technische Universität München*. Probleme der Semiotik 8. Tübingen: Stauffenberg Verlag, 1988.

Laqueur, Thomas W. *Making Sex: Body and Gender from the Greeks to Freud*. Cambridge, MA: Harvard University Press, 1990.

Larner, Christina. "Crimen Exceptum? The Crime of Witchcraft in Europe." In *Crime and the Law: The Social History of Crime in Western Europe since 1500*, ed. V. A. C. Gatrell, Bruce Lenman, and Geoffrey Parker, 49–75. London: Europa Publications, 1980.

Lea, Henry Charles. *Geschichte der Inquisition im Mittelalter*. Ed. and trans. Heinz Wieck, Max Rachel, and Joseph Hansen. 3 vols. Nördlingen: Greno, 1987.

———. *Materials toward a History of Witchcraft*. Ed. Arthur C. Howland. 3 vols. Philadelphia: University of Pennsylvania Press, 1939.

Lecouteux, Claude. *Mélusine et le chevalier au cygne*. Paris: Payot, 1982.

———. "Le Merwunder." *Etudes germaniques* 32, no. 1 (1977): 1–11; 45, no. 1 (1990): 1–9.

———. "Das Motiv der gestörten Mahrtenehe als Widerspiegelung der menschlichen Psyche." *Vom Menschenbild im Märchen*. Ed. Jürgen Janning, Heino Gehrts, and Herbert Ossowski. Veröffentlichungen der europäischen Märchengesellschaft 1. Kassel: Erich Röth Verlag, 1980.

Le Goff, Jacques. "Melusine: Mother and Pioneer." *Time, Work, and Culture in the Middle Ages*. Trans. Arthur Goldhammer. Chicago: University of Chicago Press, 1980. 205–22.

Lehmann, Hartmut, and Otto Ulbricht, eds. *Vom Unfug des Hexen-Processes: Gegner der Hexenverfolgungen von Johann Weyer bis Friedrich Spee*. Wolfenbütteler Forschungen 55. Wiesbaden: Harrassowitz Verlag, 1992.

Le Roy Ladurie, Emmanuel. "Mélusine maternelle et défricheuse." *Annales: Economies, Sociétés, Civilisations* 26, no. 3–4 (1971): 587–622.

———. "Mélusine ruralisée." *Le territoire de l'historien.* Ed. Emmanuel Le Roy Ladurie. Paris: Gallimard, 1973. 281–98.

———. *The Royal French State, 1460–1610.* Trans. Juliet Vale. 1987. Reprint, Oxford: Blackwell Publishers, 1994.

Lestringant, Frank. "Catholiques et cannibales: le thème du cannibalisme dans le discours protestant au temps des guerres de religion." In *Pratiques et discours alimentaires à la Renaissance: actes du colloque de Tours de mars 1979, Centre d'études supérieures de la Renaissance,* ed. Jean-Claude Margolin and Robert Sauzet, 233–45. Paris: G. P. Maisonneuve et Larose, 1982.

———. *Ecrire le monde à la Renaissance: quinze études sur Rabelais, Postel, Bodin et la littérature géographique.* Collection Varia 6. Caen: Paradigme, 1993.

———. *Le huguenot et le sauvage: L'Amérique et la controverse coloniale en France, au temps des Guerres de Religion (1555–1589).* Paris: Aux Amateurs de Livres, 1990.

———. "Rage, fureur, folie, cannibales: le Scythe et le Brésilien." In *La folie et le corps: études,* ed. Jean Céard, 49–80. Paris: Presses de l'Ecole normale supérieure, 1985.

Lhereté, Jean-François. "Le juge et les sorciers: un inquisiteur laïc face à la culture populaire en France au XVIIe siècle." *Cultura / letteratura popolare / dotta nel seicento francese.* Ed. P. Carile et al. Quaderni del Seicento francese 3. Bari: Adriatica; Paris: Nizet, 1979.

Liebertz-Grün, Ursula. "Das Spiel der Signifikanten in der *Melusine* des Thüring von Ringoltingen." In *Ordnung und Lust: Bilder von Liebe, Ehe und Sexualität im Spätmittelalter und Früher Neuzeit,* ed. Hans-Jürgen Bachorski, 211–29. Literatur, Imagination, Realität 1. Trier: Wissenschaftlicher Verlag, 1991.

Lienhard, Marc, ed. *Croyants et sceptiques au XVIe siècle: le dossier des "Epicuriens": actes du Colloque organisé par le GRENEP, Strasbourg, 9–10 juin 1978.* Strasbourg: Librairie ISTRA, 1981.

———. "Les épicuriens à Strasbourg entre 1530 et 1550 et le problème de l'épicurisme au XVIe siècle." In *Croyants et sceptiques au XVIe siècle: le dossier des "Epicuriens": actes du Colloque organisé par le GRENEP, Strasbourg, 9–10 juin 1978,* ed. Marc Lienhard, 17–45. Strasbourg: Librairie ISTRA, 1981.

Lindberg, David C., and Robert S. Westman, eds. *Reappraisals of the Scientific Revolution.* Cambridge: Cambridge University Press, 1990.

Lubac, Henri de. *Pic de la Mirandole: études et discussions.* Paris: Aubier Montaigne, 1974.

Lugowski, Clemens. *Die Form der Individualität im Roman.* 1932. Suhrkamp Taschenbuch Wissenschaft 151. Frankfurt am Main: Suhrkamp Verlag, 1976.

Lundt, Bea. *Melusine und Merlin im Mittelalter: Entwürfe und Modelle weiblicher Existenz im Beziehungs-Diskurs der Geschlechter: Ein Beitrag zur historischen Erzählforschung.* Munich: Wilhelm Fink Verlag, 1991.

Maclean, Ian. *The Renaissance Notion of Woman: A Study in the Fortunes of Scholasticism and Medical Science in European Intellectual Life.* Cambridge: Cambridge University Press, 1980.

Mandrou, Robert. *Magistrats et sorciers en France au XVIIe siècle: une analyse de psychologie historique.* Paris: Plon, 1968.

Markdale, Jean. *Mélusine, ou l'androgyne.* Paris: Editions Retz, 1983.

Markus, Robert A. Review of *The Rise of Magic in Early Medieval Europe*, by Valerie Flint. *English Historical Review* 107, no. 422 (1992): 378–80.

Mauss, Marcel. *A General Theory of Magic.* Trans. Robert Brain. London: Routledge and Kegan Paul, 1972.

McKnight, Stephen A. *Sacralizing the Secular: The Renaissance Origins of Modernity.* Baton Rouge: Louisiana State University Press, 1989.

McLaughlin, R. Emmet. *Caspar Schwenkfeld: Reluctant Radical. His Life to 1540.* New Haven: Yale University Press, 1986.

Mebane, John S. *Renaissance Magic and the Return of the Golden Age: The Occult Tradition and Marlowe, Jonson and Shakespeare.* Lincoln: University of Nebraska Press, 1989.

Merkel, Ingrid, and Allen G. Debus, eds. *Hermeticism and the Renaissance: Intellectual History and the Occult in Early Modern Europe.* Washington, D.C.: Folger Shakespeare Library; London: Associated University Presses, 1988.

Mertens, Volker. "Melusinen, Undinen: Variationen des Mythos vom 12. bis zum 20. Jahrhundert." In *Festschrift Walter Haug und Burghart Wachinger,* ed. Johannes Janota et al., 1:201–32. Tübingen: Max Niemeyer Verlag, 1992.

Metzke, Erwin. *Coincidentia Oppositorum: Gesammelte Studien zur Philosophiegeschichte.* Ed. Karlfred Gründer. Forschungen und Berichte der evangelischen Studiengemeinschaft 19. Witten: Luther Verlag, 1961.

Midelfort, H. C. Erik. "Johann Weyer in medizinischer, theologischer und rechtsgeschichtlicher Hinsicht." In *Vom Unfug des Hexen-Processes: Gegner der Hexenverfolgungen von Johann Weyer bis Friedrich Spee,* ed. Hartmut Lehmann and Otto Ulbricht, 53–64. Wolfenbütteler Forschungen 55. Wiesbaden: Harrassowitz Verlag, 1992.

———. "Recent Witch Hunting Research, or, Where Do We Go from Here?" *The Papers of the Bibliographical Society of America* 62, no. 3 (1968): 373–420.

———. *Witch Hunting in Southwestern Germany, 1562–1684: The Social and Intellectual Foundations.* Stanford, CA: Stanford University Press, 1972.

Mies, Maria. "Colonization and Housewifeization." In *Patriarchy and Accumu-*

lation on a World Scale: Women in the International Division of Labour, 74–111. London: Zed Books, 1986.

Mignolo, Walter D. "The Darker Side of the Renaissance: Colonization and the Discontinuity of the Classical Tradition." *Renaissance Quarterly* 45, no. 4 (1992): 808–29.

Monter, E. William. *Frontiers of Heresy: The Spanish Inquisition from the Basque Lands to Sicily.* Cambridge: Cambridge University Press, 1990.

———. Review of *The Rise of Magic in Early Medieval Europe,* by Valerie Flint. *Journal of Social History* 26, no. 1 (1992): 200–201.

Moog, Hanna, ed. *Die Wasserfrau: Von geheimen Kräften, Sehsüchten und Ungeheuern mit Namen Hans.* Cologne: Eugen Diederichs Verlag, 1987.

Mora, George, and Benjamin Kohl, eds. *Witches, Devils, and Doctors in the Renaissance.* Trans. John Shea. Medieval and Renaissance Texts and Studies 73. Binghamton, NY: Medieval and Renaissance Texts and Studies, 1991.

Muchembled, Robert. *Les derniers bûchers: un village de Flandre et ses sorcières sous Louis XIV.* Paris: Ramsey, 1981.

———. "Satanic Myths and Cultural Reality." In *Early Modern European Witchcraft: Centres and Peripheries,* ed. Bengt Ankarloo and Gustav Henningsen, 139–61. Oxford: Clarendon Press, 1990.

———. Sorcières: justice et société aux 16e et 17e siècles. Paris: Editions Imago, 1987.

Mühlherr, Anna. "Geschichte und Liebe im Melusineroman." In *Positionen des Romans im späten Mittelalter,* ed. Walter Haug and Burghart Wachinger, 328–37. Fortuna vitrea 1. Tübingen: Max Niemeyer Verlag, 1991.

———. *"Melusine" und "Fortunatus": Verrätselter und verweigerter Sinn.* Fortuna vitrea 10. Tübingen: Max Niemeyer Verlag, 1993.

Müller, Jan-Dirk. "'Curiositas' und 'erfarung' der Welt im frühen deutschen Prosaroman." In *Literatur und Laienbildung im Spätmittelalter und in der Reformationszeit: Symposion Wolfenbüttel 1981,* ed. Ludger Grenzmann and Karl Stackmann, 252–73. Stuttgart: J. B. Metzler, 1984.

———. "'Erfarung' zwischen Heilssorge, Selbsterkenntnis und Entdeckung des Kosmos." *Daphnis* 15, no. 2–3 (1986): 307–42.

———. "Melusine in Bern: Zum Problem der 'Verbürgerlichung' höfischer Epik." In *Literatur, Publikum, historischer Kontext,* ed. Gert Kaiser, 29–77. Beiträge zur älteren deutschen Literaturgeschichte 1. Bern: Peter Lang, 1977.

Murray, Alexander. "The Epicureans." *Intellectuals and Writers in Fourteenth-Century Europe: The J. A. W. Bennett Memorial Lectures, Perugia, 1984.* Ed. Piero Boitani and Anna Torti. Tübinger Beiträge zur Anglistik 7. Tübingen: Günter Narr, 1986.

———. "Missionaries and Magic in Dark-Age Europe." Review of *The Rise of Magic in Early Medieval Europe,* by Valerie Flint. *Past and Present* 136 (1992): 186–205.

Nader, Helen. "The End of the Old World." *Renaissance Quarterly* 45, no. 4 (1992): 791–807.

Nauert, Charles G., Jr. *Agrippa and the Crisis of Renaissance Thought.* Illinois Studies in the Social Sciences 55. Urbana: University of Illinois Press, 1965.

Neuber, Wolfgang. *Fremde Welt im europäischen Horizont: Zur Topik der deutschen Amerika-Reiseberichte der Frühen Neuzeit.* Philologische Studien und Quellen 121. Berlin: Erich Schmidt Verlag, 1991.

Niccoli, Ottavia. "'Menstruum Quasi Monstruum': Monstrous Births and Menstrual Taboo in the Sixteenth Century." In *Sex and Gender in Historical Perspective,* ed. Edward Muir and Guido Ruggiero. Trans. Mary M. Gallucci, 1–25. Baltimore: Johns Hopkins University Press, 1990.

Oakley, Francis. *Omnipotence, Covenant and Order: An Excursion in the History of Ideas from Abelard to Leibniz.* Ithaca, NY: Cornell University Press, 1984.

Oberman, Heiko A. *Werden und Wertung der Reformation: Vom Wegestreit zum Glaubenskampf.* 2d ed. Spätscholastik und Reformation 2. Tübingen: J. C. B. Mohr, 1979.

Opie, Iona A., and Moire Tatem, eds. *A Dictionary of Superstitions.* Oxford: Oxford University Press, 1989.

Ozment, Steven. *The Age of Reform, 1250–1550: An Intellectual and Religious History of Late Medieval and Reformation Europe.* New Haven, CT: Yale University Press, 1980.

———. "Mysticism, Nominalism, and Dissent." In *The Pursuit of Holiness in Late Medieval and Renaissance Religion: Papers from the University of Michigan Conference,* ed. Charles Trinkaus and Heiko A. Oberman, 67–92. Studies in Medieval and Reformation Thought 10. Leiden: E. J. Brill, 1974.

———. *Mysticism and Dissent: Religious Ideology and Social Protest in the Sixteenth Century.* New Haven, CT: Yale University Press, 1973.

———. *When Fathers Ruled: Family Life in Reformation Europe.* Cambridge, MA: Harvard University Press, 1983.

Ozment, Steven, ed. *Three Behaim Boys: Growing Up in Early Modern Germany, a Chronicle of Their Lives.* New Haven, CT: Yale University Press, 1990.

Pagden, Anthony. *European Encounters with the New World: From Renaissance to Romanticism.* New Haven, CT: Yale University Press, 1993.

Pagel, Walter. *Das medizinische Weltbild des Paracelsus: Seine Zusammenhänge mit Neoplatonismus und Gnosis.* Kosmographie: Forschungen und Texte zur Geschichte des Weltbildes, der Naturphilosophie, der Mystik und des Spiritualismus vom Spätmittelalter bis zur Romantik 1. Wiesbaden: Franz Steiner Verlag, 1962.

———. "Paracelsus als 'Naturmystiker.'" In *Epochen der Naturmystik: Herme-*

tische Tradition im wissenschaftlichen Fortschritt, ed. Antoine Faivre, Rolf C. Zimmermann et al., 52–104. Berlin: Erich Schmidt Verlag, 1979.

———. *Paracelsus: An Introduction to Philosophical Medicine in the Era of the Renaissance*. Basel: S. Karger, 1958.

Pagels, Elaine H. *Adam, Eve, and the Serpent*. New York: Random House, 1988.

Park, Katharine, and Lorraine J. Daston. "Unnatural Conceptions: The Study of Monsters in Sixteenth and Seventeenth Century France and England." *Past and Present* 92 (1981): 20–54.

Parkin, Nora. "Melusine." Ph.D. Diss., Washington University, 1993.

Pastor Bodmer, Beatriz. *The Armature of Conquest: Spanish Accounts of the Discovery of America, 1492–1589*. Trans. Lydia L. Hunt. Stanford, CA: Stanford University Press, 1992.

Paxton, Frederick S. Review of *The Rise of Magic in Early Medieval Europe*, by Valerie Flint. *American Historical Review* 97, no. 3 (1992): 830–31.

Pearl, Jonathan L. "Humanism and Satanism: Jean Bodin's Contribution to the Witchcraft Crisis." *Canadian Review of Sociology and Anthropology* 19, no. 4 (1982): 541–48.

Peters, Edward. *The Magician, the Witch, and the Law*. Philadelphia: University of Pennsylvania Press, 1978.

———. Review of *The Rise of Magic in Early Medieval Europe*, by Valerie Flint. *Catholic Historical Review* 78, no. 1 (1992): 270–73.

———. *Torture*. New York: Basil Blackwell, 1985.

Petzoldt, Leander, ed. *Magie und Religion: Beiträge zu einer Theorie der Magie*. Wege der Forschung 337. Darmstadt: Wissenschaftliche Buchgesellschaft, 1978.

Peuckert, Will-Erich. *Gabalia: Ein Versuch zur Geschichte der Magia naturalis im 16. bis 18. Jahrhundert*. Berlin: Erich Schmidt Verlag, 1967.

Pico della Mirandola, Giovanni. *Oration on the Dignity of Man*. Trans. A. Robert Caponigri. 1956. Reprint, Washington, D. C.: Gateway, 1991.

Pine, Martin L. *Pietro Pomponazzi: Radical Philosopher of the Renaissance*. Saggi e testi 21. Padua: Editrice Antenore, 1986.

———. "Pomponazzi and the Problem of 'Double Truth.'" *Journal of the History of Ideas* 29 (1968): 163–176.

Pintard, René. *Le libertinage érudit dans la première moitié du XVIIe siècle*. 2 vols. Paris: Boivin, 1943. Geneva: Slatkine, 1983.

Pitz, Ernst. "Diplomatische Studien zu den päpstlichen Erlassen über das Zauber- und Hexenwesen." In *Der Hexenhammer: Entstehung und Umfeld des Malleus Maleficarum von 1487*, ed. Peter Segl, 23–70. Bayreuther historische Kolloquien 2. Cologne: Böhlau Verlag, 1988.

Pohl, Herbert. *Hexenglaube und Hexenverfolgung im Kurfürstentum Mainz: Ein Beitrag zur Hexenfrage im 16. und beginnenden 17. Jahrhundert*. Geschichtliche Landeskunde 32. Stuttgart: Franz Steiner Verlag, 1988.

Pörksen, Gunhild. "Die Bewohner der Elemente nach Paracelsus' 'Liber de nymphis.'" *Nova Acta Paracelsica* 6 (1991/92): 29–50.

Préaud, Maxime. "La *Démonomanie*, fille de la *République*." In *Jean Bodin: actes du colloque interdisciplinaire d'Angers, 24 au 27 mai 1985*, 2:419–29. Angers: Presses de l'Université d'Angers, 1985.

Riezler, Sigmund. *Geschichte der Hexenprozesse in Bayern: Im Licht der allgemeinen Entwicklung*. Stuttgart: J. G. Cotta, 1896.

Robbins, Russell H., ed. *The Encyclopedia of Witchcraft and Demonology*. London: Crown Publishers, 1959.

Robisheaux, Thomas W. *Rural Society and the Search for Order in Early Modern Germany*. Cambridge: Cambridge University Press, 1989.

Roper, Lyndal. *The Holy Household: Women and Morals in Reformation Augsburg*. Oxford: Clarendon Press; New York: Oxford University Press, 1989.

Rose, Mary Beth. *The Expense of Spirit: Love and Sexuality in English Renaissance Drama*. Ithaca, NY: Cornell University Press, 1988.

Rose, Paul Lawrence. *Bodin and the Great God of Nature: The Moral and Religious Universe of a Judaiser*. Travaux d'humanisme et Renaissance 179. Geneva: Droz, 1980.

Rott, Jean. "Le magistrat face à l'épicurisme terre à terre des strasbourgeois: note sur les reglements disciplinaires municipaux de 1440 à 1599." In *Croyants et sceptiques au XVIe siècle: le dossier des "Epicuriens": actes du Colloque organisé par le GRENEP, Strasbourg, 9–10 juin 1978*, ed. Marc Lienhard, 57–62. Strasbourg: Librairie ISTRA, 1981.

Rouget, Gilbert. *La musique et la transe: esquisse d'une théorie générale des relations de la musique et de la possession*. Paris: Gallimard, 1980.

Roussineau, Gilles. "Peur et répression du mal dans la *Démonomanie des sorciers de Jean Bodin*." In *Jean Bodin: actes du colloque interdisciplinaire d'Angers, 24 au 27 mai 1985*, 2:411–18. Angers: Presses de l'Université d'Angers, 1985.

Rummel, Walter. "Soziale Dynamik und herrschaftliche Problematik der kurtrierischen Hexenverfolgungen: Das Beispiel der Stadt Cochem (1593–1595)." *Geschichte und Gesellschaft: Zeitschrift für historische Sozialwissenschaft* 16, no. 1 (1990): 26–55.

Saillot, Jacques. "Jean Bodin, sa famille, ses origines." In *Jean Bodin: actes du colloque interdisciplinaire d'Angers, 24 au 27 mai 1985*, 1:111–19. Angers: Presses de l'Université d'Angers, 1985.

Salisbury, Joyce E. *Medieval Sexuality: A Research Guide*. Garland Medieval Bibliographies 5. New York: Garland Publishing, 1990.

Salisbury, Joyce E., ed. *Sex in the Middle Ages: A Book of Essays*. Garland Medieval Casebooks 3. New York: Garland Publishing, 1991.

Schairer, Immanuel B. *Das religiöse Volksleben am Ausgang des Mittelalters nach Augsburger Quellen.* Leipzig: B. G. Teubner, 1913.

Schieder, Wolfgang. "Hexenverfolgungen als Gegenstand der Sozialgeschichte." *Geschichte und Gesellschaft: Zeitschrift für historische Sozialwissenschaft* 16 (1990): 5–7.

Schiffman, Zachary S. *On the Threshold of Modernity: Relativism in the French Renaissance.* Baltimore: Johns Hopkins University Press, 1991.

Schipperges, Heinrich. *Paracelsus: Der Mensch im Licht der Natur.* Stuttgart: Ernst Klett, 1974.

Schneider, Gerhard. *Der Libertin: Zur Geistes- und Sozialgeschichte des Bürgertums im 16. und 17. Jahrhundert.* Studien zur allgemeinen und vergleichenden Literaturwissenschaft 4. Stuttgart: J. B. Metzler, 1970.

Schnyder, André. "Johann Fischart als Bearbeiter eines mittelalterlichen Märes: Veränderungen ästhetischer Darstellungsverfahren und kultureller Deutungsmuster im 'Peter von Stauffenberg.'" *Wirkendes Wort* 39, no. 1 (1989): 15–43.

———. "Der *Malleus Maleficarum*: Fragen und Beobachtungen zu seiner Druckgeschichte sowie zur Rezeption bei Bodin, Binsfeld und Delrio." *Archiv für Kulturgeschichte* 74, no. 2 (1992): 323–64.

———. "Der *Malleus Maleficarum*: Unvorgreifliche Überlegungen und Beobachtungen zum Problem der Textform." In *Der Hexenhammer: Entstehung und Umfeld des Malleus Maleficarum von 1487,* ed. Peter Segl, 127–49. Bayreuther historische Kolloquien 2. Cologne: Böhlau Verlag, 1988.

Schormann, Gerhard. *Hexenprozesse in Deutschland.* 2d ed. Göttingen: Vandenhoeck und Ruprecht, 1986.

Schwab, Gabriele. "Seduced by Witches: Nathanial Hawthorne's *The Scarlet Letter* in the Context of New England Witchcraft Fictions." In *Seduction and Theory: Readings of Gender, Representation, and Rhetoric,* ed. Dianne Hunter, 170–91. Urbana: University of Illinois Press, 1989.

Schwerhoff, Gerd. "Rationalität im Wahn: Zum gelehrten Diskurs über die Hexen in der frühen Neuzeit." *Saeculum* 37, no. 1 (1986): 45–82.

Scott, Joan W. "Gender: A Useful Category of Historical Analysis." *American Historical Review* 91, no. 5 (1986): 1053–75.

Scribner, Robert W. "Sorcery, Superstition, and Society: The Witch of Urach, 1529." In *Popular Culture and Popular Movements in Reformation Germany,* 257–75. London: Hambledon Press, 1987.

Segl, Peter. "Henricus Institorius: Persönlichkeit und literarisches Werk." In *Der Hexenhammer: Entstehung und Umfeld des Malleus Maleficarum von 1487,* ed. Peter Segl, 103–26. Bayreuther historische Kolloquien 2. Cologne: Böhlau Verlag, 1988.

Segl, Peter, ed. *Der Hexenhammer: Entstehung und Umfeld des Malleus*

Maleficarum *von 1487*. Bayreuther historische Kolloquien 2. Cologne: Böhlau Verlag, 1988.

Shumaker, Wayne. *The Occult Sciences in the Renaissance: A Study in Intellectual Patterns*. Berkeley: University of California Press, 1972.

Simon, Manuel. *Heilige, Hexe, Mutter: Der Wandel des Frauenbildes durch die Medizin im 16. Jahrhundert*. Historische Anthropologie 20. Berlin: Dietrich Reimer Verlag, 1993.

Soldan, Wilhelm G. *Geschichte der Hexenprozesse*. 1843. Ed. Heinrich Heppe and Sabine Ries. Reprint, Essen: Athenaion, 1990.

Spini, Giorgio. "Ritratto del protestante come libertino." In *Ricerche su letteratura libertina e letteratura clandestina nel seicento: atti del convegno di studio di Genova (30 ottobre–1 novembre 1980)*, ed. Tullio Gregory et al., 177–88. Florence: La nuova Italia Editrice, 1981.

Staff, Anneliese. "Von Hexen / Zauberern / Unholden / Schwarzkünstlern / und Teufeln . . . : Bibliographie zu den Beständen der Hexenliteratur der Herzog August Bibliothek Wolfenbüttel." In *Vom Unfug des Hexen-Processes: Gegner der Hexenverfolgungen von Johann Weyer bis Friedrich Spee*, ed. Hartmut Lehmann and Otto Ulbricht, 341–91. Wolfenbütteler Forschungen 55. Wiesbaden: Harrassowitz Verlag, 1992.

Stallybrass, Peter, and Allan White. *The Politics and Poetics of Transgression*. Ithaca, NY: Cornell University Press, 1986.

Stouff, Louis. *Essai sur Mélusine: roman du XIVe siècle par Jean d'Arras*. Dijon: Picard, 1930.

Stuby, Anna M. *Liebe, Tod und Wasserfrau: Mythen des Weiblichen in der Literatur*. Opladen: Westdeutscher Verlag, 1992.

Tedeschi, John. "Inquisitorial Law and the Witch." In *Early Modern European Witchcraft: Centres and Peripheries*, ed. Bengt Ankarloo and Gustav Henningsen, 83–118. Oxford: Clarendon Press, 1990.

Tenenti, Alberto. "Milieu XVIe siècle: libertinisme et hérésie." *Annales: Economies, Sociétés, Civilisations* 18, no. 1 (1963): 1–19.

Thomas, Brook. "Stephen Greenblatt and the Limits of Mimesis for Historical Criticism." In *The New Historicism: And Other Old-Fashioned Topics*, 179–218. Princeton, NJ: Princeton University Press, 1991.

Thomas, Keith. *Religion and the Decline of Magic: Studies in Popular Beliefs in Sixteenth and Seventeenth Century England*. London: Weidenfeld and Nicolson, 1971.

Thorndike, Lynn. *A History of Magic and Experimental Science*. 8 vols. New York: Macmillan, 1923–58.

Todorov, Tzvetan. *The Conquest of America: The Question of the Other*. Trans. Richard Howard. New York: Harper and Row, 1984.

Tomlinson, Gary. *Music in Renaissance Magic: Toward a Historiography of Others*. Chicago: University of Chicago Press, 1993.

Trinkaus, Charles. In *Our Image and Likeness: Humanity and Divinity in Italian Humanist Thought*. 2 vols. Chicago: University of Chicago Press, 1970.

Truax, Jean A. Review of *The Rise of Magic in Early Medieval Europe*, by Valerie Flint. *Speculum* 68, no. 3 (1993): 768–70.

Unverhau, Dagmar. "Akkusationsprozeß-Inquisitionsprozeß: Indikatoren für die Intensität der Hexenverfolgung in Schleswig-Holstein? Überlegungen und Untersuchungen zu einer Typologie der Hexenprozesse." In *Hexenprozesse: Deutsche und skandinavische Beiträge*, ed. Christian Degn, Hartmut Lehmann and Dagmar Unverhau, 59–143. Studien zur Volkskunde und Kulturgeschichte Schleswig-Holsteins 12. Neumünster: Karl Wachholtz Verlag, 1983.

Vance, Eugene. *From Topic to Tale: Logic and Narrativity in the Middle Ages*. Theory and History of Literature 47. Minneapolis: University of Minnesota Press, 1987.

———. *Mervelous Signals: Poetics and Sign Theory in the Middle Ages*. Lincoln: University of Nebraska Press, 1986.

Van Nahl, Rudolf. *Zauberglaube und Hexenwahn im Gebiet von Rhein und Maas: Spätmittelalterlicher Volksglaube im Werk Johan Weyers (1515–1586)*. Rheinisches Archiv 116. Bonn: Ludwig Röhrscheid Verlag, 1983.

Vickers, Brian. "Analogy versus Identity: The Rejection of Occult Symbolism, 1580–1680." In *Occult and Scientific Mentalities in the Renaissance*, ed. Brian Vickers, 95–163. Cambridge: Cambridge University Press, 1984.

———. "Francis Yates and the Writing of History." *Journal of Modern History* 51, no. 2 (1979): 287–316.

Vickers, Brian, ed. *Occult and Scientific Mentalities in the Renaissance*. Cambridge: Cambridge University Press, 1984.

Walker, Daniel P. *The Ancient Theology: Studies in Christian Platonism from the Fifteenth to the Eighteenth Century*. Ithaca, NY: Cornell University Press, 1972.

———. *Spiritual and Demonic Magic from Ficino to Campanella*. London: Warburg Institute, University of London, 1958.

Wear, Andrew, R. K. French, and I. M. Lonie, eds. *The Medical Renaissance of the Sixteenth Century*. Cambridge: Cambridge University Press, 1985.

Weber, Hartwig. *Kinderhexenprozesse*. Frankfurt am Main: Insel Verlag, 1991.

Webster, Charles. *From Paracelsus to Newton: Magic and the Making of Modern Science*. Cambridge: Cambridge University Press, 1982.

Wiesner, Merry E. *Working Women in Renaissance Germany*. New Brunswick, NJ: Rutgers University Press, 1986.

Williams, George H. *The Radical Reformation*. 3d ed. Sixteenth Century Essays and Studies 15. Kirksville, MO: Sixteenth Century Journal Publishers, 1992.

Williams, Gerhild Scholz. "Altes Wissen – Neue Welt: Magie und die Entdeckung

Amerikas im 16. Jahrhundert." In *Gutenberg und die neue Welt*, ed. Horst Wenzel. Munich: Wilhelm Fink Verlag, 1994.

———. The Death of Love: *Mélusine* (1392) and *Dr. Faustus* (1587)." In *Love and Death in the Renaissance*, ed. Kenneth R. Bartlett, Konrad Eisenbichler, and Janice Liedl, 183–97. Ottawa: Dovehouse Editions, 1991.

———. "Faust verführt: Epikur in der Frühen Neuzeit." *Festschrift Walter Haug und Burghart Wachinger*. Ed. Johannes Janota et al. Tübingen: Max Niemeyer Verlag, 1992. 1:123–38.

———. "On Finding Words: Witchcraft and the Discourses of Dissidence and Discovery." In *The Graph of Sex and the German Text: Gendered Culture in Early Modern Germany, 1500–1700*, ed. Lynne Tatlock and Christiane Bohnert, 45–66. Chloe Beihefte zum *Daphnis* 19. Amsterdam: Rodopi, 1994.

———. "Frühmoderne Transgressionen: Sex und Magie in der *Melusine* und bei Paracelsus." *Daphnis* 20, no. 1 (1991): 81–100.

———. "Gemeinsame Sache: Johann Fischarts Übersetzung von Jean Bodins *Démonomanie des sorciers* (1580/81)." Forthcoming.

———. "Mélusine/Melusine: Erfahrungsdeterminierter Realismus im frühneuzeitlichen Roman." *Lili: Zeitschrift für Literaturwissenschaft und Linguistik* 23, no. 89 (1993): 10–23.

———. "Provokation und Antwort: Hans Blumenbergs Frühe Neuzeit." *"Der Buchstab tödt, der Geist macht lebendig": Festschrift zum 60. Geburtstag von Hans-Gert Roloff von Freunden, Schülern und Kollegen*. Ed. James Hardin and Jörg Jungmayr, 1:109–26. Bern: Peter Lang, 1992.

———. "The Woman/The Witch: Variations on a Sixteenth-Century Theme (Paracelsus, Wier, Bodin)." In *The Crannied Wall: Women, Religion, and the Arts in Early Modern Europe*, ed. Craig A. Monson, 124–27. Ann Arbor: University of Michigan Press, 1992.

———. "Der Zauber der neuen Welt: Reise und Magie im sechzehnten Jahrhundert." *German Quarterly* 65, no. 3–4 (1992): 294–305.

Williams, Gerhild Scholz, and Steven Rowan. "Jacob Spiegel on Gianfrancesco Pico and Reuchlin: Poetry, Scholarship, and Politics in Germany in 1512." *Bibliothèque d'humanisme et Renaissance* 44, no. 2 (1982): 291–305.

Wiltenburg, Joy D. *Disorderly Women and Female Power in the Street Literature of Early Modern England and Germany*. Charlottesville: University Press of Virginia, 1992.

Wolf, Hans-Jürgen. *Hexenwahn: Hexen in Geschichte und Gegenwart*. 2d ed. Dornstadt: Historia Verlag, 1990.

Wootton, David. "Lucien Febvre and the Problem of Unbelief in the Early Modern Period." *Journal of Modern History* 60, no. 4 (1988): 695–730.

———. "New Histories of Atheism." In *Atheism from the Reformation to the Enlightenment*, ed. Michael Hunter and David Wootton, 13–53. Oxford: Clarendon Press; New York: Oxford University Press, 1992.

———. "Unbelief in Early Modern Europe." *History Workshop: A Journal of Socialist and Feminist Historians* 20 (1985): 82–100.

Wunder, Heide. "Hexenprozesse im Herzogtum Preussen während des 16. Jahrhunderts." In *Hexenprozesse: Deutsche und skandinavische Beiträge*, ed. Christian Degn, Hartmut Lehmann, and Dagmar Unverhau, 192–204. Studien zur Volkskunde und Kulturgeschichte Schleswig-Holsteins 12. Neumünster: Karl Wachholtz Verlag, 1983.

Wuttke, Dieter. "Sebastian Brants Verhältnis zu Wunderdeutungen und Astrologie." In *Studien zur deutschen Literatur und Sprache des Mittelalters: Festschrift für Hugo Moser zum 65. Geburtstag*, ed. Werner Besch et al., 272–86. Berlin: Erich Schmidt Verlag, 1974.

Yates, Frances A. *Giordano Bruno and the Hermetic Tradition*. Chicago: University of Chicago Press, 1964.

Yoder, John. Conclusion to *Croyants et sceptiques au XVIe siècle: le dossier des "Epicuriens": actes du Colloque organisé par le GRENEP, Strasbourg, 9–10 juin 1978*, ed. Marc Lienhard, 163–67. Strasbourg: Librairie ISTRA, 1981.

Zagorin, Perez. *Ways of Lying: Dissimulation, Persecution, and Conformity in Early Modern Europe*. Cambridge, MA: Harvard University Press, 1990.

Zambelli, Paola, ed. *"Astrologi hallucinati": Stars and the End of the World in Luther's Time*. Berlin: Walter de Gruyter, 1986.

———. "Scholastiker und Humanisten: Agrippa und Trithemius zur Hexerei, die natürliche Magie und die Entstehung kritisches Denkens." *Archiv für Kirchengeschichte* 67, no. 1 (1985): 41–79.

Ziegeler, Wolfgang. *Möglichkeiten der Kritik am Hexen- und Zauberwesen im ausgehenden Mittelalter: Zeitgenössische Stimmen und ihre soziale Zugehörigkeit*. Kollektive Einstellungen und sozialer Wandel im Mittelalter 2. Cologne: Böhlau Verlag, 1973.

Zilboorg, Gregory. *The Medical Man and the Witch during the Renaissance*. Baltimore: Johns Hopkins University Press, 1935.

Index

Abortions, 16
Absolution, 44
Adam, 52
Adam and Eve, 11, 47, 52, 111
Adultery, 48
Africa, 19
Agnan (Aygnan), 77
Agrippa of Nettesheim, 7, 13, 67, 98
America, 19, 53, 77, 85
Amor and Psyche, 23
Anabaptists, 127
Anarchy, social, 130
Antiquity, 20
Apollo, 95
Apulia, 114
Arcana, magical, 103
Aristotle, 28, 46
Arthur, 29
Ascendant, 61, 62
Atheism, 4, 21, 119, 129, 140, 142
Atheists, 3, 121, 143
Auto-da fé, 105, 106, 124
Avalon, 30

Bankert, 55
Baroja, Julio Caro, 91
Basque, 17, 90, 94, 107, 110, 116
Basso, Isa Dardano, 91, 93
Behaviors, asocial, 59
Behringer, Wolfgang, 68, 76
"Belle dame," 33
Benandanti, 13
Benedictes, 112
Benzoni, Girolamo, 77

Bergerac, Cyrano de, 122
Birth, 29, 60 (*see also* Childbirth; Procreation)
  freak, 58
  triple, 52
Birthmark, 34, 38
Bishop of Pamplona, 104
Bloch, R. Howard, 19
Blumenberg, Hans, 9
Bocal, Pierre, 117
Bodies
  divine, 49
  elemental, 49, 58
  stellar, 58
Bodin, Jean, 4, 8, 47, 57, 58, 62, 65–88, 89, 90, 96, 98, 103, 104, 121, 122, 123, 124, 125, 130, 132, 135, 136
Bohemes, Bohemienne, 114
Books, miracle, 15
Brazil, 140
Broadsheets, 124
Brunfels, Otto, 142
Bruno, Giordano, 77, 143
Bucer, Martin, 127, 142

Calvin, Jean, 122, 128, 133, 143
Calvinists, 127, 129
Cannibalism, 85, 140
Cardano, Girolamo, 7, 77
Castellio, Sebastian, 142
Castration, 55, 73, 86
Catholic, 127
Céard, Jean, 93, 106

230 Index

Charron, Pierre, 48, 130
Chauveton, Urbain (Calvetus, Urbanus), 77
Childbirth, 28, 74 (see also Birth)
Children
  "bon age," 118
  possessed, 117, 119
  testimony of, 118
Clark, Stuart, 18
Claude de Sainctes, 128
Cohn, Norman, 1
Colloquium Heptaplomeres, 8, 98
Columbus, Christopher, 78, 85, 116
Conception, 55–56, 57, 59, 60, 61, 74 (see also Procreation)
Concote, 86
Confession, 125
Conjuring, of dead, 16
Conquerors, 9, 48
Control, social, 11, 12
Copulation, satanic, 114
Cosmology, 3, 14, 18
Cosmos, 16, 27, 43, 46, 65, 123
Couldrette, 24
Council of Trent, 76
Counter-Reformation, 123
Creation, third, 54
Crimen exceptum, 75
Curiosity, scientific, 9, 13, 125

D'Arras, Jean, 23–44
Dancing, 114, 115–16
De Certeau, Michel, 3, 20, 93
"De Chastel de l'Espervier," 41
De Fugueroa, Antonio Venegas, 103
De La Noue, François, 131
De la sagesse livres trois, 130
De praestigiis daemonum, 7, 8, 68, 78, 82, 99, 136
De sagis, 7
Deists, 8, 121
Delumeau, Jean, 18
Delusion, satanic, 81
Demonologists, 57, 73
Demonology, 3, 90, 138

Démonomanie des sorciers, 8, 68, 98, 121, 125, 132, 134
Denck, Hans, 142
Dependence, satanic, 59
D'Eschaux, Bernard, 93
"Devil's whores," 60
Discourse, 2, 3, 9, 11, 15, 65, 121, 126
  cosmographical, 20
  magic, 2, 4, 7, 8, 14, 17, 20, 66
  religious, 127, 144, 145
Discovery, 3, 48
Dissension, religious, 4, 138
Dissidence, religious, 3, 10, 12, 19, 133, 141, 143, 145
Dissidents, religious, 3, 10, 12, 20, 140
Dissimulation, religious, 3, 10, 12, 131, 133, 145
Diversité, 121
Diversity, religious, 3, 121–45
Divorce, 58
Dogmatization, 126
Dürer, Albrecht, 47

Ehelich, 55
Elements, 45
Engelbrecht, Anton, 142
Epicureans, 121, 131, 133, 140, 142, 143 (see also Dissenters)
Episteme, 9, 63
Epistemology, 2, 3, 6, 9, 10, 49, 67, 97, 108, 138
Espaignet, 99, 101
Europe, 6, 12, 15, 141
Evidence, circumstantial, 76

Fabelwerk, 84
Farel, Guillaume, 122
Faust, 119
Fées, 67
Femininity, 15, 56
Ferrand, Jacques, 111
Ficino, Marsilio, 6, 7, 48, 49
Fischart, Johann, 4, 8, 67, 68, 69–70, 85, 86, 87, 89, 134
Flint, Valerie, 15

Florence, Italy, 6
Force, demonic, 30
Foucault, Michel, 9
Franck, Sebastian, 142
Fratricide, 24, 30, 36, 38
Free will, 54
Frías, Alonso de Salazar (see Salazar)
Funkenstein, Amos, 9

Gender, 11, 65–87
Ghosts, 27
Giants, 27, 52
Gilbert, Neal, 20
Ginzburg, Carlos, 13
Glosses, 15
Gödelmann, Johann, 82
Goldammer, Kurt, 5
Grillando, Paul, 98
Gruet, Jacques, 143
Gypsies, 49

Hartwilerin, Johanna, 83
Haug, Walter, 19, 26
Henningsen, Gustav, 13, 94
Henry IV of France, 90, 101
Herbs, 78
Heresy, 10, 119
Hermaphrodites, 57
Hermeneutics, 2, 49
Heterodoxy, 9, 11
Hexengeister, 62
Hexenhebammen, 72, 119
Hincmar, Bishop, 16
Historiography, 12
History, family, 26, 32, 41, 42
Holy Land, 30
Honor, 39
Hossius, Stanislas, 140
Hualde, 107, 116
Hubris, 25, 48

Idolatry, 119
Illegitimacy, 55
Imaginatio, 57
Inconstance, 108, 121
Inconstancy, 100

Incubus, 16, 60, 78
Inquisition, Spanish, 103, 104
Inquisitors, 21, 71, 76, 91, 104, 126
Intercourse, 84
Interdict, 24, 27, 29, 33
  divine, 58
  social, 59
Interlangage féminin, 145
Interpreter, 108
"Invisible illnesses," 56
Irreligion, 131, 143
Iureteguia, Marie de, 106

Jean, duc de Berry, 25
Jesus Christ, 11, 25, 32, 46, 56, 128
Jewish sources, 16, 61
Jews, 49, 63, 75
"Judaizer," 87
Jurisprudence, 11
Justice, 40

King Roger, 89
Knowledge, arcane, 16
Kramer, Heinrich (Institoris), 1, 8, 65–88, 123, 124, 125, 134, 135, 144
Kuhn, Thomas S., 9

Labourdins, 91, 92, 93, 97, 109, 112, 121
Labourt, 90, 91, 94, 100, 107, 117, 130
Lakoff, George, 18
Lamia, 80
Lancre, Pierre de, 5, 8, 17, 89–119, 121, 122, 123, 124, 125, 130, 133, 135, 136
Language, 126
Laqueur, Thomas, 81
Las Casas, Bartholomé de, 116
Latenzphase, 76
Law
  canon, 76
  imperial, 75
  inquisitorial, 76
Le Loyer, Pierre, 130
Legereté, 121

Index

Lerchheimer, Augustin, 137
Léry, Jean de, 140, 141
Lesbianism, 81
Lessing, Gotthold, 9
Liberté, 121
Libertines, 4, 8, 121, 128, 129, 130, 140, 143 (see also Dissenters)
Lightness, devilish, 114
Limus terrae, 51
Lindanus, Willhelm (Guillaume Lindan), 128
Literature, travel, 19
Livre des princes, 98, 132
Logroño, 105, 106, 124
Loyalties, 39
Lucifer, 25, 47
Luther, Martin, 27, 47, 50, 126
Lutheran, 127

Macht, 14
Magia naturalis, 46
Magic, 2, 3, 4, 5, 11, 13, 15, 23, 65, 135, 141
   aura of, 24
   black, 10, 11, 50, 90
   demonic, 4
   and gender, 65–87
   and history, 26
   love, 16
   and margins, 89–119
   and myth of transgression, 23–44
   and religious diversity, 121–45
   satanic, 6, 9
   and science of man and woman, 45–63
   scientific, 21, 62
   white, 10, 49, 50 (see also *Scientia magica*)
Magistrates, 21, 132
Magus, 15, 16, 20, 48, 78, 98
Maimonides, Moses, 75
Malleus Maleficarum, the Witches' Hammer, 1, 2, 8, 15, 50, 54, 65, 68, 71, 76, 79, 87, 90, 119, 123, 134, 135
Mandrou, Robert, 18

Marginalization, 3, 9, 59, 83, 126
Margins, 11, 89, 120, 126, 89–119
Marriage, 54, 55, 58, 59, 74, 79, 126
Mary, 11
Masculinity, 15, 56
Mass, Black, 97
Masturbation, 80
Matrix, 55, 57, 58, 60
Medicine, 57, 65
Melancholy, 57
Mélusine, 5, 23–43, 45, 65, 66, 89, 125, 135 (see also Mélusine de Lusignan)
Mélusine, 5, 7, 23–43, 65, 125
Mélusine de Lusignan, 16, 23–44
Memory, 44
Menstruation, 60
Mentalities, history of, 18
Mentality, early modern, 3
Metaphysics, 50
Midelfort, H. C. Erik, 1, 2, 10
Monster, 27, 58, 60
Monstra, 52, 53, 57, 60
Mörfinnen, 67
Morgana, Faye, 29, 41
Muchembled, Robert, 18
Multiplicité, 108
Mysticism, 14
Myth, 67, 95, 135
   founding, 25
   of transgression, 23–44

Narrative, 2, 26, 28
Nathan der Weise, 9
Natives, New World, 10, 12, 19, 20, 85, 102, 141, 145
Navarra, 91, 103
Neo-historicists, 26
Neuber, Wolfgang, 19
"New creatures," 53
"New people," 52, 77 (see also Natives)
New World, 3, 4, 6, 9, 12, 84, 85, 100, 126, 144 (see also Natives)
Nicodemism, 131, 132, 140, 142

Nympha, 52
Nymphen, 45, 52

Olaus Magnus, Bischoff von Upsal, 85
Old World, 6, 13, 141
"One-sex model," 81
Order
  cosmic, 16 (*see also* Cosmos)
  political, 12
Orthodoxy, religious, 4, 6, 11, 12, 94, 104, 121, 123, 127, 135, 140, 143, 144

Padua, Italy, 6
Pamplona, bishop of, 126
Paracelsus, 5, 7, 8, 13, 45–63, 65, 88, 99, 127, 133, 135
Paradise, 48
Paré, Ambroise, 60
Parliament of Bordeaux, 87, 90, 93, 96, 101
Patrimony, 33
"Peinlich Befragung," 134
Peter, Edward, 1
Philosophia
  adepta, 46
  sagax, 8, 51
Philosophy, 11, 18
Physicians, 48
  charlatan, 49
Pico della Mirandola, Gianfresco, 7, 13
Pico della Mirandola, Giovanni, 7, 13, 48, 49, 50, 98, 130
Pitz, Ernst, 70
Pomponazzi, Pietro, 6, 129
Pope Innocent VIII, 70
Pope Paul III, 4
Portents, 24, 36
Possession, 70
Post-Reformation, 6, 9, 123
Praetorius, Antonius (Schultze) (*see* Scultetus, Johann)
Predestination, 54, 58
Prescience, 37
Prisca theologia, 16

Procreation, 55, 59 (*see also* Birth; Conception)

Rabelais, François, 8
Radicalism, religious, 131
Realism, experiential, 18, 19, 21, 26, 66, 100, 144
Religion, 5, 65 (*see also* Orthodoxy)
Ringoltingen, Thüring von, 24, 26, 65
Ritterspiegel, 35
Ritual, pagan, 78 (*see also* Sabbath)
Rudolf of Hochberg, 24

Sabbath, witches', 16, 85, 95, 100, 103, 104, 106, 107, 114, 117, 135
Sacraments, 74
Salazar, 91, 103, 104, 105, 106, 119, 126
Salvation, 32, 44
Sancerre, siege of, 85
Saracens, 63
Satan, 4, 10, 11, 58, 61, 62, 65, 68, 71, 77, 84, 89, 98, 100, 101, 104, 108, 113, 117, 118, 124, 130, 139
Satanic Other, 102
Satanism, 21, 98
Schnyder, André, 2
Science, occult, 6, 7, 18, 66
Scientia magica, 5, 6, 11, 48, 49, 55, 65, 98, 123
Scott, Joan, 11
Scultetus, Johann, 82, 137, 138
Secularization, 13
"Seductive Otherness," 20
"Semantics of deceit," 14
Semiotics, 6, 17, 66
Seneca, 48
Sermons, German, 1
Serpent, 39
Servetus, Michael, 143
Sexuality, 11, 15, 59, 60–61, 73, 81, 133
  deviant, 124
Signs, astrological, 24

234 Index

Skepticism, 4, 62, 63, 67, 87, 104, 126
Skeptics, 138
"Small world," 27, 52, 55, 56
"Sodomites," 58
Sorcerers, 69
Sorcery, 139
Spee, Friedrich, 82
Spirits
   elemental, 27, 52
   evil, 61, 62
   water, 45, 67, 68
Spiritualists, 127
Sprenger, Jakob, 70, 77
St. Bartholomew's Day Massacre, 128, 141
Staden, Hans, 140
State, absolutist, 8
Strasbourg Formula of Concord, 142
Succubus, 5, 16, 27, 60, 78
Supremacy, judicial, 136
Supreme Council, 106
Swan Knight, 89
Synchretism, 15

Tableav de l'inconstance, 8, 89, 91, 98, 113, 124, 132
Telecha, Ieanne de, 106
Theology, 11, 18
Thevet, André, 77
Tobacco, 92
Tomlinson, Gary, 6
Torture, 76
Tractatus de immortalitate animae, 129
Transgression, 25
   myth of, 23–44
Translator, 108
Treatise on Love, 111
Trials, witch, 8, 17, 66, 68, 75–76, 83, 100, 108, 124, 134
Tupinamba, 140
Turks, 63

Unbelief (*see* Atheism)
Unehelich, 55
Universe
   closed, 27, 49
   finite, 12
   planned, 50

Vance, Eugene, 19
Vanini, Giulio, 143
Vaults, sublunary, 45
Venegas, 103
Virginity, 55
Von Hohenheim, Theophrastus Paracelsus (*see* Paracelsus)
Von Hutten, Ulrich, 123
Von Sponheim, Trithemius, 7, 67, 98

Wagner, Christoph, 119
Wars, religious, 85, 96, 131, 140
Wende, 9
Weyer, Johannes, 4, 7, 8, 47, 49, 50, 56, 58, 65–88, 96, 98, 104, 124, 135, 136
Wisdom
   esoteric, 7
   folk, 18
Witch craze, 136
Witch(es), 12, 20, 62, 71, 95, 100, 111, 124
   hunts, 1, 17
Witchcraft, 6, 7, 10, 15, 18, 65, 68, 85, 87, 90, 112, 113, 134, 135, 138, 139, 141
   decriminalization of, 8
Wittgenstein, Ludwig, 18
Wootton, David, 122
Worldview, magical, 42, 43

Zozaya, Marie, 106
Zwinglian, 127